Praise For *On Thin Ice*

On Thin Ice *is a fascinating and compelling story about one person's journey in law enforcement and a thoughtful, intricate, and insightful roadmap of the steps needed to address the problems in American policing. Jeff and I worked at LAPD during a time of upheaval and change. We saw firsthand how organizational negligence and the old way of doing things impact not only public trust but officers' physical and mental health. As a retired lieutenant and current police best practices expert, I not only recommend this book to those outside of the profession but firmly believe it should be essential reading for those starting a career that is incredibly rewarding, if done the right way. Thank you, Jeff, for having the courage to speak the truth.*

—Adam Bercovici, Lieutenant, LAPD (Ret.)

On Thin Ice *is a powerful and passionate testament to Jeff's three decades in law enforcement, spanning from his early days at the LA Sheriff's academy to his role as a respected LAPD lieutenant and nationally recognized consultant. By sharing his deeply personal stories and lessons, Jeff provides a trusted guide for law enforcement professionals at every rank. This book is both an inspiration and a call to action for anyone committed to excellence, accountability, and building lasting trust with the communities they serve.*

—Ralph Ornelas, Former Chief of Police, Westminster PD and Commander, LA Sheriff's Department (Ret.)

On Thin Ice *is a riveting and honest account of one LAPD veteran's transformation from hockey player to law enforcement leader. With gripping personal stories and hard-earned insights, Jeff challenges us to reimagine the future of policing in America at a critical time in our history. This book isn't just a memoir; it's a bold blueprint for justice, accountability, and change.*

—Dr. Michael Ayalon, CEO of Greek University

On Thin Ice *is an unflinching, necessary call to rethink how we police, how we lead, and who we serve. Having personally spent more than two decades in law enforcement, I recognize myself—and the culture I came up in—on every page. Jeff is deeply committed to confronting the difficult conversations law enforcement too often avoids, exposing the systemic failures that have long gone unchallenged while pushing us toward meaningful change. This is a must-read for anyone in public safety who believes that real courage lies not just in holding the line, but in the willingness to change.*

—Michelle J. Caron, Inspector, DC Metropolitan PD (Ret.)

ON THIN ICE

An LAPD Veteran's Journey
To Reimagine Policing

JEFF WENNINGER

Populous Publishing

Populous Publishing, LLC
Ohio, USA

Cover design by RS Creative&Design

ISBN 979-8-9994515-0-7, 979-8-9994515-1-4

Printed in the United States of America

Dedication

I am overwhelmed with gratitude for the people who have shaped me, supported me, and helped me bring this book to life. It's not simply my story. It's the culmination of countless voices, lessons, and influences that have guided me along the way.

First, I want to honor my mother, Nancy Wenninger, and my father, Eugene Wenninger. You gave me the foundation I stand on, the voice to tell this story, and the strength to navigate the complexities of life and leadership. Mom, your unwavering encouragement and belief in me instilled the confidence I needed to share my experiences openly and honestly. Dad, your integrity and wisdom taught me the value of speaking out when it matters most. Together, you gave me not just a voice but the courage to use it to make a difference.

To my son Kristoffer: You are my greatest motivation. Every day I strive to set an example of integrity, resilience, and accountability, just as my father did for me. Watching you grow has been one of my greatest privileges, and I hope the lessons in this book inspire you as you inspire me to pursue what is right.

To my good friend, Ronald Siegel, whom we lost last year: Thank you for your friendship, your sharp mind, and your shared insights on the social and governmental complexities of life, honed through over eighty years of living in Los Angeles. Your encouragement and wisdom were invaluable, and while you are no longer with us, your influence lives on in these pages. You reminded me of the importance of holding a mirror to society and speaking the truth, even when it's uncomfortable. I dedicate these words, in part, to your memory.

And to those who've questioned my character or tried to tarnish my name, your words are a reminder of exactly why this book matters. That very mindset is part of what's afflicting the profession I care so deeply about. It's not about self-serving manipulation of the narrative. It's about honest reflection and confronting where we truly stand. I've come to understand that speaking up invites criticism—even personal attacks from some. But to cower in the face of antagonism only helps protect what's broken.

My mother, whose quiet strength and courage during her battle with cancer taught me resilience and grace in my most challenging moments. (Portrait by Juli Munson)

My father, the steadfast voice of wisdom, guided me through life's toughest challenges and shaped my sense of integrity.
(Portrait by Juli Munson)

My dear friend Ronald Siegel, whose wisdom, encouragement, and insight into life's complexities continue to inspire me—your influence lives on. (Portrait by Juli Munson)

TABLE OF CONTENTS

Prologue

Far and away the best prize that life offers is the chance to work hard at work worth doing.

—Theodore Roosevelt

I begin with Theodore Roosevelt because, before he became the twenty-sixth president of the United States, he served as the New York City Police Commissioner. In May 1895 Roosevelt was appointed president of the board of commissioners. He radically overhauled a police force riddled with corruption, partisanship, inefficiency, and lack of accountability. In only two years' time, Roosevelt implemented sweeping changes that created a more honest, efficient, and technologically advanced police force. He wrote an essay in the September 1897 edition of *The Atlantic* to describe what he had learned:

> *Our experience with the police department taught one or two lessons which are applicable to the whole question of municipal reform. Very many men put their faith in some special device, some special bit of legislation or some official scheme for getting good government. In reality, good government can come only through good administration, and good administration only as a consequence of a sustained—not spasmodic— and earnest effort by good citizens to secure honesty, courage, and common sense among civic administrators. If they demand the impossible, they will fail; and, on the other hand, if they do not demand a good deal, they will get nothing.*

I've written this book to demand a good deal, a better deal, for the police departments and the public they serve throughout the United States. I invoke the spirit of Teddy Roosevelt as we begin our journey, because I am not demanding the impossible. I am advocating for what is necessary and achievable. If we fail to enact meaningful change, we will fail, not just as police departments but as a society. The urgency is real, and this is the thin ice we stand on today.

I offer my thoughts and insights as someone with over three decades of firsthand experience in law enforcement. I retired as a lieutenant after serving in some of the most challenging and significant assignments in Los Angeles policing, including the Rodney King riots, the LAPD elite Metropolitan Division, and the Rampart gang unit. I later oversaw the investigation and adjudication of officer-involved shootings, a role that exposed me to the brutal truth of both pervasive failures and opportunities for improvement.

How did I end up here? Ironically, I never intended to become a cop. My initial goal was to follow in my father's academic footsteps by becoming a professor of criminal justice. The plan was simple: spend five years on the streets of Los Angeles, gain practical experience, and return to academia equipped with real-world insights to fuel my research and teaching. But as with so many people, life had other plans. Five years turned into over thirty as my mission shifted from teaching to making policing better.

You could say that my journey, my career in law enforcement, began when a hockey friendship, college bar hopping, and a few heavy-handed police converged to change the trajectory of my life. It started innocuously enough but escalated in a way that offered me a firsthand view of the very issues I would later dedicate my career to addressing.

"Hey, motherfucker, let's see your identification," was the conversational prelude to what was to come and to what would prove to be a life-altering encounter.

Early in life I stumbled plenty. Hardship was my constant companion as I worked to find my footing. I've faced my share of critics and haters, some who doubted me and others who hoped I would fail. But even in those early days I developed a relentless drive for excellence, a commitment that started on the ice. Hockey was where I first found a purpose, a place to channel my energy and prove that I was more than capable. I wasn't just good, I had a knack for finding the net, an instinct that can't be coached.

For four years I poured all my energy and focus into playing on an elite youth travel team, honing my skills and learning the discipline that only comes from unrelenting competition. At sixteen I left home to play junior hockey in Canada, embracing a challenge that demanded maturity and resilience far beyond my years. Later, I joined the United States Hockey League, a premier training ground for collegiate and professional prospects where the competition is fierce, and every game a proving ground. My time there earned me an athletic scholarship to play Division I collegiate hockey, a dream that would have opened the door to a promising professional career if not for the injuries that sidelined me and stifled my aspirations.

Still, hockey was more than just a sport; it was the influence that shaped and strengthened my character. The discipline I gained from early-morning practices, the ethics instilled by playing on a team, and the camaraderie built through shared victories and defeats all built the foundation of who I was and who I would become. And that foundation didn't just help me on the ice; it became critical in my survival and success as a police officer. Those lessons in discipline, teamwork, and resilience shaped how I approached every challenge, on the ice or in the line of duty.

But I wasn't thinking about any of that on a warm fall evening in Kent, Ohio, back in 1986 when a former hockey teammate and I were just hanging out. We were of legal drinking age, so on Labor Day weekend we visited an iconic bar called Robin Hood. It had begun as The Robin Hood Tea Room in 1927 and was wildly popular with college faculty and students alike. Many years later it evolved into a bar and grill. I was there that fall evening to enjoy a drink or two from its famous buckets of beer.

When the bar closed, the crowd flooded out the exit, packing the sidewalk with far more people than it was designed to accommodate. It was not long before my friend and I, along with many other students, were standing in the street.

Suddenly, a car carrying four young women approached and tried to force its way through the mass of people clogging the street. As the car inched forward, my friend thought it would be funny if he hopped onto the car's hood, likely motivated by the girls' good looks, a desire to get their attention and, perhaps, a phone number. Remember, this was the eighties. There weren't any dating apps. When you saw a girl you liked, that was your chance.

But my friend's flirtatious gesture fell flat, just as he would in a very real way only moments later. The driver, unamused, braked suddenly, causing my friend to fall off the hood. As he fell, he grabbed the car's antenna, which snapped off in his hand. He wasn't hurt and, to the contrary, appeared to be relishing what he saw as a harmless prank, but the situation soon changed. A police officer who had seen the whole thing approached, grabbed my friend, slapped handcuffs on him, and threw him in the back seat of a police car.

My focus immediately became intentional as our carefree night veered in a direction unfamiliar to me, and I thought, *This might not end well*. I was the guy who held a beer at parties just to fit in, sneaking off to pour some out so it looked like I was drinking. My evenings usually involved working out, lifting weights, or playing pickup hockey. If not for my friend's urging, I wouldn't have been hanging out with the bar crowd that night at all.

Interacting with the police was not something I was accustomed to either. My only prior experience was when I received a speeding ticket. But I felt a sense of responsibility to my friend. I needed to know how to assist him to ensure he got home safely following his arrest. So I approached the officer to ask where he was taking my buddy, when he would be released, and how much the bail would be. The officer was immediately hostile and barked at me, "Listen, asshole! Get back on the sidewalk, or you're going to jail too!"

Although I'd been drinking, I had my bearings and was keenly aware of the officer's arrogance. I had been polite, and my questions were reasonable. But the officer's threat to take me to jail, too, made it clear that he saw me as more than someone simply inquiring about how to help my friend. He viewed me as the enemy. His offensive demeanor made it clear that he had a distorted view of reality. I knew further interaction with that cop would not likely go well. My gut said, "Walk away."

I did as the officer commanded and returned to the sidewalk. Then two more cops showed up, and the officer who had barked at me pointed directly at me which, in hindsight, should have been a clue to what was about to occur.

The two cops who had just arrived headed toward me. At first, I felt a sense of calm. One was a sergeant, and I assumed his rank meant he'd bring a level of logic and professionalism to the situation. I couldn't have been more wrong. The sergeant was the first to speak, and his opening line was, "Hey, motherfucker, let's see your identification."

When I reached to retrieve my ID from my rear pants pocket, I was met with an onslaught of punches, kicks, and knee strikes from both officers. It obviously was not their first time beating an unassuming individual. All I had done was reach for my ID as directed.

I'm a big guy, six feet tall and, at the time, 200 pounds. I was also a hockey player who had been in his share of fistfights. The sucker punch that landed on my chin was as effective as any I had experienced on the ice, and it accomplished what sucker punches are supposed to do, knock me off balance.

At that moment I became acutely conscious of my movements, as I needed to defend myself, but I didn't want to be perceived as aggressive or combative toward the officers. Ultimately, I assumed a squatting fetal position. I was no threat. And yet those officers went to town on me. After suffering a split chin and a total pummeling, I felt the unmistakable shock of cold metal handcuffs around my wrists as the cops took me to the city jail and booked me for disorderly conduct, resisting arrest, and interfering in official police business. The realization that I had been badly beaten for making an innocent inquiry to an officer who saw me as an "asshole" began to set in.

While I was being booked I asked about my friend's whereabouts. They told me they'd let him go. The ridiculousness of the situation overcame me. My friend had made a playful gesture and been cuffed. I'd merely asked about his well-being, but in the end I was the guy who was beaten by the cops and charged with several crimes.

I spent the next seventy-two hours in the Kent Police Department lockup. It was a long weekend. I used those hours to ponder in disbelief how the cops had beaten me and then manufactured the circumstances to substantiate the bogus charges against me.

It was the end of a long summer I had spent working hard at the Kent Water Treatment Plant. It was apparent I would have to spend all the money I had earned to pay for an attorney. Although I felt powerless to hold the police accountable, I wasn't going to let them get away with the character assassination inherent in the charges.

My mother had been a Kent City Council member. My father was a highly regarded sociology professor and administrator at Kent State University. My family was well-known in the community, so I realized if this could happen to me, it could happen to anyone.

A major part of my parents' view of their parental role was a commitment to personal responsibility. My father believed his job as a parent was to raise me to be accountable and independent. He made decisions that pushed me to take responsibility for my actions and learn from my mistakes. He later explained that he left me in jail because he trusted I could handle it and believed the experience would teach me valuable lessons for my personal growth.

I admit my father was outside the norm, unconventional even, but he was wise. He often said, "No worthy lesson is learned without some sort of hardship." Although I was wronged by the police, there was much I could learn from the experience. If confronted with a similar circumstance again, I would do things differently. I would allow the events to unfold and make my inquiries via phone, an example of how I applied insights for personal growth that translated well to my law enforcement career.

But back then, I was handcuffed and taken to court in a police van with my split and badly bruised chin, injuries that usually would have happened at a hockey game, not at the literal hands of the police. I was arraigned on the charges and released on my own recognizance, meaning I signed a promise to appear in court instead of posting bail. But that signature represented something far more profound to me: it was my promise to fight those fraudulent charges.

I refused to agree to any of the plea deals offered because I knew I had done nothing wrong. I took the proceedings to a jury trial where the prosecutor offered to adjudicate the case with a citation for a "minor misdemeanor" (essentially a traffic ticket) and a $60 fine. With that, the original charges were dropped.

At the time I thought that if this could happen to a white male from a well-established family within the community, what could happen to someone from a family of lesser influence or an individual of reduced financial means? They might have been made to serve jail time for all kinds of reasons.

My father often said, "Sometimes it's not enough to be right." And those words had never been more poignant. The experience made me want to combat the injustice I had endured from an unbridled police force that abused power, mistreated the public, and showed a general lack of respect for those they were supposed to protect and serve. The police abuse began with the way the officer first spoke to me, continued when the officers beat me, and culminated when they falsely accused me. Suddenly, the police were far from the friendly protectors I had grown up believing they were.

That incident changed my life trajectory. I started taking criminal justice classes in the hope of attending law school. A neighbor and friend of my parents was a judge, and I sought her advice. She discouraged me from becoming an attorney, telling me that I lacked the academic credentials to be accepted to a top-tier law school, adding that I would likely only get accepted to schools characterized as "attorney factories." I would be one of a million attorneys in an already saturated profession. Even so, I contemplated a career in law enforcement. Perhaps I was best suited to make an impact from within the police ranks themselves.

Then, in the "You cannot make this shit up" file that we all have, the City of Kent Police Department, the same one that had beaten, arrested, and falsely charged me, announced that it was seeking correctional officers for the city jail. I half-heartedly applied without any expectation that I would seriously considered. I was hired.

That job served as the ultimate exoneration of any wrongdoing. What occurred the night of my arrest was so insignificant that the police department that arrested me had hired me to work in their jail. Had there been any credibility to the arrest, I never would have been hired, and what had been deeply impactful and unsettling to me, the police department dismissed as trivial.

Even more ironic, the guy who delivered the initial blow to my chin was a sergeant then and had been promoted to lieutenant. I worked for him. I actually came to like him and his keen sense of humor.

That said, I vividly recall the time he summoned me to his office. After some friendly banter, he brought up my arrest. He explained that when police officers encounter a large group of students who have been drinking and identify someone exhibiting what they perceive as belligerent behavior, that would be me simply asking a question, their priority becomes getting that person out of the situation. In their eyes, my beating was justified as a way to prevent the situation from escalating into something more dangerous.

Kent was predominantly white, so in this instance, the enemy wasn't a specific minority. It was the students. The officers operated under a "them versus us" mentality, believing that making an example of me would maintain control of the situation.

This was the first time I truly understood that some cops are biased—not always because of race, but against anyone they choose to dominate. In my case, the force used was completely unjustified, but I accepted the lieutenant's explanation. That encounter marked the beginning of a theme that would recur throughout my career, actions being excused by the mindset that "the end justifies the means." It's a slippery slope, and far too often it leads to abuse of power in law enforcement.

We need the police. Law enforcement has been a cornerstone of organized society for over 5,000 years. The first formal police organization was established in Egypt around 3000 BCE. While I'll delve deeper into the history of policing later, the essence of the role, as defined by Sir Robert Peel, remains the same: preventing crime and disorder and maintaining public safety.

That said, there's significant room for improvement in modern policing, so much so that what I've witnessed and experienced during my career drove me to write this book.

But this book isn't just about identifying what's wrong; it's about envisioning what policing should be. Law enforcement often is seen as an aggressive, unaccountable force that wields absolute authority over the communities it serves.

The critical questions: *What can police be? What should they be?*

Policing can and should be a force for good, the bedrock of every community, a force focused on protection, trust, and support. In this book I will explore how we can get there. It's not about reforming law enforcement; it's about completely reimagining its role in a way that's better for all. That's the goal I'm promoting, the message I'm always advocating.

Before delving into actionable steps, I'd like to share more of my personal journey, my personal and professional experiences, the lessons I've learned, and why I chose to stay in the profession. Those experiences have shaped the perspective I bring to these pages and inform the ideas I'll share.

I'm not here to complain or point fingers. I'm here to help forge a new path forward.

My hope is that this book will spark clarity, inspire meaningful conversation, and facilitate lasting change, whether you're a law enforcement officer, a policymaker, or a concerned citizen. Together, we can build a system of policing that serves everyone with fairness, trust, and respect.

Section I:
How My Experience Shaped My Perspective

Chapter 1:
The Roots of My Resilience

*Our experiences shape us; appreciate them, for you would not
be the person you are without them.*

—Unknown

Kent, Ohio, is a picturesque Midwestern town about forty miles
south of Cleveland that's best known as the home of Kent State
University. My father was a professor of sociology at the
university, and my mother worked as a chemist for DuPont
before choosing to dedicate herself to raising a family. Like
much of the town, our neighborhood was a mix of university
professors and their families, progressive in its outlook but not
without its own hidden complexities. Kent was a great city and
university, but both became infamous in 1970 as focal points of
Vietnam War protests.

Kent, for all its charm, will forever be marked by one of the
most infamous and tragic events in American history. The Kent
State shootings refer to the killing and wounding of unarmed
Kent State University students by the Ohio National Guard on
May 4, 1970. Students and faculty had gathered between classes
for a peace rally to oppose President Richard Nixon's order to
expand the war in Vietnam into neighboring Cambodia.

Twenty-eight National Guard soldiers fired approximately
sixty-seven rounds in just thirteen seconds, killing four students
and wounding nine others, one of whom suffered permanent
paralysis. The killings triggered immediate and massive outrage

on campuses around the country. More than four million students participated in organized walkouts at hundreds of universities, colleges, and high schools as the killings at Kent State further polarized the political climate.

Kent State symbolized the growing divide between a disillusioned youth and a government many believed had overstepped its bounds. The tragedy further influenced public opinion against the Vietnam War and marked a pivotal shift in the national conversation.

My father was there that day, immortalized in one of the iconic photographs. One image captures the moment when National Guardsmen opened fire on the students while my father stood with others atop a rooftop in the background, a glimpse of calm in the chaos. I was too young to grasp the enormity of what had happened, but as I grew older, the significance of that moment and my father's proximity to history became indelible.

The shooting's impact reached far beyond the Kent campus and community. Once a quiet college town, Kent became ground zero for a national reckoning and fodder for debates over war, government authority, and the limits of power. May 4, 1970, wasn't just about the past. That day was a lens through which we would come to understand so much about the present and the future.

I remember countless conversations with my father about the differing perspectives on the causes and accountability surrounding the shooting. Reserved and contemplative, my father rarely shared his feelings about that day. Instead, he challenged us to think critically about the world around us, encouraging us to form our own opinions about the complex interplay of justice, power, and responsibility. His approach was a reflection of his character: a man of quiet strength who grew up in the modest town of Bucyrus, Ohio. Its unassuming motto, "The Small City in the Middle of Everywhere," mirrored his humble beginnings and steady resolve.

Born to teenage parents during the Great Depression, my father's early years were anything but idyllic. For the first two years of his life he lived with another family in Toledo, Ohio, while his young parents worked to stabilize their situation. The arrangement ended abruptly when the family caring for him sent a letter demanding his parents make the agreed-upon payment. When my great-grandfather intercepted the letter, it set off a chain of events that led to my father's reunion with his parents, a bittersweet beginning that would shape his life.

Despite those early hardships, my father found success. He worked during his youth to help support his family, eventually earning an ROTC scholarship to Ohio State University, as it was known then. As an undergraduate, he displayed the discipline and determination that would define his life. After graduating, he served as a lieutenant in the Air Force during the Korean War, a chapter of his life that instilled a deep sense of duty and calm.

He met the woman who would become my mother in an Ohio State chemistry class. Shared values marked their relationship: a commitment to education, civic responsibility, and progressive ideals. Together, they built a life that reflected those principles, a life dedicated to their family and the betterment of their community.

My father was a thoughtful, learned individual who, when he spoke, had wisdom to share. The love he had for his family was evident. The loving looks he shared provided all the reassurance we needed. He never raised his voice, remaining poised under circumstances that would cause others to lose control.

He was a man whose simple presence commanded respect. There was no need for loud shows of force or grand gestures. He also had an innate ability to distill complex issues into thought-provoking questions. When I voiced an opinion, he never dismissed it outright but, instead, would ask, "What makes you think that? What evidence supports your conclusion?" Those questions weren't meant to discredit me; rather, they were an invitation to be more discerning, to challenge my assumptions, and to refine my thinking.

He modeled his philosophy and method in everything he did. He believed that understanding comes not from shouting the loudest but from listening carefully, questioning thoughtfully, and speaking deliberately. Through those interactions, my father awakened in me a critical thought process that would become an essential element of my identity and serve me well in my law enforcement career.

Yet, there was more to my father than his intellect and quiet wisdom. His life was a testament to perseverance and adaptability. Raised in an environment that didn't always nurture his potential, he carved a path of his own, one defined by integrity, hard work, and an unwavering sense of purpose. He never sought recognition or accolades, but his impact was felt in every interaction and every life that he touched.

The lessons my father imparted were not always overt; they were often embedded in how he lived his life. I deeply admired and sought to emulate his poise in the face of adversity, his ability to maintain a calm demeanor, and his commitment to fairness and justice. He showed me that true strength lies in restraint and that wisdom comes from the willingness to question, learn, and grow.

In many ways, the things my father taught me became the foundation upon which I built my career in law enforcement. The principles of accountability, fairness, and critical thinking were not just ideas, they were the fundamentals instilled in me by a man whose quiet persona contradicted the depth of his influence. For me, the discussions about May 4 were never just about history, they were about understanding the complexities of power, justice, and humanity—lessons that my father, without ever saying so explicitly, had been teaching me all along.

My parents didn't just talk about progressive values, they lived them daily. They weren't simply ahead of their time, they were light years ahead. After marrying in 1956, they dreamed of having four children, each a year apart. When they struggled to conceive, they decided to pursue adoption to make their dream a reality. Ironically, just as they were approved to adopt, my mother became pregnant with my sister Holly.

Not knowing if my mother could have more children, they moved forward with the adoption process. I was placed in their home just before Christmas 1966. Since they had already adopted me, a White child, the agency asked if they would consider adopting a minority child next. My parents didn't hesitate. They adopted my brother, Dorn, who is half-Japanese, and later my African American foster sister, Vanessa, became part of our family.

Vanessa joined our family through a foster program designed to help children from under-resourced families. She was the youngest of many siblings in inner-city Cleveland, and her family didn't have the financial resources to provide her the opportunities she needed to thrive. Between the ages of two and eight, Vanessa lived with us intermittently, becoming an essential part of our lives. Her energy, warmth, and sense of family enriched us all. Vanessa's presence expanded what my family already represented—that love and connection transcend bloodlines.

My mom ensured we connected with Vanessa's family during those years. Mom would often take my siblings and me to visit Vanessa in Cleveland, a city vastly different from our quiet Midwestern town. Those trips are etched in my memory, not just for the contrast between our worlds but for the lessons my mom imparted during those visits. Vanessa's neighborhood was rough, and the environment far removed from what I was used to in Kent, yet my mom was never hesitant or judgmental. She had a quiet confidence and street smarts that allowed her to navigate all spaces with grace.

Those visits weren't just about staying connected to Vanessa, they were formative experiences for me that helped develop my empathy and understanding. My mom's commitment to nurturing that connection taught me the importance of being there for others, regardless of the circumstances.

Family, as I learned, isn't defined by geography, economics, or circumstance. It's defined by understanding, encouragement, and the willingness to be there for each other. My mom's strength and openness left a lasting impression on me, shaping how I view relationships and responsibilities to this day. She taught me that family is about embracing differences and finding commonality, no matter how different our worlds may be.

In our family, race has never been a point of contention. Back then it wasn't even a topic of discussion. My parents raised us to be respectful of all people. They didn't sit us down for lectures about equality or tolerance. They didn't need to. They modeled those values, and we absorbed them naturally. To me, my brother wasn't defined by his heritage, nor was my sister defined by her skin color. They were just my siblings, and we treated each other the way any siblings would, playing, laughing, and, of course, occasionally arguing.

In the 1960s and 1970s a multiracial family like ours wasn't common, especially in a town like Kent. Looking back, our family life would have made a great sitcom. But despite the challenges, my parents embraced diversity and were committed to building a family that was as inclusive as it was unique.

But while race wasn't something we focused on at home. It was obvious that those outside our family saw things differently. The whispers and stares at the A&P grocery store were part of our routine. My mother, poised as ever, would stroll past the gawkers with her head held high, refusing to let their ignorance disrupt our lives.

I distinctly remember one woman who approached my mother in the store, smiling with a thin veneer of politeness that couldn't hide her condescension: "All your children look so much alike!"

My mother, with the grace and strength that defined her, didn't attempt to win the woman's favor. She ignored the remark, finished shopping, and walked out with her dignity intact.

Yes, prejudice reared its ugly head, even in a college town as progressive as Kent. I remember when a Black professor and his family moved into our neighborhood. It should have been a moment of progress, a sign that the town was moving toward the inclusive ideals it often claimed to represent. Instead, it became a stark reminder of how far there was to go. The family faced subtle but unmistakable hostility, glances that lingered too long, invitations that never came, and whispered words that weren't meant for them to hear. It wasn't overt, but it was enough. Before long, they left. I was young and naïve, unaware of what had driven them out, but even then I sensed that something wasn't right.

Looking back, I recognize the quiet racism that pushed them away. It wasn't the kind of hatred that grabs headlines. Instead, it was insidious, the kind that hides behind polite smiles and unspoken barriers. It was the kind of prejudice that sees itself as harmless yet is anything but. I was faced with the reality that at least some of my neighbors were not as I perceived them. Kent was a forward-thinking town for its time, but beneath the surface the rot of stereotypes and judgments still led to discrimination.

I have to acknowledge what wasn't readily spoken; Black families primarily lived on the south side and didn't patronize most of the White restaurants or social gathering spots. Perhaps that's why we rarely ate dinner out. Instead, my mom would pick up food to serve at home. Despite it all, we had a carefree childhood, unaware of the social realities, but I'm sure my parents were always on guard.

It wasn't lost on me, even as a child, that my family's story was different. My parents weren't just raising children; they were making a statement, whether they wanted to or not. Their actions showed us that not only family but individuals shouldn't be defined by skin color, nationality, or socioeconomic status, and that we all should have a commitment to something greater than ourselves.

* * *

As a child I attended Kent State University School, a 240-student laboratory school attached to the university. Liberal in its thinking and child-centered in its approach, the school was far ahead of its time. A laboratory school functions as both a learning environment for children and a research and training site for university students and faculty, blending traditional education with hands-on observation and innovative teaching methods.

The environment exposed me to more racially and culturally diverse classmates than usual, as most students were children of Kent State faculty who resided in cities outside of Kent, such as Akron and Cleveland. But I struggled in school. I faced obstacles that many of my classmates didn't. I had a speech impediment that required therapy, and I wore white leather corrective boots because I was severely pigeon-toed. But my greatest challenge was that I simply couldn't seem to get the letters in the right order. Luckily, the school didn't use traditional grades. Instead, we received in-depth, narrative-based evaluations. Even with that more flexible system, I wasn't doing well. When my mother discussed my difficulties with my teachers, they reassured her that children develop at different rates. But I knew I was different.

By fifth grade I was only reading at a first-grade level. My younger brother, Dorn, scored higher than I did and well above his grade level. Dorn was what Dairy Queen calls "the full meal deal." Incredibly bright, he achieved academic scholarships for undergraduate and graduate school, majoring in Spanish and international business. He speaks English, Spanish, Portuguese, and French fluently and has completed multiple Ironman Triathlons and marathons. Among his achievements are winning both the Antarctica and North Pole ultramarathons and completing seven marathons in seven days on seven continents. While Dorn played hockey, he didn't reach the elite level I did, primarily because he didn't have the same physical attributes. He was small in stature at just eighty-nine pounds as a high school freshman. But Dorn was one of the most strategic hockey players I've ever seen, and his deep insight into life's challenges rivals that of my father. I respect him immensely.

At the time, though, I just felt inferior. I remember sitting on the woodpile beside our house after school and crying. My mother sought me out and asked what was wrong. I told her I felt stupid. I'd wrestle with the words on a page, but no matter how hard I tried, I couldn't comprehend what I had just read. I acted up in school to avoid reading aloud, knowing that my stammering would draw laughter from my classmates.

My mother explained that we all have our strengths and weaknesses. All she and my father ever asked of me was to do the best I possibly could in anything I sought to achieve. She said that while my brother excelled as a student, I excelled as an athlete. She put it all into perspective for me: fulfill what is inside you, and don't worry about what is outside. But the outside world ultimately came to my rescue.

It wasn't until seventh grade that my reading teacher said, "Hey, I'd like you to come in during lunch if you would be so kind as to do some testing." I agreed, and the results confirmed her suspicions.

At the time, dyslexia wasn't as well understood or addressed as it is today. Fortunately, my teacher figured out my problem and had me come in at lunchtime when she taught me to read. Her work helped me achieve better results in high school and, eventually, make it to college. I had to learn in a way that worked for me, and thanks to that teacher, I did.

I was also supported by my best friend, Randy. His father was a physics professor at Kent State, and we met when I was six. He's been like an older brother to me, valuing academics and sports and encouraging me to strive for excellence in school and student activities. His influence even extended to my son who currently serves as an eighth-grade principal's advisory council member, something I'd also done in high school, thanks to Randy's example. My son calls him "Uncle Randy."

Randy lived in my neighborhood and played a significant role in getting me into hockey. When I met him I was a figure skater. I thought the patches on his hockey jacket were cool, and I wanted some of my own. Randy went on to play hockey at Ohio State and later became a brilliant aerospace engineer for McDonnell Douglas in Los Angeles. He's now retired from the Air Force space program, where he served for several years in a civilian role.

Randy and his two older brothers led me into ice hockey, but I also remember watching them go to college and pursue a master's degree. All three exemplified the essence of a student-athlete, setting a standard that reinforced what my parents always emphasized, the importance of education. Their example and my parents' guidance taught me that academics and athletics could coexist, and that both were vital to a well-rounded life.

At the time, hockey seemed to be my future, but my father often reminded me, "College hockey scholarships are few and far between." While he recognized my skill on the ice, he emphasized the importance of a solid education as a foundation for life beyond the rink. After all, the average length of a professional hockey career is a short five years.

My experience as a figure skater gave me superior skating ability. Still, my parents were cautious about investing in hockey equipment until I demonstrated a commitment to the game. I'll never forget my first season, playing in figure skates, blue jeans, and standard winter gloves. My only hockey equipment included shin guards, elbow pads, and a helmet. But by the second season, after scoring all seven goals in a 7-0 win in our first game, my parents committed to buying me all the gear I needed. At that moment I felt like a real hockey player.

Both of my parents instilled a moral compass that has influenced my sense of right and wrong. Their example has compelled me to stand up for what I believe to be right despite it being unpopular or coming with certain personal hardship.

Those lessons became the substance of who I am. My parents' quiet defiance in the face of prejudice and their unwavering belief in the dignity of all people laid the foundation for the values I carried into my adult life. Their example taught me to stand firm in my principles, even when it's uncomfortable, even when the world around me doesn't yet understand.

My mother's influence on my life was as profound as it is enduring. She was a remarkable woman whose accomplishments and values left a permanent impression on me. An AAU Ohio State Champion in the breaststroke, she was a fierce competitor who could hold her own against anyone, even the fastest male swimmers at Ohio State. Unfortunately, competitive swimming for women didn't exist at the collegiate level then, so she joined the synchronized swimming team instead, a testament to her adaptability.

But swimming was just one facet of her athleticism. My mother also was a dedicated runner who competed in marathons well into adulthood. Her physical strength was matched only by her inner fortitude, a force that guided her through the many challenges she faced and one I would lean on as I navigated my own life. My father shared her passion for running and competed in countless 10K and marathon road races, showing the same dedication and determination that defined our family.

My mom's strength extended beyond her athletic pursuits. She was deeply committed to civic engagement and the betterment of her community. She served as president of the League of Women Voters and, as I previously mentioned, as a city council member in Kent. In the 1970s, alongside my father, she cofounded the Kent Environmental Council, a forward-thinking initiative that remains active today. She believed in creating a better world, not just for her family but for everyone, and she approached that mission with tireless dedication and purpose.

Her principles were unshakable, even when it came to family, a lesson she taught me in one unforgettable moment. We were confronted with bigotry during a trip to San Antonio to visit her grandfather, a retired Army colonel. He was ill and didn't have long to live.

When we arrived, he was unwilling to see my brother, Dorn, because of his Japanese heritage, harboring lingering prejudices from his experiences in World War II. My mother didn't hesitate. She turned around, gathered us back into the car, and spent the day with us at the Alamo instead. For her, standing by her values—equality, dignity, and respect—was more important than maintaining ties with someone who refused to see the humanity in all people. That moment left a lasting impression. It showed me that principles matter, even when it means making difficult and painful choices.

My mother was resolute in her sense of principle, placing her values above all else, even her personal needs and family ties. This characteristic was ingrained in me through her example although, at times, it has been to my detriment. There have been instances in my personal and professional life when I've been misunderstood, criticized, opposed, accused, and rejected in the pursuit of doing what I believe to be right. But I know no other way.

Her strength was most evident during the most challenging battle of her life, her fight against glioblastoma, a highly aggressive brain cancer. In 1982, after suffering from debilitating headaches and other serious symptoms, she was misdiagnosed with a mild stroke. It wasn't until her condition worsened and she returned to the Cleveland Clinic late on a Friday night that the devastating diagnosis became clear. My mother faced the news with the same courage she brought to every aspect of her life.

She was scheduled for brain surgery the next Monday morning. But I will never forget being awakened by the phone ringing on Saturday night, and my father knocking on my bedroom door to tell me to get dressed. We were heading to the hospital because my mother needed emergency surgery.

I remember standing next to her hospital bed and crying, not knowing if this was goodbye. My mother had always been full of energy and involved in all types of selfless endeavors. To see her reduced to the confines of that hospital bed with barely enough strength to lift her head was devastating.

But she maintained her awareness of those around her, the people she loved, and made their wellbeing her focus: "Jeffrey," she said, "I can't remember the last time I saw you cry." I had acquired a tough exterior reminiscent of a hockey player, but her words influenced an emotional transformation that led to the empathy I would demonstrate in my law enforcement career.

She went on to undergo surgery, chemotherapy, and radiation, enduring the grueling treatments with determination and grace. Even during her illness my mother continued to live with purpose. That summer she astonished everyone by completing a 10K just months after her initial brain surgery. Watching her push through her physical limitations to achieve something so remarkable reinforced the values she had always instilled in me: perseverance, determination, and the belief that no obstacle is insurmountable.

If my father knew of Mom's bleak prognosis, he didn't share it with us children. And we, for better or worse, didn't have the internet to conduct our own medical research. In hindsight, I'm glad I was allowed to have hope.

But Mom's cancer returned in October 1982. Despite the prognosis, my mother remained steadfast. She continued to focus on her family, encouraging me to pursue my hockey dreams, even as her health deteriorated. So in May 1983, I attended an invitational tryout for a junior hockey team in Canada, the country that invented the game I loved.

While at the tryout and unbeknownst to me, my mother's condition worsened to the point that she was not going to be with us much longer. When I arrived home she appeared unconscious as I stood next to her bed with tears in my eyes. Having learned from her that toughness and tears can coexist. I wasn't sure she knew I was there. But as I held her hand and told her I loved her, she gently squeezed my hand; it was the reassurance I needed.

Thirty minutes later, she passed away. It was Mother's Day, which has since taken on a deeply personal significance for me. Every year I dedicate that day to honoring her memory and recommitting myself to the values she instilled: strength, compassion, and unwavering integrity.

Her death was a profound loss, but her life was an even greater inspiration. My mother's resilience built the foundation of who I am. She taught me that true strength is measured not by how loudly you speak but by how consistently you act in accordance with your values. Above all, she showed me that empathy, in its purest form, is the driving force behind every meaningful choice we make. Her legacy lives on in me, not just in the lessons she taught but in the person she helped me become and in the person I am helping my son become. She was more than a mother, she was my guiding light, and she still is. She's the one I strive to honor in everything I do.

My mother's inspiration manifested in many ways. The mere thought of the pain she endured from her brain tumor causes me, even to this day, to experience a surge in adrenaline that, when properly channeled, can result in instances of extraordinary athletic performance. Throughout her illness I played hockey for my high school team and started getting attention in the media. As my mother recovered in the hospital from brain surgery, I found motivation in knowing she was watching me on television. That's why the media described my performance as "playing like a man possessed."

I saw this in my brother Dorn, too. Years later, I had gone to watch him compete in his first marathon in Napa Valley, California. As he approached the finish line, his running gait was noticeably distressed. His face bore a grimace that we would later learn was caused by the pain of a stress fracture sustained during the race. His first words to me as he fought back tears were, "I did it for Mom."

We all grieved differently. Holly was off at school, and I was at home, grateful to be near my dad and brother. Losing my mother at sixteen was a defining moment. It was a loss that forced me to confront the realities of mortality far earlier than most of my peers. While they were preoccupied with school dances, dating, or the latest teenage drama, I found myself wrestling with more profound questions about life, responsibility, and my place in the world.

During that first year after my mother's passing, my father began dating Cheryl, a lovely woman who would become a transformative figure in all our lives. Cheryl was an economics professor at Kent State, and from the moment she entered our family, she brought a warmth and an intelligence that complemented my father's steady presence. My father, always a good judge of character, chose not just a great partner for himself but also a remarkable stepmother for my siblings and me.

Cheryl was as instrumental in shaping me as my mother had been. She became a source of strength and wisdom, offering guidance during the formative years of my early adulthood. Her marriage to my father, rooted in mutual respect and shared values, lasted thirty-five years until my father's passing from cancer in 2018. Cheryl followed him the next year, but the legacy of their love and partnership is a cherished chapter in my family's story.

* * *

At just fourteen I was invited to the regional tryouts for the 1984 U.S. Olympic team. It was a big deal, especially for an aspiring professional hockey player like me. The Mid-American III Hockey Conference, covering Ohio, Pennsylvania, West Virginia, and Kentucky, held its tryouts in May 1981. We were still inspired by the underdog story of the 1980 "Miracle on Ice" U.S. hockey team that had upset the Soviet Union and gone on to win gold at Lake Placid. Only twelve skaters would advance from the Mid-American tryouts to Colorado Springs for the chance to make the team. My age prohibited me from moving on. Even so, I was honored to have been considered to play at that level.

As a high school freshman I played for my school team, which clinched the Ohio State Championship. The thrill of that victory and my performance on the ice began to spark interest from college recruiters, and I couldn't help but wonder what might come next. That answer came sooner than I expected. At just sixteen I was encouraged to take the leap and play junior hockey in Canada, a move that promised to elevate my game. My potential had surpassed the level of competition that Ohio's hockey scene could offer, and this opportunity was the chance to test myself against the best.

Leaving home at such a young age was difficult, but the extraordinary opportunity made the decision easier. It marked the start of an evolution that would challenge me to grow both on and off the ice.

Canada was a rude awakening. The game was faster and unapologetically brutal. It was also deeply ingrained in Canadian culture, and as the lone American on the team, I was often singled out by opposing teams, not for my skills but for my nationality. They saw me as an outsider, and their rough play reflected their disdain.

In that environment I quickly learned that skill alone wasn't enough. Hockey in Canada had its own culture of unwritten rules, and fighting was an essential part of the game. It was a stark contrast to the more refined style I had grown up with in Kent where the sons of professors prioritized finesse over physicality. But on the cold, unforgiving Canadian ice, holding your ground often meant dropping your gloves and raising your fists.

My initial attempts at fighting were awkward, clunky, and unsuccessful. But I adapted, learning to protect myself and hold my own against opponents who were often older, stronger, and far more experienced in that aspect of the game. Those clashes taught me more than just how to defend myself physically. I learned to stay focused in the heat of conflict and remain calm even when confronted with others' attempts to intimidate me.

Those were lessons I would remember long after I left the rink, lessons that would shape how I approached stressful altercations during my law enforcement career.

Off the ice I continued to process the heavy loss of my mother, a grief that shaped every decision I made during that time. The experience of losing her made me acutely self-aware that some decisions must be guided by responsibilities greater than myself. That sense of duty to my family as we navigated our collective grief ultimately led me to return home before completing the season in Canada.

As adults we understand that grief isn't something you simply "get over" or move past—it becomes a part of you, a shadow that lingers. But as a young man, that was a lesson I had yet to learn. My naïveté manifested in a desire to withdraw from the unnecessary drama found in teenage life. I chose not to connect with friends and people my own age whose priorities felt trivial. I attended school events, social gatherings, and even athletic events alone, preferring the quiet company of my thoughts to the noise and nonsense of teenage antics. I became more introspective, reserved, and focused on what mattered to me.

The United States Hockey League (USHL), a premier developmental league for collegiate and professional hockey, provides an essential stepping stone for players striving to reach the sport's highest levels. In 1984 I joined the Dubuque (Iowa) Fighting Saints, one of the standout teams in the USHL. Under the expert leadership of coach Jack Barzee, the Fighting Saints had built a tradition of excellence since their relocation from Waterloo, Iowa, in 1980. The team had won two national championships, two playoff titles, and two regular-season crowns in just four seasons. Being part of such a storied program was both an honor and a significant step in my development as a player, offering me the opportunity to compete at an elite level in one of the most respected leagues in North America.

Barzee was a coach unlike any I had encountered. He innately understood his players, recognizing not just their athletic skills but also their unique personalities. He had a knack for motivating each individual in a way that resonated with them personally. That ability to connect with people left a lasting impression, one I carried into my police career. I'll never forget my first regular season game with the Fighting Saints. I was eager to make an impression, but nerves got the best of me, and I wasn't playing my best. During a break Jack put his arm around me, leaned in and said, "Hey, buddy, I hope you realize there are nearly a billion people in China, and not one of them gives a fuck about this game."

His words, laced with humor and perspective, had the intended effect. They broke through my tension, allowing me to relax and play the way I knew I could. Jack's leadership wasn't about barking orders or demanding perfection; it was about understanding what each player needed to perform at their best. It's a philosophy that stuck with me long after I hung up my skates and picked up the badge.

That season turned out to be decisive for me. Playing for Dubuque gave me a taste of what it meant to compete at an elite level, and I thrived in that environment. We captured another Clark Cup title as playoff champions and finished as the runner-up at the national tournament. I had a breakout season, earning Rookie of the Year and catching the attention of college and

NHL scouts alike. One of those scouts was David McNab of the Hartford Whalers whose interest in my potential validated all the hard work I had put into the sport.

The rink became my sanctuary, a place where I could channel my grief and find control in all the uncertainty. Hockey wasn't just my escape. Hockey was my lifeline. Every practice, every game, and every goal was a way to honor my mother's unwavering belief in me. Even in her absence, she was still my biggest supporter, her voice a quiet, internal encouragement to excel.

With scholarship offers in hand I chose to continue my hockey career at Western Michigan University, a Division I program with a reputation for excellence. I was particularly drawn to the assistant coach who had been the head coach at Kent State. His familiarity with my game gave me confidence that I could make an immediate impact.

After training camp the head coach posted numeric rankings for each player. To my surprise and pride, I was ranked number one, ahead of seasoned veterans and star players. But that recognition, instead of fostering camaraderie, created tension within the team. My upperclassman teammates saw me as a threat to their playing time and professional aspirations, and their resentment quickly became apparent.

One day I walked into the locker room to find my gear packed into an equipment bag soaked with urine. It was a humiliating experience that revealed just how far some were willing to go to make a statement. Fighting, which had become a necessary skill in Canadian hockey, reentered my life in a bitterly ironic way. In practice I was forced into physical confrontations, not with opponents but with teammates who resented me. The constant hostility wore on me, and though I continued to perform well, scoring my first collegiate goal against the Canadian National Team and helping deliver key wins against rivals like the University of Michigan, the joy I once felt for the game began to dissipate.

I was playing a game I no longer found rewarding. I knew that if I left Western Michigan, my chances of playing professionally could be irrevocably damaged. But I needed to remain true to myself and preserve my passion for the game. I was steadfast in my decision to transfer to Kent State to play out my college hockey days. While Kent State was a Division I hockey school, it wasn't a top-tier powerhouse like Western Michigan. But I was willing to potentially forfeit my professional hockey aspirations to restore my love for the game.

At Kent State I discovered a more supportive environment that allowed me to thrive. I was honored to be named team captain and wasted no time making my mark. In my debut game for the Golden Flashes I delivered a standout performance, scoring a hat trick against Notre Dame, proving I still could compete at the highest level. But hockey, a brutal mistress, had more lessons in store for me…

The play happened in an instant, but the aftermath lingered for years. I was skating full speed in a race for the puck that had been dumped into the offensive zone. When I reached for the puck, a defender collided with me, hurtling me headfirst into the unforgiving end boards. The sound was dull, almost surreal, as my helmet hit the boards. In an instant, my shoulder violently tore from its socket, and pain shot through me at an intensity I had not felt before. I lay crumpled on the ice and in excruciating pain. I knew in my gut that this wasn't just another hit.

The diagnosis was as grim as the injury felt: a dislocated shoulder. The path back to the ice would be steep, but I was determined to make it. My days were consumed by rehab, grueling sessions designed to rebuild strength and protect against further injury. The harness strapped around my shoulder served as both a physical limitation and a mental reminder of my vulnerability. Still, I pushed through, focusing on one goal, returning to the game I loved.

But hockey can be ruthless, not just in its physical demands but in the calculated way opponents exploit weakness. I returned to competition with cautious optimism, eager to contribute to my team once again. Then it happened. I squared off with an opposing player who didn't bother with pretense; his intentions were as clear as his actions. He grabbed my arm, the one bound by the harness, and yanked it downward with brute force. The pain was instant and excruciating, a sickening echo of my first injury. My shoulder dislocated again. I knew then my season was over.

The surgery that followed was invasive and final, a Bristow procedure that left a screw permanently embedded in my shoulder. Recovery was a battle up an endless incline. Each session in physical therapy tested not just my body but my spirit. Still, I pushed forward, refusing to give in to despair. Slowly, I clawed my way back into playing shape, determined to prove that I wasn't done yet.

But once more, fate had other plans. Just as I began to regain my confidence on the ice, disaster struck. This time it was a full tear of the ligaments in my left knee, a devastating injury that demanded yet another surgery and another long rehab. I fought through it, only to endure another hit that tore the same ligaments. The cycle was cruelly repetitive; each recovery was met with a new injury, and each step forward was followed by two steps back.

Eventually, I had to face the truth my body was telling me: I couldn't keep doing this. My shoulder was scarred, my knee barely holding together, and my quickness, the attribute that defined my game, was no longer what it was. Hockey skill is measured in fractions of a second, and I could no longer perform at the level I was accustomed to. The game I loved, the one that had given me so much joy and purpose, was taking more than it was giving. The realization hit me like a slapshot to the face—my hockey career was over.

It's often said that elite athletes face two deaths: the one at the end of life and the moment they realize it's time to walk away from their sport. For me, that moment came far earlier than anyone expected, making it even harder to accept. I couldn't shake the feeling that I was a serious underachiever.

Hockey wasn't just a sport to me. It was my identity, my refuge. It had been there for me through the hardest times in my life, a place where I could channel everything I had into something meaningful. To lose it felt like losing a part of me.

But my parents had always taught me that life is about more than just one thing, no matter how important it may seem. My father's constant reminders about the value of education echoed in my mind while my mother's resilience served as inspiration. Both lived lives of purpose that were driven by values far beyond personal ambition. Their example gave me the strength to pivot, to take the lessons I had learned on the ice and carry them into whatever came next. Hockey had shaped me, but I soon realized that it didn't define me.

The values my parents instilled in me, coupled with the discipline and determination I honed through hockey and the adversity that came with it formed my compass as I prepared to navigate an entirely new world. Leaving the familiarity and comfort of the rink behind was no small feat, but I knew I wasn't walking away from those hard-earned lessons. They were synonymous with my character, ready to guide me as I took my first steps into law enforcement, shaping how I would approach the challenges and triumphs that lay ahead.

Chapter 2:
The Identity and Integrity
Behind the Badge

What is right is not always popular, and what is popular is not always right.

—Albert Einstein

My father, the professor, believed five years in law enforcement was enough to gain the practical experience I'd need before pursuing a doctorate in criminal justice. That timeline felt right to me as well because, by my late twenties, I could return to academia with a solid foundation of real-world insights. If I was going to gain that experience, I wanted to do it in a large, dynamic city. The Los Angeles Police Department (LAPD) wasn't just one of the largest police forces in the country. LAPD was a cultural institution immortalized in countless movies and TV shows as the epitome of action, bravery, and honor. But what captivated me most wasn't Hollywood's glamour but the department's complexity, its vast specialization opportunities, and the chance to learn in one of the most diverse cities in the nation.

I was also intrigued that the LAPD had created SWAT (Special Weapons and Tactics), a world-renowned unit known as one of the premier tactical teams in law enforcement. Its legacy is not just in its tactical brilliance but in how its practices and principles influence the training of all department personnel. This represented the chance to be part of a force that sets standards for law enforcement agencies across the globe. It wasn't just a career; it was a calling shaped by inspiration and the promise of having a meaningful impact.

By the time I moved to Los Angeles to join the LAPD I was accustomed to living independently. It was my father who had instilled in my siblings and me the importance of self-reliance from an early age. After graduating high school, he gave us the summer to remain at home, but after that it was time to forge our own paths. While Dad provided financial assistance when needed, the expectation was clear: We were to work hard and make it on our own. Visits home weren't for raiding the fridge or having our laundry done for us, they were about reconnecting.

As my father often emphasized, higher education was about more than academics. It was a proving ground for independence where you learned to manage the day-to-day realities of life without the safety net of home. So when I packed my bags for Los Angeles at the age of twenty-three, it felt like an exciting and natural next step rather than a daunting leap into the unknown.

Once settled in I went through the hiring process for both the LAPD and, as a backup, the LA County Sheriff's Department. To my surprise, I was offered a job by both. The sheer size and density of Los Angeles were intimidating. Driving on the freeways for the first time left my palms sweaty. The city's endless sprawl was overwhelming to navigate. But I was determined to make it work. I was ready to prove to myself, and anyone watching, that I could succeed.

Even though pursuing this path had been at my father's urging, he didn't hold back his cautionary advice. He knew the realities of policing all too well, warning me that my expectations might not align with the reality of the job. "You'll probably be disappointed," he said, speaking with the clarity of someone who understood what I was walking into. My father had studied the police extensively while working on his PhD dissertation, and his research had given him a deep understanding of the flaws and limitations of law enforcement.

What I didn't know then was just how accurate his words would be. I was about to get a front-row seat to the challenges, complexities, and shortcomings of a profession I had idealized for so long. Despite his warnings, I pushed forward, convinced that this was my calling and determined to find my own way through the realities of the job.

I doubt that my college professors ever saw me as a future police officer or a civil servant. They envisioned something different for me, perhaps shaped by how I approached learning. Being dyslexic, I learned best through active engagement. I sat in the front row, asked a lot of questions, and cultivated a dynamic relationship with my professors. This approach allowed me to excel despite the challenges dyslexia presented and, ultimately, I earned a General Studies degree. My customized curriculum was the equivalent of undergraduate degrees in sociology, psychology, and criminal justice, minus the foreign language requirement, which I couldn't pass due to my dyslexia.

Of all those fields, sociology captivated me the most. I think that was mainly due to my father's influence and the many conversations we'd had growing up. But what my professors didn't know was my deeper motivation. I wasn't heading into law enforcement just to gain experience. I wanted to learn, grow, and eventually influence how law enforcement could be improved. This wasn't just a career choice. This was a reflection of the values my parents had instilled in me. Through the way they lived their own lives, they taught me that progress requires engagement and action.

* * *

My plan was clear: I would join the LAPD. But an unsolicited conversation at police headquarters gave me pause. A sergeant, noticing that I also had been offered a position by the LA County Sheriff's Department, stopped me and said, "You're a fool if you don't take that job." His words surprised me. "The LAPD used to be the best, but that's no longer the case."

That conversation planted seeds of doubt, especially since it wasn't the first time I'd heard criticism of the LAPD from insiders. Previously, a candidate for the LA County Sheriff's Department told me that his father, who was a retired LAPD sergeant, would not allow him to apply to the LAPD. When I asked why, he encouraged me to come over and have a beer with his father to find out. I figured it was best to hear it straight from the source, so I took him up on his invitation.

The retired sergeant I spoke with came from a different era, and his views reflected that. He harbored resentment toward the Affirmative Action programs Los Angeles had implemented for hiring and promotion. As a White male, he believed those programs had cheated him. His bitterness was palpable, but because of the way I was raised, and the diversity within my own family, I saw things differently. To me, merit was and is the ultimate equalizer. I believed that if I achieved the highest score or demonstrated the most skill, no one could deny me an opportunity or a promotion. But looking back, I recognize now that my thinking may have been naïve and aspirational.

Those conversations forced me to reevaluate my decision. Could I make the kind of impact I wanted in an organization that even its own members questioned? The decision before me became much more complex, and I seriously considered whether the LA County Sheriff's Department might offer a better path forward than the LAPD would.

I wondered if the complaints about the LAPD were just the usual comments from disgruntled current and former employees, or if they were valid warnings about deeper institutional problems. Ultimately, I chose to wear the tan and green uniform of a deputy sheriff with the LA County Sheriff's Department instead of joining the LAPD.

In hindsight that was likely the right decision, and not just because of the complaints I'd heard about the LAPD. It was more a matter of perspective and scale. As you know, I grew up in a town of just 24,000 people. Before moving to Los Angeles, the largest city I had lived in was Dubuque, Iowa, population 62,000. Transitioning to Los Angeles, with nearly three and a half million residents, was an entirely different experience, both culturally and logistically.

LA's extremes were staggering. Vast differences in wealth created neighborhoods that felt like different worlds, and its sprawling geography stretched across more than 500 square miles. Policing a city so massive and diverse would have been unlike anything I'd ever experienced. I relished the challenges it promised, but I also knew it would take time to adjust to LA's sheer scale and complexity. My choice to start with the sheriff's department allowed me to ease into that entirely new world while still immersing myself in the work I was passionate about.

Joining the LA County Sheriff's Department began with the academy, and it wasn't for the faint of heart. Of the 157 recruits who started with me, only 107 graduated. Nearly a third of the class quit or was dismissed for failing to meet training standards. Often, resignations were encouraged when no legitimate grounds for dismissal existed with subjective judgments from training staff determining who couldn't cut it.

My ambition in the academy didn't go unnoticed, though not always in a positive way. "All you need is a 70 percent to pass," some of my peers would say, as if mediocrity were the goal. But my parents had instilled in me the importance of integrity and striving for excellence. I worked hard, earning a 98.7 percent academic average, the highest in the class. I also earned the highest physical fitness scores and demonstrated the second-highest firearms proficiency despite not having fired a gun before entering the academy. At graduation I was honored with the Certificate of Merit, recognizing the recruit who exemplified the highest level of achievement. What made that award so meaningful was that it wasn't just about scoring the highest. It was also a recognition of leadership, as recipients were selected by both academy staff and peers. It wasn't just an acknowledgment of my performance, but the respect I earned through my work ethic, discipline, and leadership ability. This acknowledgment meant the world to me, even if I knew academic performance wasn't always valued in the field.

* * *

Los Angeles County Men's Central Jail opened in 1963 as a concrete behemoth in a warehouse district just outside downtown LA. The Inmate Reception Center was part of this complex and home to my first assignment. It was through those doors that all male inmates entered the jail system to begin their incarceration. As the inmates were processed they were searched, ordered to strip and shower, thrown jail clothing wrapped inside a towel, and given a meat and cheese sandwich before being escorted to their housing in the general inmate population.

The conditions were appalling. Many of the toilets didn't flush, so they served as receptacles for standing excrement. Inoperable shower drains caused dirty shower water to pool on the shower floors for hours. But the worst was the inconsistent cooling system that made extreme heat the norm. The lack of proper ventilation increased the humidity so that it seemed the stench could be cut with a butter knife.

One day I was assigned to escort a prisoner to his permanent cell. He already had been in state prison for another crime, but he had been sent to the county jail to face other charges.

The inmate was a white power gang member with a shaved head and tattoos that broadcast his hatred. As I escorted him down the hall, he made his feelings toward law enforcement unmistakably clear by spitting directly in my face. It was as deliberate and insulting as the sucker punch I'd taken years earlier outside that bar in Kent.

I immediately spun him around and pushed him against the bars of the nearest cell. I requested additional personnel to assist in the escort to discourage any further recalcitrant behavior. But when the other deputies arrived, to my surprise they put the boots to the inmate, who was swiftly taken away for medical treatment.

Meanwhile, the sergeant of the watch asked to speak with me in private: "You're not going to cut it in law enforcement, son…unless you understand some simple truths." He then explained that when somebody spits in your face, it constitutes an assault upon your person. He pleaded, "You have one free shot," which he characterized as a "reflexive response" to the assault. And as he began to spar an imaginary foe, he performed an elbow strike and said, "Ideally breaking his nose."

Then, as he demonstrated a hip throw, a takedown technique that was taught in the academy, he continued: "Remember, he's handcuffed with his hands behind his back, so you step in front of him, and you take him down, face first, and plant his skull on the concrete floor." He justified such action by saying, "You're putting him on the floor to prevent any further assault. That's how we do business. That's how we keep control of things."

I had done as we were taught in the academy and used only the amount of force necessary to overcome the resistance posed by the white supremacist after he spat in my face. I was accustomed to being in physical altercations from my hockey days, and I was never known to back down from a fight on the ice, so I was confident in my abilities to handle myself, but only when I needed to do so. But the sergeant was explaining the realities of how an application of force, or lack thereof, would be viewed in my law enforcement career. He not only detailed what force I was expected to use but provided the justification for it. To me, the other deputies had used unnecessary force, the kind that erodes public trust; they had done so in the belief that you maintain control by intimidation, by beating people. It was clear I would have detractors, and as long as men like this sergeant were in positions of influence, perhaps I didn't have a place in law enforcement after all, but I had no intention of conforming. I would not break the law to enforce the law.

Regardless of whether you're trying to enforce the law or break the law, an underlying protocol still needs to be maintained between the law enforcement officer and the "bad actor." If that breaks down, then you get retributive justice through unwarranted police violence that undermines public trust and gives policing a lousy name. A law enforcement officer's oath is a sworn commitment to uphold both the law and the dignity of all individuals, whether criminal or law-abiding.

I saw law enforcement's code of ethics breached too often. This code is meant to be the motivating and essential principle that governs how officers perform their duties with integrity, fairness, and respect for the rights of all people. The code of ethics in law enforcement is not just taught in the academy; it's shaped through a combination of formal instruction, hands-on experience, and professional development and education throughout an officer's career.

The insular culture of policing often demonizes specific groups. This mentality can be so pervasive in law enforcement that it hijacks the profession's stated and intended values, beliefs, and behavioral norms.

Don't get me wrong. Most law enforcement professionals are committed public servants who work within the confines of the law, but there is a subculture, an underbelly of systemic abuses. I've heard it argued that these abuses are necessary, theoretically because "law enforcement is often ugly."

This is not to say that I believe police officers should be pacifists when provoked. There is a time when violence is necessary, when you must get your hands dirty in defense of yourself or others. But part of the problem with police violence, especially when it appears grossly disproportionate to the threat, is rooted in a lack of appropriate training and a culture that undermines what officers should be doing when under stress.

Poorly trained officers often default to the instinctual "fight or flight" response when a threat is perceived. But training alone isn't enough; there's a disconnect between what officers are taught and how they respond in the field. Even well-trained officers can abandon their training and revert to what the culture allows or encourages them to do.

Cracking someone's head open because they spat on you is not a response born of proper judgment. The response is one shaped by a deeper systemic failure, one in which both inadequate training and a toxic culture allow aggression to replace restraint.

* * *

The LA riots didn't emerge from a vacuum. They were the result of decades of systemic inequalities, racial injustices, and the long-standing tension between law enforcement and marginalized communities. For me, they were an awakening to the complexities and failings of the institution I was part of, and they left a lasting influence on my career and perspective.

The immediate spark for the unrest was the LAPD's brutal beating of Rodney King, a Black man, after a high-speed chase in March 1991. King was struck with batons and kicked repeatedly while lying on the ground. The attack, captured on video by George Holliday and first aired by KTLA, shocked the nation when it became one of America's first viral videos. King's injuries were severe—a broken leg, skull fractures, and permanent brain damage. Yet the LAPD initially showed no interest in the video, leaving Holliday to turn to someone who would listen: the media.

Public outrage was swift and intense. Communities in Los Angeles, across the United States, and around the world condemned the excessive force displayed in the footage. In response Mayor Tom Bradley, the city's first African American mayor, formed the Independent Commission on the Los Angeles Police Department and named former FBI Director Warren Christopher to lead it. The Christopher Commission's report, released in July 1991, condemned the LAPD's discriminatory practices and revealed a deeply ingrained culture of racism and excessive force that particularly targeted Black communities. For residents of those neighborhoods, the findings were not revelations but confirmations of what they had lived for decades.

At a press conference Los Angeles Police Chief Daryl Gates said, "We believe the officers used excessive force taking him [Rodney King] into custody. In our view, we find that officers struck him with batons between fifty-three and fifty-six times." The LAPD initially charged King with "felony evading" while driving under the influence of alcohol but later dropped the charge.

The Los Angeles County District Attorney subsequently charged the four LAPD officers, including one sergeant, with assault and use of excessive force.

Despite the overwhelming evidence against the officers, the legal system seemed poised to fail the very people it was meant to protect. The trial of the four LAPD officers was moved to Simi Valley, a predominantly White suburb of Ventura County, where the jury also was predominantly White, angering many and further deepening the public's distrust in the judicial system. The decision reinforced the belief that justice was not for all but was tilted in favor of law enforcement, fueling the outrage that would soon boil over.

On April 29, 1992, after seven days of deliberation, the jury acquitted all four officers of assault and acquitted three of the four on charges of excessive force. The fourth officer's excessive force charge ended in a hung jury.

"The jury's verdict will not blind us to what we saw on that videotape," Mayor Tom Bradely said. "The men who beat Rodney King do not deserve to wear the uniform of the LAPD." President George H. W. Bush said, "Viewed from outside the trial, it was hard to understand how the verdict could possibly square with the video. Those civil rights leaders with whom I met were stunned. And so was I."

Many officers argued that the denunciations of the verdict, broadcast nationwide, provoked the civil unrest. Although the wisdom of making these public statements during such a tumultuous time is open to debate, to assert causation was insidious, a willful aim to detract from any responsibility for the deteriorated relationship between the LAPD and many of the Black communities it serves.

It takes an introspective person to acknowledge and then grasp the significant impact the shameful, racist history of this country has had in stifling the academic and economic opportunities of minorities. The vast majority of officers attributed racial discrepancies to minorities' allegedly low intellect, bad choices, and laziness. As studies have shown, violence is easily rationalized when inflicted on people the oppressor considers inferior. Too many cops lacked an understanding of the influences the years of racial and economic inequalities and authoritarian police practices had on minority communities, priming the city to combust.

When the verdicts were announced, I was having dinner at *Tony Roma's* in Glendale, an LA suburb. The news broke on every television in the restaurant, and chaos unfolded on the screens within minutes. A news broadcast ordered all law enforcement personnel to report to their assignments immediately, a marked contrast to today, as we had neither cell phones nor pagers then. By the time I arrived at my division, riot gear was being distributed. I was deployed to South Los Angeles, specifically the Firestone Station that borders LAPD's 77th Street area, the epicenter of the riots that had erupted at the intersection of Florence and Normandie.

Driving into South LA was something that remains burned into my memory. It was a surreal, unnerving experience. To avoid the most volatile zones we took the 710 Long Beach Freeway and entered the area from the east. From the elevated freeway, the devastation was unmistakable. Fires raged unchecked across the city, their orange flames merging ominously with the fading light of the setting sun. Thick plumes of black smoke twisted skyward, creating a dystopian skyline that suffocated the horizon. The city I had sworn to serve and protect was unrecognizable, transformed into a war zone of chaos and fury. It was unlike anything I had ever witnessed.

When we finally exited the freeway, the reality on the ground was even more shocking. At one point we drove past a strip mall where looters brazenly emptied stores, carrying big-screen TVs, stereo systems, and armloads of clothing. Our marked sheriff's buses, filled with deputies in full riot gear, did nothing to deter them. The looters barely glanced in our direction, their defiance speaking volumes about the fractured relationship between law enforcement and the community. It was a moment that forced me to confront an uncomfortable truth: The authority of the badge meant little to people who had lost all faith in the system it represented.

As the days wore on, the scale of the destruction became more evident. Entire neighborhoods were reduced to ashes with more than 7,000 fires reported and nearly 3,100 businesses destroyed. The financial toll approached $1 billion, but the human cost was far greater: 63 lives lost, over 2,000 injuries, and countless families displaced or devastated.

Being on the ground during that unrest exposed me to some of the most harrowing realities of law enforcement. I witnessed instances of police brutality that mirrored the very issues that had sparked the riots. Looters were beaten and left bleeding in the streets while officers searched for new targets. Some officers even referred to the riots as a "target-rich environment," a phrase that is still unsettling to this day. Those officers weren't concerned about restoring order. They wanted retribution.

The media, politicians, and even some law enforcement officials painted a simplistic narrative, portraying the rioters as criminals without legitimate grievances. President George H. W. Bush, in a public address, blamed the violence on gang members and criminals, dismissing it as "the brutality of a mob, pure and simple." The president's rhetoric ignored the deep-seated inequalities and systemic failures that had driven people to the breaking point.

The state's response during the riots was equally troubling. Immigration agents conducted sweeps, arresting and deporting hundreds of undocumented residents. Of the 16,291 arrests made during the riots, over 1,200 were undocumented immigrants. The LAPD reported it had adhered to the stated policy of not making arrests based on immigration status, a commendable stance amid the chaos. But many of those detained were ultimately handed over to immigration for immediate deportation, a practice that further alienated vulnerable communities. Regardless of your stance on immigration, those mass deportations tore families apart, deepened fear, and reinforced the sense that law enforcement was an occupying force rather than a protector.

In the aftermath of the riots Mayor Bradley appointed former CIA and FBI Director William Webster to lead another commission to evaluate the LAPD's response. The Webster Commission's report, released on Oct. 21, 1992, criticized the department's lack of preparation, poor intelligence, and inability to control the unrest. Yet, like the Christopher Commission before it, the report fell short of confronting the deeper systemic issues in law enforcement that fueled the widespread anger and mistrust. The official responses leaned heavily on punitive measures, focusing on restoring order rather than on understanding the root causes of the riots. That approach missed a critical opportunity to rebuild trust and address the systemic failures that had brought the city to the brink.

The riots were more than a moment of reckoning for Los Angeles, they were a wake-up call for me. They exposed the weaknesses in the relationship between law enforcement and the communities we are sworn to protect, fractures that had been overlooked, dismissed, or willfully ignored for far too long. Those six days of disorder didn't just devastate the city, they forced me to question how policing needed to change to build trust and create lasting safety. The riots underscored the vital importance of law enforcement understanding the communities they serve, addressing their concerns, and fostering relationships built on mutual respect. Without those elements, the cycle of violence and mistrust will persist, leaving cities like Los Angeles vulnerable to future eruptions.

For those of us in law enforcement this challenge goes beyond professional duty. It is a moral imperative. We owe it to the communities we serve to face these hard truths and act on them. The lessons of 1992 remain as urgent today as they were then: Justice for all requires accountability, empathy, and the courage to embrace systemic change. Without it, we're not just failing our profession, we're failing the very people who need us most.

* * *

I recently re-read a letter I had written to my father back in 1992 during my time with the LA County Sheriff's Department. I was telling him about things I was doing with the department, particularly work that dealt with an issue law enforcement still struggles with today: racial diversity in both policing and the communities it serves. Even in the early stages of my career I was drawn to engaging with the community and gaining a better understanding of people whose upbringing, socioeconomic status, and opportunities were vastly different from mine.

Of course, my father and mother had instilled that perspective in me. My father constantly challenged me to think deeper about community issues. I would share with him experiences I had in the field, things I thought I had figured out, only to realize, through his insight, that I had barely scratched the surface. Those conversations weren't about dictating how things are but about exposing me to a more in-depth thought process that would lead to a more comprehensive understanding of the issues.

In a way, this book is a continuation of that conversation with him, even though he's no longer with us. He would ask me two essential questions:

If the community is at the heart of any law enforcement mission, what is the unique contribution of the organizational managers?

What can the people who lead police departments do to engage with their communities as partners and not as prohibitors?

My father's influence stayed with me as I navigated my early years in policing, pushing me to see beyond the badge and look deeper at the impact of institutional decisions.

Transitioning from the structured environment of the academy to life as a deputy working in the jails required more than just professional adaptation. It required a conscious effort to balance work and personal life, especially in a field that often demands so much of its personnel. I was well-liked at work but deliberately compartmentalized my job from my personal life. I intentionally tried diversifying my friendships, spending most of my off-duty time with non-law enforcement friends. This choice helped me maintain a sense of identity beyond the badge.

During that time I began dating a fellow deputy sheriff named Teri. What stood out to me about her wasn't just her beauty, strength, and intelligence. We shared understanding of the importance of keeping work and personal life separate.

That ability to compartmentalize is a key aspect of emotional intelligence. It allows us to manage stress, maintain focus, and stay balanced by giving each area of life its proper attention. For those of us in law enforcement, this skill isn't just helpful; it's essential for coping with the job's emotional and mental toll while preserving personal well-being.

Teri and I formed a deep connection over this shared perspective, and though our romantic relationship eventually ended, our respect and friendship endured. To this day we remain close, and I often make a point to visit her when I'm in Los Angeles. She's even met my son, which speaks to the lasting value of the bond we built.

As a Black woman, Teri was more attuned than I was to how others viewed our interracial relationship. Perhaps because I had grown up with racially diverse siblings I was better at tuning out the noise of racism, or perhaps I was unaware of my perceived White privilege. In my heart, the prejudice wasn't something to dwell on, but that didn't make it any less real or disruptive.

One night Teri took me to a comedy club in Hyde Park, just off Crenshaw Boulevard. It was an eye-opening experience. I was the only non-Black person, and it didn't take long for the comedian to go off-script and zero in on us. He began patronizing Teri, questioning why she was dating "Whitey" when there were so many good Black men around. Teri, tough as ever, sat through it for a while, but she eventually nudged my arm, signaling that we should leave.

That night underscored the complexities of interracial relationships and navigating racism from both sides. For Teri, the challenges were often louder and more direct. For me, they were something I was only beginning to understand. But those experiences also reinforced what my parents had always taught me: relationships, like families, are defined by commitment and respect, not by others' narrow-minded judgments.

* * *

It eventually became apparent that being a deputy sheriff wouldn't live up to my expectations. Historically, deputies were transferred to patrol assignments after a year, but budget cuts had significantly slowed that process. Many deputies were stuck in the jail system for five or six years before they ever set foot in a police car. Working in the jails felt like I was serving a sentence of my own, and I needed to be paroled.

Jails are a toxic environment, not just for the inmates but for those working within their walls. Fresh out of the academy, many deputies were eager to prove themselves, subscribing to an unspoken tradition of violence to maintain control over the inmate population. That mindset was reinforced by a belief deeply embedded in law enforcement culture—that the public, and especially the inmates, were fundamentally opposed to them. When left unchecked, such a belief creates a justification for abusing authority and engaging in acts of senseless violence.

One moment of my jail time still stands out. I was assigned to the release desk with a senior deputy. Our job was to process inmates being released, ensuring their fingerprints matched those taken when they arrived. During one shift an inmate sucked his teeth in a show of disrespect to the senior deputy. In response, the deputy swung his ASP, a leather impact device reinforced with steel, across the inmate's face, breaking his jaw.

Instead of walking free, the inmate was transported to the medical ward on the thirteenth floor of the University of Southern California Medical Center. The violence was unnecessary, and it wasn't what I believed police work should be. Yet this kind of force was amazingly common and accepted among the deputies because it was seen as maintaining control.

I struggled with how to respond. I knew that reporting the incident to a supervisor would fall on deaf ears, considering the scolding I had previously received when the white supremacist spat in my face. It was clear that supervision endorsed violence as a means of control. Speaking up in a system that tolerated, or even encouraged, such behavior was risky. I turned to my father for advice, and his guidance helped me understand the complexities of my situation.

I decided to confront the senior deputy privately, and in no uncertain terms, I said, "Listen, I'm not cool with what happened. It's never going to happen again...not in front of me." My tone, posture, and expression left no room for doubt. If it happened again, I wouldn't hesitate to report him. The consequences might not be good for either of us, but I wouldn't stand by and allow abuse to continue.

But it wasn't about just that one deputy or that one incident. It was about the culture. Too often deputies lacked the skills to handle physical confrontations appropriately. When fights broke out between inmates, some deputies would respond with indiscriminate violence, swinging metal flashlights wildly and striking anything within reach. It was less about restoring order and more about punishment and degradation, a dangerous gauntlet that eroded respect for law enforcement and fueled retaliation from inmates. The cycle of violence makes it more unsafe for anyone wearing the uniform.

That culture of unchecked aggression wasn't unique to my experience. Thomas Parker, a former FBI agent and assistant special agent in charge of the bureau's Los Angeles Field Office, once assessed the Los Angeles County Jail system. His findings were damning:

Of all the jails I have had the occasion to visit, tour, or conduct investigations within, domestically and internationally, I have never experienced any facility exhibiting the volume and repetitive patterns of violence, misfeasance, and malfeasance impacting the Los Angeles County jail system.

Parker's words underscored what I already knew: I couldn't continue to work in such an environment.

When I decided to leave the LA County Sheriff's Department I wasn't giving up on law enforcement, I was still searching for a path toward making a positive impact on it. This decision brought me full circle back to the LAPD, which itself had become infamous for the systemic issues that had been laid bare for the world to see. Still, I believed that if there was any department where change could start, it had to be this one.

The second time through the hiring process was challenging. At the time, the LAPD based its hiring decisions on the percentage score achieved during interviews. I scored the maximum, 100 percent. But candidates with military experience were awarded an additional five points, allowing them to score as high as 105 percent. My perfect score wasn't enough for someone without a military background.

Each month, candidates gathered at the LAPD headquarters for hiring certification. We were divided into lines based on gender and race. Once at the front of the line, we provided our names and interview scores. Despite attending several certification sessions, I wasn't hired, and I finally decided to ask why.

The explanation was clear but deeply frustrating: The positions allotted for White male candidates were filled by individuals whose scores exceeded 100 percent due to military service, while candidates of other races were hired with significantly lower scores than mine.

I deeply respect military veterans and their sacrifices, but excluding fully qualified candidates like me felt wrong. I thought it undermined the principles of fairness and equal treatment that law enforcement is supposed to uphold. A White male without military experience need not apply. If such biases existed within the hiring process, how could the department claim to treat citizens equitably in the communities it served? It was a contradiction I couldn't ignore.

Determined to fight for what I believed was right, I expressed my frustration with the hiring process and explained that I intended to consult legal counsel if necessary. Shortly afterward I was hired as a lateral officer, a candidate transferring from another law enforcement agency, and the next chapter of my career began.

Joining the LAPD as a lateral officer came with its own challenges. My training group was small, just seven of us, and our academy focused on the LAPD's unique policies and procedures. We also had to demonstrate proficiency in defensive tactics, firearms manipulation, and marksmanship. It wasn't long before I encountered one of the starkest examples of how insular the law enforcement culture could be.

One of my first observations was the conflicting firearms training philosophies between the LAPD and the LA County Sheriff's Department. At the sheriff's department, we were taught that untrained suspects were likely to "slap the trigger," causing their shots to go high and to the right, often over an officer's left shoulder. But the LAPD trained its officers to expect suspects to "mash the trigger," leading to shots going low and to the right of the officer. The sheriff's department had taught me to step to the right when firing, but if the LAPD's premise was correct, that practice could inadvertently place an officer directly in the line of fire.

Both methods couldn't be correct, so I couldn't help but question the disparity. Was there conflicting data, or had each department simply developed its own approach based on anecdotal evidence? I wanted answers, not just for the sake of clarity but because the stakes couldn't be higher. When I brought up my concerns, I expected a constructive conversation. Instead, I was met with resistance. My inquiry was perceived as challenging the LAPD's authority rather than an opportunity to reconcile conflicting approaches.

"Who are you to question the methods of the LAPD?" was the response I received.

That reaction was another example of law enforcement's insular culture. Instead of fostering an environment where ideas and experiences could be shared to improve practices, the department seemed more concerned with maintaining its own authority. This wasn't just about conflicting shooting stances; it was emblematic of a deeper unwillingness to embrace critical thinking.

Despite the resistance I faced during training, I was determined to succeed as an LAPD officer. But I knew that the real challenges were ahead, not in the academy or training sessions, but on the streets of Los Angeles, those same streets that had burned during the LA Riots, those same communities that were still simmering with tension.

As I stepped into my role I carried with me the lessons I had learned in the jails, the academy, and my previous experience as a deputy sheriff. But nothing could have fully prepared me for the realities of policing in a city as vast and complex as Los Angeles.

The LAPD was a department under a microscope, its actions scrutinized by a public that had lost trust in its ability to serve and protect without bias. This was the environment in which I began my next chapter, one that would test not only my skills but also my values and my belief in what law enforcement could be and should be.

I knew that asking tough questions and challenging the status quo wouldn't always be welcome. But I also knew that change doesn't happen by staying silent.

My journey with the LAPD was just beginning, and it would push me to confront the realities of a profession I had once idealized, forcing me to grapple with the complexities of policing in one of America's most challenging urban environments.

Chapter 3:
Reflections from the Field

Productivity is never an accident. It is always the result of a commitment to excellence, intelligent planning, and focused effort.

—Paul J. Meyer

I began my life as a probationary officer with the LAPD in 1993 at the 77th Street Division, the epicenter of the Rodney King riots just a year earlier. The weight of those events lingered heavily over the community and the department. Tensions were high, and in many ways the police were seen as the enemy. What I hadn't anticipated but soon came to understand was that the public was the enemy to many officers too. One of those officers was about to make that attitude abundantly clear.

I worked with this officer only once. I'll call him "The Shadow," not because he carried any real mystery but because his presence revealed a darker side of the profession. The Shadow embodied the attitudes that festered in the margins.

Everything was going as expected until we drove past an interracial couple, a Black woman and a White man. Without hesitation or thought, he muttered, "My parents taught me better than that." When I asked him to explain, he left me stunned: "My parents taught me never to have sex with animals." The "animal" he referred to was the Black woman.

Not only did I have an African American foster sister, but for two years I had been dating Teri, a distinguished LA County

Sheriff's deputy who happened to be Black. Teri, a Los Angeles native, had opened my eyes to the strained relationship between law enforcement and the Black community in ways I never could have understood on my own.

I was welcomed into her world with open arms, including regular Sunday dinners at her Aunt Edna's house in Inglewood. Those evenings were filled with laughter, peach cobbler, and an abundance of love, much like the way I was brought up. The warmth and close bond of her family were worlds away from the hateful nonsense I encountered on the job.

Teri had always been candid about the challenges faced by the Black community in Los Angeles, especially when it came to law enforcement. Growing up in LA, she had endured her share of slurs and indignities at the hands of police officers, experiences that shaped her understanding of how racism thrived in environments of indifference. To her, meaningful change would require nothing less than a complete cultural overhaul, a daunting task that wouldn't come easily or quickly.

Hearing my LAPD partner's words that day left me with a mix of surprise, concern, and disbelief. His casual racism, spoken with the confidence of someone who assumed I shared his views, was a harsh introduction to the culture I had stepped into. He wrongly believed that because we wore the same uniform and shared the same skin color, I shared his racist views. All I could think was, *You're a fuckin' idiot.* I immediately knew I didn't want to work with him again, but I also suspected he wasn't the only one in the department with those views. Beliefs and attitudes influence judgment and behavior, and as my partner, he would be perceived as a reflection of me, which made me uncomfortable.

He acted as if his racist belief was a universally accepted truth, and that forced me to confront some uncomfortable questions. Could I, just one officer, effect change while wearing a uniform that, to many, represented racism and brutality? Was the racist image of the LAPD deserved? Had racism been allowed to remain unchecked for decades?

The racial overtones of that remark spoke volumes. The comment came from an officer serving in a community where racial tensions had erupted into violent riots just a year prior. I couldn't shake the thought that this very mindset, the ignorance and bigotry on display, had fueled the anger that led to the unrest in the first place. Nothing had been learned. That realization pushed me to consider a different path, one where I could drive change through promotion and the greater scope and scale of influence it provided.

Little progress has been made. Recently, LAPD officers from the department's Recruitment and Employment Division had been unknowingly recorded saying racist and sexist remarks in relation to police applicants, the very people they were to be considering for hire. Although Chief Jim McDonnell was quoted as saying to the *Los Angeles Times,* "We don't tolerate that type of behavior in the workplace," it demonstrates that, although progress has been made, the systemic reality of racism still plagues law enforcement. The difficult truth is that within this organization, the culture was so permissive that officers of various ranks felt comfortable engaging in this degrading behavior with seemingly no fear of consequence. Although likely meant as an attempt at humor, it underscores the inability to regulate behavior in relation to societal expectations.

Teri supported my ambition to rise through the ranks, firmly believing that real change could only be achieved from positions of leadership. Yet, as my career progressed, I noticed a growing distance between us. Eventually, as I mentioned before, we went our separate ways, though we remain close friends.

Later, Teri revealed the real reason for our breakup: She believed our interracial relationship would hinder my ability to rise within the department. The "good ol' boy" culture of the LAPD wouldn't look kindly on the White officer who was dating a Black woman.

Her decision hurt, but looking back, I see that she was probably right. Our relationship might not have prevented me from being promoted, but it likely would have made it more difficult. Yet, had I been allowed to choose between Teri and career advancement, without hesitation, I would have chosen Teri.

It wasn't just personal relationships that were subject to the racist culture. The department's leadership was thought to reflect the same narrow mindset. Assistant Chief Robert Vernon, the second-in-command to Chief Daryl Gates, was a well-known figure within the LAPD. He was also a controversial one, accused of allowing his fundamentalist Christian beliefs to influence his decisions, creating an atmosphere of intolerance that trickled down through the ranks. Vernon oversaw more than 80 percent of the department's daily operations, and his influence was palpable.

According to a 1987 *Los Angeles Times* article, union officials believed that fundamentalist Christians received favorable consideration for promotions and transfers under

Vernon. His widely circulated audiotapes, recorded over two decades, were criticized for espousing intolerance toward women, homosexuals, and others.

As I navigated those early days, I saw the issues weren't confined to individual officers or isolated incidents. They were built into the culture that prioritized power over accountability, loyalty over integrity, and silence over excellence. Like my partner's comment, the culture assumed complicity and punished dissent. If I was going to make a difference, I knew it wouldn't be easy. I also knew that doing nothing wasn't an option.

* * *

Transitioning from the personal challenges I faced as a probationary officer to the broader realities of the job, I quickly learned that the dangers of law enforcement weren't always as straightforward as responding to a crime scene or engaging with a suspect. Policing demanded a constant balancing act: decisive action under pressure, split-second decisions, and the ability to adapt to unpredictable circumstances.

On one particular day, my partner, "The Car Commander," was driving, and I was "keeping the books," a term for the officer responsible for writing reports and managing the information coming through the car's computer. Tactical responsibilities were clearly defined. The driver made the initial contact during public interactions, whether on a radio call or spotting suspicious activity, while the officer keeping the books acted as the cover officer, scanning the area for secondary threats. The division of duties was designed to ensure the safety and efficiency of every interaction, though it would soon be tested in ways I hadn't experienced.

The radio dispatcher's voice crackled with an urgent code-three call—lights and sirens on full alert. "Assault with a deadly weapon in progress. Shots fired." The words sent an immediate surge of adrenaline through my body. Policing is inherently high stakes, requiring officers to respond to rapidly evolving, sometimes life-threatening situations. Split-second decisions are the norm, and the weight of those decisions can mean the difference between life and death. Even before we arrived, I could feel the tension mounting. Those types of calls test every ounce of your training, resolve, and ability to think under pressure. They also expose the gap between textbook tactics and the messy, unpredictable reality of the field.

The address led us to a two-story duplex on an east-west street. As we approached, I noted the positioning dictated by our route. The direction we were driving would place my partner closest to the duplex and the armed suspect. The details of the call painted a grim picture. A domestic dispute had escalated into violence. A man armed with an AK-47 had shot his fleeing girlfriend in the leg, thwarting her escape and shattering her femur. She lay bleeding on the front porch; blood streaked across the sidewalk where he had dragged her back toward the house. The reality of what awaited us hit harder with every second.

What happened next would underscore the critical nature of tactical decision making in law enforcement. It would also reveal how even a momentary lapse in judgment could put lives, including our own, at risk. The scene we rolled into would soon become one of the most intense and defining moments of my career.

From a tactical standpoint, we made an error. Partners are to communicate to ensure the best and safest decisions are being made, but we pulled directly in front of the suspect's duplex and stopped on the apron of the driveway. While my partner controlled the vehicle, we shared responsibility for this tactical misstep.

We should have stopped our vehicle a few houses down from the duplex, exited the vehicle, and alternately moved to positions of cover in a gradual approach to the location, all the while broadcasting our observations to the other responding units and requesting additional resources if needed. That was no longer an option. Our position left us vulnerable and so exposed that, for the suspect, it would be like shooting fish in a barrel.

Police cars didn't have ballistic door panels at the time, but even if they had, they wouldn't have stopped a round from an AK-47. The rifle has the capacity to fire up to 600 rounds per minute, but it also can fire single shots or bursts of two or three to increase accuracy. The only thing that would stop an AK-47 round was our car's engine block.

We had to get out of the car as quickly as possible and keep the car as a barrier between us and the approaching suspect. The passenger side was our only escape option. I opened the door and threw myself out, landing with my legs up on the seat and my shoulders on the concrete pavement of the street. Serving as a makeshift ramp, I pulled my partner over the top of me. He then hurried to the rear of the car, presumably because it was farthest from the suspect.

But that position provided the least cover. A basic rule in police tactics is to know the difference between cover and concealment. Cover provides protection from bullets while concealment only prevents observation. So I took a position against the front passenger tire, which afforded me the cover of the engine block. And I thought, *Holy shit, where is this guy? Is he advancing on us?*

In stressful confrontations, my perception is that time slows down, allowing me to have entire conversations with myself in just a few seconds. I remember thinking, *Well, I don't really want to look over the hood of the car, because a mistimed peek could be messy.* And I thought, *I can't do that to my dad.*

Then I looked from under the car, hoping I could see the suspect's legs as he approached. That would help me decide how to respond tactically and neutralize him as a threat. Unfortunately, the yard and driveway were elevated from the street, so my line of sight was limited to just beyond the sidewalk, and the suspect would be nearly on top of me by the time I could see his position.

I anticipated that the shooter would likely come around the front of the car. That was my gut feeling. So I lay on my back and aimed up over the front of the car. I even had the presence of mind to thumb-cock the hammer of my handgun. In other words, I manually cocked the hammer back in single-action mode to maximize accuracy, as it greatly reduced the amount of trigger pressure necessary to fire a round. I would have time for one or two shots, and I would need to make each one count. A headshot was needed, or my time would run out, and things would end badly.

As we waited for backup and reassessed our options, the arrival of the LAPD Air Support Division was the turning point we desperately needed. The helicopter, piloted by a Vietnam

War veteran, quickly shifted the suspect's focus. A commanding voice boomed above us, "Hey, motherfucker, look up here!" The blunt approach was startlingly effective. The suspect's attention snapped away from us, redirecting his fire toward the helicopter, giving us the critical moment we needed to redeploy and avert the immediate threat.

Under fire, the pilot displayed remarkable skill in executing swift evasive maneuvers. He flew straight up the driveway, rapidly climbed, and then sharply descended into a tight right turn, disappearing behind nearby buildings and out of the suspect's view. The maneuvers were flawless. His courageous act likely saved our lives and led to the helicopter personnel being recognized with the Police Medal, the second-highest honor for valor.

We moved from the car to a safer position behind some trees. The shooter, unaware of our new location, returned to the porch where he had earlier dragged his wounded girlfriend. She was bleeding heavily. The duplex had two front doors, and one led directly to a stairwell inside their unit. Leaving the door open, the suspect sat on the stairs with only his legs visible and used a landline phone to communicate with the police dispatch center. While he wasn't an immediate threat, we were still pinned down in the hot zone, armed only with our 9mm Beretta semi-automatic handguns.

A tactical alert was issued because this was considered an incident of significant importance and required the mobilization of citywide personnel and resources. All hands were on deck; nobody was going home. Although we were pinned down, there was a flurry of police activity around us. Traffic was being redirected, neighboring residences were being evacuated, containment was being established, and witnesses were being identified and interviewed, a masterful example of LAPD's skill in handling such chaos.

Since 1967, SWAT has served as the LAPD's specialized response unit for high-risk incidents, deploying only in situations that exceed the capabilities of standard patrol officers. In this instance, the suspect was armed, posed a significant threat to the lives of the public and police personnel, and was afforded elements of cover and concealment at his position on the stairwell. The SWAT personnel arrived and systematically replaced the patrol officers on interior containment and hurriedly deployed sniper teams into concealed positions. A sniper can see what others making tactical decisions cannot. So a sniper's job includes intelligence gathering through observation while remaining prepared to fire and take a life to save a life.

As the suspect became visibly agitated and began to stand, the police dispatcher, who had remained on the phone with the suspect, broadcast, "He's going to shoot her in the head!" As the suspect left the concealment afforded him on the stairwell, shots rang out from the evacuated homes directly across the street. The suspect instantly toppled forward and landed in a contorted position at the base of the steps. He was hit three times, in the knee, in the chest, and in the neck, before collapsing like a top-heavy sack of potatoes. He was dead. It seemed like we had been pinned down forever, and the entire incident is ingrained in my head for life.

Of course, we had to give a statement as part of the investigation into the shooting. By happenstance, I eventually became officer-in-charge of the detectives responsible for investigating officer-involved shootings and lethal force incidents. But back then, the investigations were elementary. The interviews were casual conversations in which investigators shared their understanding of the events rather than an impartial inquiry intended to gather the facts.

In essence, the justification for the shooting was elicited through closed-ended questions that required a simple "yes" or "no" answer. There was no question the shooting was justified. The suspect was trying to kill my partner and me, and if that LAPD chopper had not arrived when it did, he might have done so. His actions and statements over the phone made it reasonable to believe he was about to kill his girlfriend. The shooting was in immediate defense of her life.

It turned out that the shooter had full-blown AIDS, making him the most dangerous of all suspects—he had nothing to lose. We didn't know that until later, of course, and there were other lessons, many of which were about the reality of the environment I was policing. I have long said that police officers are not paid for what they do every day but for what, God forbid, they may have to do.

Afterward, the weight of what had happened began to take its toll. The stress of the situation left its imprint on me in ways I couldn't ignore. I dealt with persistent digestive issues, struggled to sleep, and felt an exhaustion that no amount of sleep seemed to remedy.

The events of that day didn't just alter how I approached my work. They fundamentally reshaped the focus of my career. I had always been ambitious, striving for excellence, but that experience highlighted the crucial importance of not just being capable but also commanding a full range of skills. Our tactical misstep had made us dangerously vulnerable to the point of risking our lives. That realization changed everything.

For my partner, the aftermath was even more life-changing. The experience led him to a non-field assignment with limited public interaction. His was a deliberate choice to step away from the type of danger we'd faced.

Soon after the life-threatening standoff with the armed suspect, I found myself confronting another, albeit different, challenge that defined the streets of Los Angeles: the pervasive influence of gang culture. Policing the Rollin' 60s Neighborhood Crips required not only vigilance but also a deep understanding of the environment.

The Rollin' 60s and its rival gang, the Bloods, embodied the cycle of violence and crime that had festered in the city since the 1960s and 1970s. While the Bloods wore red, the Crips wore blue, colors that signified not just gang allegiance but a violent criminal element. The Rollin' 60s originated in 1976 from the Westside Crips and expanded their reach nationwide. It was in their territory that I responded to a gruesome drive-by shooting in which a Rollin' 60s member was killed while sitting on a bus bench at Crenshaw Boulevard and Hyde Park. The victim was riddled with rounds from an AK-47, his life violently cut short by the cycle of retaliatory shootings that defined gang wars.

As the junior officer, I was tasked with maintaining the crime scene log. That experience was only the beginning of how deeply those encounters would shape my perspective as I aimed to command all aspects of police work.

* * *

No one succeeds alone, especially in law enforcement. As officers, we work within our organizations, surrounded by highly individualistic and often egotistical personalities that shape the culture. My partner at the time, "The Linebacker," was a rare exception. He was smart, steady, and physically and mentally strong, a reliable presence on the otherwise unpredictable streets of Los Angeles. He had a way of cutting through the noise and confusion. He was always ready to act with purpose.

He grew up in a housing project in South LA and overcame the enticement of gang life by channeling his energy into athletics and, eventually, law enforcement. Built like an NFL linebacker, he exuded quiet confidence, the kind you couldn't fake. He never bragged about his abilities; he didn't have to. He simply applied them when needed.

I'll never forget the day I learned about his martial arts expertise. We had a suspect turn violent, and before I could react, The Linebacker had him on the ground and cuffed faster than a cowboy roping a steer. When I told him I had no idea about his martial arts background and his ability to be so agile in taking a violent person into custody, he just shrugged and said, "Those who can't...talk. Those who can, well, they just do."

Although we had nearly no interaction after working as partners, I'll always hold the utmost respect for him. His actions spoke louder than words ever could, and his presence set a standard of professionalism that I've carried with me ever since.

What defined us as partners wasn't just our shared commitment to the job but also our mutual dedication to fitness.

It wasn't about vanity; it was about readiness. The way we presented ourselves mattered. Our appearances influenced how the public perceived us as officers and directly affected our abilities to perform under pressure. We even dedicated our meal breaks to working out, demonstrating how we prioritized our physical conditioning. Our commitment to fitness and personal discipline didn't just make us stronger. Our fitness may have saved our lives.

One night while on patrol, we observed a known Rollin' 60s gang member loitering in a parking lot and glancing into parked cars, a behavior that matched the profile of an auto burglary suspect. Without hesitation, The Linebacker swooped our patrol car into the lot. As I exited the passenger door, the gang member's eyes met mine. He was sizing me up and calculating whether to comply, run, or fight.

Instantly, my partner and I noticed a bulge in his waistband, a common spot for concealing a gun. We took cover behind separate parked cars and ordered him to the ground at gunpoint. A pat-down for weapons confirmed our suspicions. He was armed with a fully loaded .357 Magnum revolver, a firearm with a muzzle velocity far greater than the 9mm handguns we carried at the time. His weapon offered greater penetration, increasing the potential to incapacitate or kill.

A noticeable trait of officers who perform well under pressure is their acquaintance with an arrestee after the offer prevails over the stress of an inherent threat. We want to better understand the mindset of a criminal, especially to enhance officer safety. The tactical failure of putting ourselves in close proximity to an armed gang member could have cost us our lives, as it has so many LAPD officers, so it prompted The

Linebacker to ask the gang member why he chose not to shoot it out with us.

The answer was both enlightening and confirming: "Trust me. I thought about taking you out. But look at you guys. I could tell you both can get it done," (vernacular for an ability to succeed in a deadly confrontation). "If I took one of you out, I knew the other would have killed me."

The importance of our commitment to physical fitness, which was so often ridiculed by our peers, provided a command presence and uniform appearance that may have saved our lives that day.

* * *

For a few months I was partnered with an officer we'll call "The Translator." He had grown up in Nickerson Gardens, the largest public housing project west of the Mississippi River. Known as the birthplace of the Bounty Hunters Bloods gang, Nickerson Gardens was a community shaped by hardship, history, and culture. My partner, having lived that life firsthand, understood the nuances of the environment in ways I never could. His ability to navigate both the streets and the badge made him an invaluable bridge between two worlds.

That day we responded to a radio call of a felonious assault. The victim was easy to spot, standing in the driveway with a bloody gash on his forehead. I asked him what happened, and his response left me baffled: "I came here to get some stank on my hang low, and the bitch hit me upside the head with a smoothie." I stood there perplexed, trying to process what I'd just heard. My thought was, *What does that even mean?!*

My partner, far more fluent in the cultural vernacular, laughed and shook his head. Recognizing my confusion, he smirked and offered a translation. The victim, he explained, had come to have sex and ended up getting hit over the head with a clothes iron, which he referred to as a "smoothie" because it smooths out wrinkles. Suddenly, the entire scene became clear, and I couldn't help but laugh at my own ignorance.

On another occasion, we were dispatched to an "unknown trouble" radio call. Upon arrival it became apparent we were dealing with a medical emergency where a man had fallen unconscious after suffering a seizure. While his wife tended to him, I asked if he was on any medication. "Yeah," she said, "peanut butter balls." Thinking I had misunderstood, I asked again, only to receive the same answer, "peanut butter balls."

Once again, The Translator laughed at my bewildered look. "She means phenobarbital," he explained, referring to the drug commonly used to manage epileptic seizures.

Experiences like these underscored how much I had yet to learn, not just about the job but also about the people I was sworn to protect. The Translator's cultural fluency went beyond mere words; he possessed an understanding of the lived experiences and the unspoken rules of a world I hadn't grown up in. He didn't just translate for me. He taught me the value of listening, learning, and meeting people where they were.

* * *

In law enforcement, we train for optimal outcomes when navigating stressful, rapidly unfolding scenarios. We train to chase suspects. We run drills. We talk tactics. We practice coordination and vehicle control. What we don't train enough for is the development of risk-analysis skills that prevent avoidable tragedies.

There's a line I remember clearly from a former partner, whom I'll call "The Wise One.": "I'm not dying in this car." That wasn't fear. That was wisdom earned through experience. His tenure made him familiar with what happens when officers justify recklessness through self-imposed urgency. During code-three responses, he came to a full stop at every intersection. Lights on. Siren blaring. But still, full stop. Because if you crash, you've become the problem and are no longer part of the solution.

His philosophy resonated with me through a lesson I had already learned from an avoidable traumatic incident early in my career.

I was part of a stolen vehicle pursuit that went horribly wrong. The suspect blew through an intersection and slammed into a family vehicle. Two young children were ejected from the vehicle and died at the scene. I can still see them. I still remember the mother's screams, the image of two lifeless bodies, her children lying dead in the street. The world just stopped in that moment. An entire family was devastated. Gone in seconds. And for what? Nothing more than a suspected property crime.

The impact of that day never left me. I carried it into every future decision I made, especially when I found myself in the position of calling off a pursuit. While we often imagine police pursuits as cinematic, adrenaline-filled races to justice, the reality is far more complicated and far more deadly.

These incidents are often dismissed as unavoidable evils or as necessary evils, but they are not unavoidable or necessary. In many cases, these incidents are predictable consequences of outdated policies, unchecked impulse, and a persistent cultural belief that letting suspects get away is worse than risking everything to stop them.

According to the National Highway Traffic Safety Administration, 577 people were killed in pursuit-related crashes in 2022. More officers died that year in pursuits than in shootings. The National Law Enforcement Officers Memorial Fund confirms this trend. The job is dangerous enough. We don't need to be creating more danger through decisions that lack solid justification.

Not just officers are at risk. A *San Francisco Chronicle* investigation revealed that from 2017 to 2022, over 3,300 people were killed during police chases. Over half of them weren't suspects. They were passengers, pedestrians, or completely uninvolved members of the public. People walking to school. People on their lunch breaks. People in the wrong places at the wrong times, paying the price for someone else's decision.

That alone should stop us in our tracks. It often doesn't.

In recent years, some jurisdictions have rolled back pursuit restrictions, believing that more lax pursuit policies will deter suspects from fleeing, but the data tells a different story. According to *Stateline*, after Milwaukee loosened its restrictions, police chases increased fifteenfold. Still, there was no corresponding drop in crime. The only measurable increase was in risk to officers, to the public, and to the reputation of the department.

Here's the hard truth. Researchers from academia and law enforcement widely accept that thirty-five to forty percent of all vehicular police pursuits end in a collision. Most of these chases aren't for violent felonies. Statistically, only about one in fifteen pursuit-related fatalities involve someone wanted for a violent crime. The rest involve property crimes, traffic infractions, suspicion of a stolen car, or, in some cases, nothing at all beyond someone's gut instinct that a driver looked suspicious and refused to pull over.

We have to ask ourselves: Is that worth it?

What actually deters crime isn't the fear of being chased. It's the belief that if you commit a crime, you'll ultimately be arrested, even if not at that moment. That doesn't require a dangerous pursuit. It requires sound investigative work, coordinated follow-up, and strong clearance rates. In many cases, we already have the tools. License plate readers. Surveillance footage. Interagency cooperation. What we lack is the discipline to pause and use them instead of defaulting to the gas pedal.

This isn't about going soft. It's about being smart. It's about shifting the internal compass from, "Did we follow protocol?" to "Was this pursuit necessary?" "Did it serve our mission?" "Could we have achieved the same result with less risk?"

That's the shift that leadership must champion. Because officers under pressure will fall back on training, instincts, and department culture. If we continue to glorify the chase and equate hesitation with weakness, we are detracting from developing the judgment essential to ensure safer outcomes.

Real courage doesn't always come with sirens. It shows up in the ability to say no, even when the adrenaline is telling you to go. It shows up in the supervisor who calls off a chase when it's safer to regroup. It shows up in the officer who resists the impulse to win in the moment and instead focuses on winning long-term through restraint, accountability, and preserving life.

This isn't just a policy issue. It's a mindset issue. A cultural issue. It's about embedding judgment into every level of the chain, from rookie officers all the way up to the chief.

Pursuits will always be part of policing, but they should be rare, well-reasoned, and followed by serious review. If they aren't, then we're not protecting the community. We're endangering it. And no one joins this profession to add names to a memorial wall unnecessarily.

Police are responsible not only for the people they chase, but for everyone they pass along the way.

* * *

After working nearly two years at the 77th Division, I transferred to the Central Traffic Division and became a traffic accident investigator. While the roles differed significantly, my commitment to understanding and engaging with the community remained the same. I was intentional with my time between calls and often went into the projects, fully uniformed, to play basketball or throw the football with the kids. Spending time with them wasn't just an outlet for me to blow off some steam and stretch my legs. It was a chance to connect with the people I served, to build trust and break down barriers. It helped me learn about the culture and relate to the realities of life in those neighborhoods. More importantly, it showed those children that the police were not their enemy, and they weren't the enemy of the police.

It reminded me of playing with my foster sister, Venessa, and the other kids in her inner-city Cleveland neighborhood when I was a kid. The laughter and camaraderie felt like home. While many of my peers ridiculed me for taking the time to engage that way, I didn't let that stop me. I thought, *If these interactions influence just one child to resist the pull of the gang lifestyle, my efforts would be well worth it.*

Those little athletic breaks reminded me why I chose a law enforcement career in the first place. Sometimes, the most impactful work happens outside the official duties of the badge, and athletics is an excellent way to facilitate that. When you get into organized sports, and the families of these kids start getting involved, the real magic happens. When I was on the LAPD hockey team, we would often set up charity games against celebrities and organize other events to benefit different causes.

Meeting the kids and seeing their faces light up as they spent time with the team was a reminder of the impact we could have, whether we were in our patrol uniforms or our hockey jerseys. Whether on the ice with NHL legends like Luke Robitaille and Dave Taylor, or alongside celebrities like Chad Lowe, Cuba Gooding Jr., and Dave Coulier, those games were about more than just cops playing sports. Whether in a professional arena or a neighborhood park, they offered a chance to show the human side of law enforcement and build connections in communities that needed those connections most.

And it's not just my story. Some of the most iconic athletes in American history credit *caring police officers* for helping them find the right paths. In a candid Fox News interview, George Foreman, when speaking of his experience and those of other fighters like Muhammad Ali and Joe Frazier, recalled, "The police rescued us. The police, they were our buddies." When the interviewer pushed back, saying that's not what people say about the police today, Foreman didn't waver, sharing, "No, but they rescued us, Muhammad Ali, George Foreman, Joe Frazier. We're products of caring police."

That kind of quiet influence is a reminder that the work we do outside the scope of enforcement matters just as much, if not more, than the work we do in uniform. Whether it's picking up a kid for a ride to the gym, handing back a recovered bicycle, or lacing up skates to play a charity hockey game, small acts build the kind of community trust no police enforcement activity ever could. I furthered my commitment to this philosophy by volunteering with Big Brothers Big Sisters of Los Angeles during my early years at the LAPD.

* * *

The violence that comes with police work often exacts an obvious physical toll, but sometimes the stress and danger of the job come from the most unexpected places. One such incident nearly killed me. It was June 21, 1996, and I was working as a field training officer (FTO) at the Wilshire Division, one of the most impactful roles an officer can hold. In this role, I wasn't just responsible for training academy graduates or probationers on properly enforcing the law; I was shaping their understanding of what it means to serve and protect. Probationary officers spend their early career partnered with someone like me, learning how to apply the lessons from the academy to the unpredictable realities of the streets.

Policing the diverse neighborhoods in the Wilshire Division meant navigating cultural differences and language barriers in daily interactions with victims, witnesses, and members of the public.

Trust was the foundation of everything I taught. Without it, police-community relations crumble, and any chance of real connection or meaningful service disappears. I emphasized lawful, ethical practices and adaptability, recognizing that Wilshire's diverse communities demanded cultural awareness and strong communication skills.

The job was relentless, not only because of the communities we served but because of the hours. Wilshire was one of several patrol stations on a compressed work schedule, and I had become accustomed to the twelve-hour shifts.

For my partner, "The Probationer," and me, sticking to a routine was essential, and a dinner break at *Jan's*, a diner on the southeast corner of Beverly Boulevard and Croft Avenue, became a regular part of ours. The diner offered a short reprieve where we could decompress from the weight of the day's calls, but that June evening was far from routine. It was about to teach me that the risks of this job don't always come in the form of a suspect with a gun or a gang turf war. Sometimes the danger is hidden, waiting to strike when you least expect it.

About dusk we were driving eastbound on Beverly Boulevard to eat at *Jan's* when, without warning, we heard a loud blast that rocked our police car and showered our windshield with shattered glass. Our attention was immediately drawn to the ground floor of a multistory building on the north side of Beverly Boulevard. Smoke and flames billowed from an opening where the floor-to-ceiling window had been blown out by the intense heat of the fire.

I immediately broadcast a request for the fire department to respond and for additional police personnel to manage the scene. It wasn't until the arrival of the LAPD helicopter that I realized the magnitude of the threat the fire posed to public safety. A good friend and LAPD hockey teammate was assigned to the Air Support Division. When the helicopter arrived overhead, he broadcast to me, "Hey, you know this is a convalescent home, right?"

There was no time to wait for the arrival of the fire department. My thought was that one of the elderly residents had been smoking in bed, fallen asleep, and inadvertently started the fire. We needed to get people out because many of the residents were physically disabled or otherwise bedridden. So we crouched low and proceeded down the hall to the room where the fire had originated. I was comfortable doing that because, as a deputy sheriff, I had gone through fire training at the LA County Fire Academy.

LAPD officers don't receive fire training. Deputies were the frontline responders to fires in jails, so we received training on fire behavior as well as the use of turnout gear, firefighters' protective equipment, and breathing apparatus. In our training the instructor threw a set of jail keys into a room engulfed in flames, and we had to retrieve it. That training allowed me to observe how fire spreads and how it reacts in different environments. More importantly, it conditioned me to think clearly and act calmly when lives are at stake and seconds count. We didn't have turnout gear or breathing apparatus that night, but standing by wasn't an option.

The hallway was quickly filling with smoke, yet I felt in control. We moved toward the room where we believed the fire had started and found the door partially open. Thick black smoke billowed out, obscuring everything inside. Dropping to our knees, I told my partner I would "run the walls" to check for anyone inside. He was to stay at the door, my lifeline, ready to guide me back if I became disoriented. Keeping my left hand firmly on the wall, I crawled forward, ensuring I could retrace my path to safety. I held my breath and stayed as low as possible. The heat intensified quickly, though, and the smoke grew so dense that I realized there was no way forward. Turning back, desperate to reach the door, I followed the wall.

When I did finally reach the door, it was closed. My lungs screamed for air. Rising to my knees, I fumbled frantically for the door handle. Beginning to feel disoriented, I dropped to the floor, knowing the air would be slightly cooler and cleaner there. I cautiously inhaled a small breath only to feel immediate irritation in my nose, mouth, and throat. The air burned, but it gave me just enough clarity to open the door and crawl into the hallway.

As I emerged I saw my partner nearby, unaware the door had closed while he had helped the room's occupant. Unbeknownst to me, because of the thick smoke and continuous loud beeping of the fire alarm, the occupant exited the room after I entered but before I reversed course to find my way out. What could have been a fatal misstep turned into a close call, but the experience would stay with me, a reminder of the thin margin between life and death in moments like those.

We got the elderly man outside and met other responding officers. We were afraid other senior residents could still be trapped in burning bedrooms, so we formed a human chain and reentered the building. We struggled through the intense smoke and heat, crawling along the first floor, but found no occupants. The heat and smoke forced us to leave and regroup. We then entered to evacuate the second story. As we crawled along the second floor we could hear pleas for help. After knocking down several doors we located additional residents and guided them to safety. Some of them were in adult diapers and had to be carried out. In the end, more than eighty senior citizens were rescued.

I began experiencing nausea, shortness of breath, and dizziness before I collapsed and was rushed to the hospital. Carbon monoxide toxicity occurs after breathing in excessive levels of the gas. When you breathe in carbon monoxide, it replaces the oxygen in your bloodstream, causing the heart, brain, and body to become starved of oxygen. Red blood cells carry oxygen throughout the body. But red blood cells take in carbon monoxide faster than oxygen and, at high levels, carbon monoxide prevents oxygen from being transported throughout the bloodstream. The problem is that your organs need oxygen to sustain life.

The carbon monoxide in my system from the fire prevented my body from circulating the oxygen I was being given. If my body couldn't absorb the oxygen that I was being administered, I could suffocate. I had a pounding headache and found little comfort in being told my prognosis was unknown and would not be known until it was determined whether my carbon monoxide levels had plateaued or would continue to rise. There I was in the emergency room, staring at the ceiling, and nobody knew if I was going to die.

I remember telling them not to contact my father unless things looked bleak. My father was still working at Kent State, having been awarded the President's Medal in 1995. He often had me teach his classes when I was home visiting. He would give me the subject material and ask that I relate the sociological concepts being taught to my experiences policing the streets of Los Angeles. I just hoped to get another chance to return to his classroom as a guest instructor. I survived, but not without long-term health damage called exertion-induced asthma. My lungs begin to constrict when I push my physical limits beyond a certain point. I can still play hockey and run races, but I need to use inhalers, and if I allow myself to reach that certain point, breathing becomes a struggle. I have experienced that point, and it's quite frightening.

I was awarded the Medal of Valor for my actions that night, as were the other officers who helped rescue the senior citizens. The Medal of Valor is the LAPD's highest honor. It's awarded to those who distinguish themselves by performing an act of extraordinary courage while facing imminent peril. I was awarded the medal by LAPD Chief of Police William Bratton at the annual Medal of Valor awards ceremony. So I know firsthand the dangers police officers willingly put themselves in every day, and my criticism of policing in this book is not directed at them or their courage.

* * *

The bond between officers is forged in the shared experiences of navigating danger, uncertainty, and the weight of community responsibility. But that bond also carries the burden of loss, an ever-present reality in law enforcement. For me, no story embodies this more deeply than that of Officer Filberto Cuesta, whose tragic death serves as both a heartbreaking reminder of the risks we face and a call to examine the fractured relationship between law enforcement and the communities we serve.

I worked alongside Officer Cuesta at both the 77th Street Division and the Central Traffic Division. Later, he transitioned to the Southwest Division Crime Resources Against Street Hoodlums (CRASH) gang unit, a team tasked with combating gang violence in some of LA's most challenging neighborhoods. On August 9, 1998, Officer Cuesta and his partner were in their patrol car, awaiting backup to manage a sizable gang-related gathering. In a tragic and cowardly act, an 18th Street gang member approached from behind the patrol car and fired, striking Cuesta in the back of the head, killing him.

Officer Cuesta was only twenty-six years old. He had dedicated four years to the department, was married, and left behind two young daughters, one eighteen months old and the other only four weeks old. His death was devastating, a sobering reminder of the dangers officers face every day. The shooter was later identified, convicted, and sentenced to life in prison, but no verdict could ever undo the heartbreak of Cuesta's loss or the ripple effects it caused. In the aftermath of his death, the walls of the alley where Cuesta was killed became a canvas for the gang's grievances. Scrawled in graffiti was a chilling message, both defiant and reflective of the deep animosity toward law enforcement:

ALL WE EVER ASKED FOR WAS A LITTLE RESPECT. YOU BELITTLE OUR FATHER (and) MOTHER. KILL OUR BROTHERS, SISTERS. BATTER OUR PRIDE AND STEP ON DIGNITY. RETRIBUTION WAS INEVITABLE. YOU CALL US ANIMALS AND HOODLUMS. ANIMALS ARE THOSE WHO ABUSE POWER AND AUTHORITY. WE'RE SURVIVORS. WE PUSH WHEN PUSHED UPON. THE BLUE TERROR IS AT ITS END. AN EYE FOR AN EYE. A BROTHER FOR A BROTHER.

When asked about the message, a sergeant's response was blunt and dismissive: "Gutless, spineless punks. They have no redeemable values. All they do is tear apart the neighborhoods they're in, tear apart the city and the community. It's almost not worth giving attention to. But they've declared war on us."

This exchange encapsulates the entrenched cycle of violence, mistrust, and misunderstanding between law enforcement and the communities they serve. Yes, the act was undeniably horrific, a senseless, premeditated murder, but the sergeant's response, steeped in anger and a lack of reflection, missed a critical opportunity to address the underlying issues driving such hostility. The writing on the wall spoke volumes about how the gang members viewed the police, not as protectors but as oppressors. Even the name of the CRASH unit itself (Crime Resources Against Street Hoodlums) embodied the casual dehumanization that fuels resentment. To the gang members, being labeled "hoodlums" wasn't just an insult, it reinforced their belief that law enforcement saw them as less than human.

This toxic dynamic isn't just about semantics. It illustrates how police culture can inadvertently perpetuate the very animosity and violence it seeks to quell. Without meaningful introspection and change, tragedies like Officer Cuesta's death will continue in the relentless cycle of distrust and retaliation.

* * *

The most powerful images of law enforcement personnel that stir my emotions are those of officers running headlong into danger while the rest of the world scrambles to escape. The scenes from 9/11 are seared into our collective memory, first responders with faces marked by both determination and exhaustion, their eyes reflecting the weight of the moment but their bodies pressing forward without hesitation. Ash and smoke clung to their uniforms, and though uncertainty was evident in every step, their resolve burned brighter. Those men and women understood the odds, they knew the risks, and yet they pushed ahead. They embodied the best of the human spirit, a courage so profound that it outweighed fear and reason and physical limitations. They were running into the unknown, driven by a singular purpose: to protect, save, and serve. That imagery is the essence of honor and sacrifice.

To serve in such a capacity, a role in which you're duty-bound to confront danger when everyone else is running away, is a privilege and an honor. I have more than earned my street cred: the "admired qualities of an officer, built through extensive knowledge and experience policing the streets." This credibility comes not just from seeing action and surviving life-threatening situations but also from the lessons I've gained in administrative roles.

But aside from all that, my combined experiences give me a unique perspective to outline a plan to Reimagine Policing™ in America and suggest ways it can evolve. The goal is to create a system that better supports both the officers on the front lines and the communities they serve.

Chapter 4:
Leading in Turbulent Times

Injustice anywhere is a threat to justice everywhere.
—Martin Luther King Jr.

Effective law enforcement leadership isn't just about policing or analyzing crime statistics; it's about upholding integrity, earning trust, and committing to the well-being of those we serve and those who serve alongside us. But those qualities are tested most during times of turmoil when cracks in the system threaten to undermine the foundation of public safety.

In the late 1990s I was working in the LAPD's elite Metropolitan Division. With just over six years of field experience, my decision to remain in law enforcement rather than pursue graduate school was driven by a conviction that I could affect greater change through direct action. My sights were set on promotion, as it would expand my scope of influence and allow me to help shape the department's culture from within.

The U.S. Justice Department had been investigating allegations of excessive use of force since 1996 as part of the ongoing follow-up to the Rodney King beating and subsequent riots. The soon-to-break Rampart scandal would provide further momentum for change.

Rampart Division, one of the largest operational commands in the LAPD, was the epicenter of this transformation. Though it covered just 7.9 square miles, about 36,000 people lived in every single one of those square miles, giving it the highest population density in Los Angeles. Rampart was home to some of the city's most violent street gangs, which led to many of the city's highest crime rates, from homicides to violent robberies. Rampart officers not only faced a staggering volume of calls for service, but they also worked within a unique demographic.

Significant portions of Rampart residents were undocumented immigrants from Central America, many of whom spoke only Spanish and carried a deep-seated mistrust of law enforcement. Their experiences with the police in their home countries often shaped their perceptions, creating a complex environment for the LAPD. The residents' distrust presented challenges for every new commanding officer assigned to the division. Even at that time, efforts to address Rampart's challenges went back decades. In 1986 the LAPD executed a mass transfer of officers, infamously called the "Easter Massacre," because the orders were delivered on Easter Sunday. The department hoped to root out the toxic culture, but a decade later, the situation was even worse.

The toxic police culture was enabled by supervisors and command staff who turned a blind eye to abuses. Use-of-force incidents were routine, but they often went unreported under the pretext that officers were "too busy to do things right." The department's failure to address those issues led to an environment where corruption could thrive unchecked.

* * *

The Rampart scandal began with a crime that seemed almost too audacious to believe: a bank robbery committed by police officers. On November 6, 1997, two suspects entered a

Bank of America branch in Los Angeles, posing as customers. One of the suspects pulled a gun and confronted Errolyn Romero, the bank's customer service manager.

According to the Los Angeles Police Department's *Board of Inquiry into the Rampart Area Corruption Incident Public Report* by Chief Bernard C. Parks, dated March 1, 2000, here's how it all unfolded:

> *Two suspects entered the Bank of America, 985 West Jefferson Boulevard, Los Angeles, posing as customers. One of the suspects pulled a gun and confronted Errolyn Romero, the bank's customer service manager. The suspect walked Romero to the vault area where two other bank employees were working. The suspect pointed his gun at the employees and demanded money that had been delivered earlier by an armored carrier. The suspect then grabbed three plastic bags containing $722,000 and left the bank along with his accomplice. The two suspects ran to a white van driven by a third suspect and escaped before the police arrived.*

> *The preliminary investigation conducted by LAPD's Robbery Homicide Division's Bank Detail discovered that Errolyn Romero had ordered $722,000 the day before the robbery. Her order was suspicious because it generated a large amount of unnecessary currency in the bank, as well as the fact that her order was for unusual denominations of bills.*

Romero, along with two other bank employees who had been present during the robbery, agreed to undergo polygraph tests. The examinations for the other two employees, conducted on December 9, 1997, indicated no signs of deception, but when

Romero took the test on December 16, 1997, the results revealed inconsistencies, labeling her "deceptive."

Faced with mounting pressure, Romero eventually confessed to her involvement in the heist. She disclosed that her boyfriend, Officer David Mack, was one of the perpetrators. LAPD detectives acted swiftly, arresting both Romero and Mack for their roles in the crime.

The Rampart scandal wasn't just a case of individual misconduct. The Rampart scandal was a systemic failure. The cultural issues within the LAPD allowed corruption to flourish. Officers who bent or broke the rules were often rewarded with silence, if not outright complicity, from their supervisors. Such normalization of unethical behavior revealed the urgent need for accountability.

The follow-up investigation revealed that Mack traveled to Las Vegas, Nevada, two days after the robbery. On that trip he was accompanied by two of his best friends, Officer Rafael Perez and another officer, both assigned to Rampart. Perez was born in Puerto Rico and served in the Marines before joining the LAPD. He was a squad leader in the academy and well liked. He worked undercover narcotics assignments with Mack. He went by "Ray" and maintained a strong uniform appearance. He also had the stereotypical cop mustache, a facial accessory I had never chosen to wear.

Interviews with Perez and the other officer failed to provide any pertinent information regarding the bank robbery, but their interviews became important later as Perez's own criminal activity came to light. On February 26, 1998, Officer Brian Hewitt, a member of the anti-gang unit CRASH in Rampart brought 18th Street gang member Ismael Jimenez to the

Rampart Police Station for questioning. CRASH operated on the front lines of LA's gang wars, taking on the city's most volatile criminal networks.

Hewitt handcuffed Jimenez and, allegedly, beat him, hitting him in the chest and stomach, causing him to vomit blood. After being released, Jimenez visited the hospital where officials notified the LAPD of his injuries and complaints. Subsequent internal investigations led to the firing of both Hewitt and another officer, Ethan Cohan, who the department determined knew about the beating but failed to report it.

One month later, officials in the LAPD property room discovered that six pounds of cocaine, seized as evidence, were missing. Days later, detectives focused their investigation on Perez, a member of the Rampart CRASH unit, and Mack.

A further audit of the LAPD property room revealed another pound of cocaine was missing, evidence that had been booked on a prior arrest made by Detective Frank Lyga, an undercover officer who had shot fellow officer, Kevin Gaines, in self-defense during a road rage incident. At the time, investigators speculated that Perez may have stolen the cocaine booked by Lyga in retaliation for the Gaines shooting.

Investigators also believed the original six pounds of missing cocaine had been checked out by Perez under another officer's name and sold on the streets of Rampart through a girlfriend.

In December 1998, Perez faced trial on charges of possessing cocaine with intent to distribute, grand theft, and forgery. After deliberating for five days the jury reached an impasse, an 8-4 vote favoring conviction. As investigators prepared to strengthen their case for a retrial, they uncovered eleven more questionable instances involving cocaine evidence. Through meticulous examination, detectives identified a pattern of "dope switches" in which Perez had signed out cocaine from the property room and substituted it with Bisquick, the powdered baking mix, in a half-assed attempt to cover his tracks.

The true extent of the issues at Rampart became glaringly apparent when Perez struck a deal with prosecutors. He pled guilty to stealing cocaine and, in return for a reduced sentence of five years in prison, provided detailed information about two "bad" shootings and implicated three other CRASH officers in various illegal activities. As part of the agreement, Perez was granted immunity from further prosecution, excluding charges of murder.

One of Perez's earliest confessions exposed how he and his partner, Nino Durden, had shot and framed Javier Ovando, an unarmed gang member, and falsely testified against him. The incident left Ovando paralyzed and, at the time of Perez's admission, Ovando was serving a twenty-three-year sentence for allegedly assaulting the two officers. Following Perez's revelation, the LA County District Attorney's Office filed a writ of habeas corpus to overturn Ovando's conviction, leading to his release after serving two and a half years in prison.

Perez's cooperation marked the beginning of a nine-month confession spree during which he met with investigators on over fifty occasions, generating more than 4,000 pages of sworn testimony. His disclosures implicated approximately seventy officers in various forms of misconduct, ranging from wrongful shootings to on-duty drinking. The fallout from his allegations and subsequent investigations by the Rampart Task Force led to the overturning of nearly one hundred additional convictions.

Chief Parks formed a Board of Inquiry composed of LAPD command staff to analyze what went wrong regarding management and how deep the corruption ran. The report, released in March 2000, blamed lax departmental management for allowing misconduct within the Rampart Division to run wild. The report offered 108 recommendations, including improvements in hiring practices, supervisory oversight, and police training.

By then the DOJ was well aware of the problems in the LAPD, so it sent a "notice of investigations" letter in May 2000. In that notice the DOJ said the LAPD had been aware of problems since at least 1991 but had done little to address them, so "federal action was now required." The city and the DOJ arranged for the LAPD to accept a "consent decree," a state of affairs by which the organization under the decree must abide by certain provisions to avoid an escalation of the matter into the courts, which the City of Los Angeles most certainly didn't want. The decree runs ninety-three pages, but this is the essence:

> *The City, by and through its officials, agents, employees, and successors, is enjoined from engaging in a pattern or practice of conduct by law enforcement officers of the LAPD that deprives persons of rights, privileges, or immunities secured or protected by the Constitution or laws of the United States.*

As the investigation of the LAPD intensified, I was assigned to the elite Metropolitan Division, serving alongside the LAPD's most highly trained tactical personnel. I was a member of A Platoon, a citywide tactical response team that performed violent crime suppression patrol, high-risk search warrant service, surveillance, bank robbery stakeouts, and riot control. Other specialized functions included dignitary protection and the training of department personnel in tactics.

* * *

On April 20, 1999, when the Columbine school shooting occurred, I was still serving in the Metropolitan Division. A contingency of SWAT officers was sent to study the Columbine incident to devise tactics for a better police response and to develop Immediate Action Rapid Deployment (IARD) tactics that are used to this day in mass shooting scenarios.

Columbine changed the way cops respond to active shooter incidents. Before that tragedy, the practice was to secure the area and wait for SWAT to respond. Basically, tactical concepts at the time required one to contain the location, control access, call SWAT, and wait. Columbine, however, demonstrated the need for law enforcement to create a more immediate and proactive response to save lives. The idea of waiting for SWAT was replaced. The training focus evolved to rapid response, coordination, and decision making under stress.

Shortly thereafter, we in the Metropolitan Division implemented into our training the Immediate Action Rapid Deployment tactics born from the lessons learned through the Columbine massacre. Then four short months later, I was a member of the tactical team that responded to an active shooter incident at the North Valley Jewish Community Center. We entered the fast-paced, uncontrolled, chaotic environment to locate the white supremacist who had fired seventy rounds from an Uzi submachine gun. He wounded five, including three children.

At the time of the shooting, more than 200 children were on the playground. I saw the immediate aftermath of a mass shooting: bullet impacts, furniture overturned, and splattered blood.

The image of a large pool of blood on the floor is a snapshot ingrained in my consciousness, and the traumatized faces of the children and staff who witnessed the shooting left me with an immense sadness and a heavy heart. I wondered how children in a civilized society could be exposed to such violence. At the same time I felt a great sense of pride in representing the strength that stands between evil and goodness, the observable, tangible evidence that told the kids things would be okay.

Our new training played a critical role in quickly securing the scene and shifting our response as we learned the shooter had fled the scene and killed a U.S. Postal Service carrier and carjacked a woman at gunpoint. He then dumped the vehicle at a nearby motel where I spent hours in a sniper position, believing he was holed up there. Staying one step ahead of us, he had fled and taken a taxi all the way to Las Vegas. He later turned himself in to the FBI and confessed. He was sentenced to two consecutive life terms and an additional 110 years.

The shooter, a white supremacist, had a history of mental illness and was found in possession of five rifles, two pistols, and 6,000 rounds of ammunition. This tragedy underscores the pressing need for legislation to prevent individuals with serious mental health concerns from accessing weapons. Yet, more than two decades and countless mass shootings later, we as a nation continue to struggle with actionable, practical solutions.

This recurring stagnation reflects broader challenges within law enforcement and public policy. While specialized tactical training is essential for successful outcomes, it cannot shield officers from the influence of long-standing subcultures within policing.

* * *

Policing has long been a profession steeped in codes and tradition, written and unwritten. The unwritten can define a department's culture, for better or worse, and Metropolitan Division was no different. One afternoon during roll call, I was reminded of that reality in a way that left a lasting impression. Speaking to all of us, a sergeant casually advised, "Sanitize your vehicles." He wasn't talking about disinfectants. The directive wasn't aimed at me, but the implications were unmistakable. His advice was an acknowledgment that some officers carried items they had no business possessing: narcotics, unregistered "throw guns," and other items used to manipulate or fabricate evidence. A throw gun is an unregistered firearm stashed until needed at the scene of a questionable officer-involved shooting. Planted as evidence, it could be used to validate self-defense claims or justify an otherwise unjustifiable lethal use of force.

The sergeant's advice was further indication that a harmful subculture had proliferated within the LAPD, one that normalized bending or breaking the rules to achieve results. Supervisors didn't just know about it. Their tacit approval allowed it to persist.

In the field, phrases like, "Are you down for the cause?" circulated as casual tests of loyalty. They weren't innocent questions but coded challenges. The subtext was clear: Would you bend the law, maybe even falsify evidence, to ensure that suspects deemed "bad actors" ended up behind bars, evidence or probable cause be damned? For too many the answer was "Yes."

A few days later, presumably following the sergeant's directive to sanitize, I overheard an even more chilling story. It centered around an officer allegedly burying a throw gun in his backyard. What struck me most wasn't the content of the story but the way it was shared. It wasn't framed as an accusation or a shocking revelation. Instead, it was recounted almost in jest as if such acts were a bleak but tolerated part of the job. Such a cavalier attitude toward something so deeply unethical spoke volumes about the culture within the department.

While I never personally witnessed evidence being planted, there was an unspoken awareness of the officers who operated in the shadows. Those individuals weren't isolated, they were tolerated, an institutional failure that left an insoluble blemish on the reputation of the organization.

Years later I encountered that culture in the harshest terms while reviewing an officer-involved shooting. I couldn't reconcile the presence of a suspect's gun at the scene with the other evidence. Something didn't add up. The possibility of misconduct was unsettling, and it forced me to confront the realities I had long tried to avoid. Most of the officers I worked alongside were honorable, law-abiding professionals who upheld their oaths. But there was no denying the subversive element within the department. It thrived in the blind spots, quietly eroding the public's trust in law enforcement. That the misconduct continued without accountability was as frustrating as it was concerning.

* * *

As I said, I was fortunate to work alongside some incredible, honorable officers, including one I'll refer to as the "Old Timer." He was a study in contrasts, short in stature but built like a brick house, tough as nails on the outside, yet kind-hearted and grounded at his core. At fifty-six he carried the wisdom and grit of a seasoned veteran.

On my first day with the Metropolitan Division I was sitting on the steps outside my condo when the Old Timer pulled up in our patrol car. He rolled down the window, leaned over the passenger seat, and shouted, "Whatcha doin'? You look like you're waiting for your mommy." His hearty laugh told me everything I needed to know: We were going to get along just fine.

His legacy looms large in the memory of the Metropolitan Division. His courage under fire and unwavering integrity earned him the respect of peers and supervisors alike. He was considered one of the last of a dying breed of old-school officers who understood the delicate balance between toughness and compassion. If you've ever experienced the humanity of a cop, you know exactly what I mean.

In 1995, while working a crime suppression detail in South Los Angeles, the Old Timer and his partner responded to an armed robbery in progress. While scouring the area, they spotted a man matching the suspect's description. As they prepared their tactical approach, the suspect drew a handgun. Without warning, he shot the Old Timer's partner in the back and arm as he exited the patrol car. The Old Timer's response was nothing short of heroic. Exiting the driver's side, he engaged the suspect in a fierce gun battle over the roof and hood of the vehicle.

A bullet grazed his left temple, knocking him to the ground. Later he would recount with characteristic grit, "All that did was piss me off." Bleeding and injured, he stood, reengaged the suspect, and ultimately neutralized the threat. The suspect, riddled with gunshot wounds, died in the street. The Old Timer's actions were not only courageous but also tactically sound, meeting the standard of "objectively reasonable" force outlined in the landmark Supreme Court case *Graham v. Connor*.

The Old Timer's story highlighted a critical truth about law enforcement: though the profession's power and authority can tempt some officers down a dangerous path, over time, the pressures and rationalizations inherent in policing can erode even the strongest ethical foundations. The Old Timer, though, insulated me from those temptations. He wasn't just a reliable partner; he was a moral anchor who reinforced the importance of staying grounded. He worked within the law and refused to compromise his principles in the absence of probable cause to arrest.

When an investigation didn't yield sufficient evidence, he would routinely say, "Well, not today, but perhaps tomorrow." He would never compromise his integrity to make an arrest.

Yet the reality was undeniable: Some officers, driven by a sense of serving the greater good, succumbed to a toxic mindset. Left unchecked in a department, this mentality will spiral into outright corruption. I consciously avoided that slippery slope by surrounding myself with ethical peers and mentors.

But just as I didn't want to be around corrupt cops, they didn't want to be around me. You could say we choose our flock, but if not for my father keeping me grounded and the fortuitous circumstance of working with good partners I, too, may have succumbed to this toxic mindset.

I talked to my dad about everything because he gave me judgment-free, insightful considerations to ponder when confronted with an ethical dilemma. I would often ask him a question, and he would not respond, as if he hadn't heard me, only to blurt out his answer a few days later. He liked to think before he spoke. My father once told me with a smirk that he started running for exercise when we children came along. It gave him time to think. Well, I got that from my father because, during that time in my career I would wake at 4 a.m. every Sunday and run ten to fifteen miles. Today, I do my best thinking on long walks.

* * *

The LAPD operated under the consent decree from 2001 until July 17, 2009, marking a significant transformation in the department. Federal Judge Gary A. Feess lifted the oversight only after the LAPD demonstrated substantial compliance with rigorous mandates aimed at eliminating behaviors and practices associated with racial profiling, excessive force, and corruption. Those changes didn't happen overnight. They required years of systemic changes, new training protocols, and cultural shifts within the department.

When the consent decree was imposed, I was a sergeant assigned to the Rampart Division that, as you know by now, is synonymous with corruption and scandal but also with hope for redemption. The commanding officer at Rampart was assembling a leadership team committed to navigating the division through that turbulent period and restoring its integrity. I was handpicked to be a part of this team. My assignment placed me at the forefront of implementing the requirements of the consent decree.

Balancing the demands of high-risk operations with the need for cultural and procedural improvement shaped my professional growth during that critical chapter. It forced me to innovate, adapt, and reconsider how law enforcement could rebuild trust in the communities it served.

Some lessons come quietly over time. Others are like a punch to the gut. That period was full of gut punches. The oversight revealed deep flaws within the department and highlighted what was possible when leadership and accountability were taken seriously. Those experiences laid the groundwork for the challenges I would face later in my career, reinforcing the importance of deliberate and ethical leadership.

Violent crime was soaring, but the era of unchecked misconduct, excessive force, false arrests, and illegal searches was coming to an end. The regime change marked a new beginning: corrupt officers would no longer be tolerated, and the department would restore its accountability.

On March 12, 2000, all CRASH units were disbanded citywide as part of the overhaul. Once seen as the model to address gang crime, the CRASH units had devolved into a culture of secrecy and impunity. Supervisors avoided asking hard questions, prioritizing results over ethics and granting officers excessive latitude to combat gang violence. While the program was initially effective, the lack of oversight allowed corruption to fester.

As CRASH dissolved, the rise of gang-related crime demanded a new solution, one built on transparency and legality. The LAPD introduced two specialized units: the Gang Enforcement Detail and the Narcotics Enforcement Detail, each reporting directly to a lieutenant under the division captain. The new structure brought the department its much-needed accountability. I was assigned as the officer-in-charge of the gang detail and was tasked with charting a new path forward. I was determined to clean things up, but not everyone welcomed the changes.

Gang violence in Los Angeles is persistent. Drive-by shootings, robberies, and territorial disputes inflamed by gang rivalries wreak havoc on communities. Gangs compete for dominance over open-air drug markets and street-level prostitution, frequently resorting to violence in a city with more active gangs than any other in the nation.

As someone with a mission to reimagine policing, I symbolized a shift from the favored intimidation-based policing of the time. My approach was purposeful and preventative, focused on reducing crime through strategic engagement rather than intimidation. Some officers resented the elimination of CRASH, while others seethed at how I ran things. Resistance was inevitable, but I knew change was necessary.

The first step in this transformation was selecting the right officers to serve in the unit. Working in the gang unit was a coveted assignment. Officers in this role were not tied to radio calls, allowing them to focus on crime prevention instead of reacting to crime.

Traditionally, entering the unit required a sponsor, a current member of the unit to vouch for the applicant. That process struck me as eerily similar to how gangs recruit and maintain loyalty among their members. Gangs identify those who are susceptible to indoctrination, those who will place the gang above everything else. Often, allegiance is fostered through intimidation, making it hard for members to leave. Initiation rites, such as committing crimes or enduring violent acts, are common and make members unlikely to betray the gang.

In law enforcement, the stakes for allowing this kind of insular selection process are just too high. Relying on personal endorsements risked perpetuating the corrupt culture. Instead, I ensured we were building a team capable of confronting gang violence without resorting to the very behaviors we sought to eliminate.

I looked for officers who demonstrated excellence in various law enforcement activities, interpersonal and administrative skills, and an unwavering commitment to integrity. To ensure transparency, a formal interview process was implemented to evaluate candidates thoroughly. One interview stands out. The candidate had an impressive résumé and strong credentials, but I couldn't shake my uneasy feeling about him. His demeanor hinted at darker motivations, and I trusted my instincts.

During the interview I asked a simple but revealing question: "What separates you from the other candidates being considered for this position?"

He casually referenced a willingness to "drop the hammer," implying a chilling, nonchalant attitude toward shooting someone. He further shared his propensity for violence by casually sharing detailed accounts of his involvement in significant force incidents.

I knew immediately that he wasn't right for the unit. His misguided motivations were troubling, and my decision not to select him was validated years later when it became clear that his answer had foreshadowed even more serious issues.

In building a team I followed a clear mantra: "Do the right thing at the right time for the right reasons." I encouraged the officers to challenge the status quo and embrace creative approaches to crime reduction. The unit soon was recognized with the Department Meritorious Unit Citation. The honor acknowledged our innovative approach to significantly reducing gang crime, including novel initiatives such as the first multi-gang injunction, the mandatory qualification to be a gang expert in court, and enforcement efforts that targeted the most violent gangs. The unit was the model for all others to emulate.

At the heart of this transformation was trust. I understood that my role as a leader required more than just selecting the right officers My role demanded empowering them to identify creative crime reduction strategies and allowing them the autonomy to implement their ideas. The success of the unit was not a reflection of autocratic leadership but of the officers' ingenuity, dedication, and commitment to excellence. While I was deeply focused on reducing violent gang crime, I was equally committed to fostering the growth of future leaders within the department. Their innovation and integrity paved the way for the unit's success and set a standard for what law enforcement leadership should aspire to achieve.

* * *

Gang associates made for easy arrests, but they had minimal impact on the larger problem. For every gang associate arrested, two more were waiting to take their place. My philosophy was simple: Results were achieved through the strategic use of personnel and resources, not the volume of arrests. I emphasized information-gathering missions over mass arrests, focusing on building solid cases that would succeed in court. My officers weren't just enforcers of the law, they were experts in gang culture, laws, and psychology.

I knew modern police work could no longer focus solely on making arrests to solve modern crime problems. To create safer communities, we needed to identify and shut down potential points of violence and theft before crimes happened.

A case at the Wilshire Financial Tower demonstrated this required shift in thinking. The courtyard, framed by flower beds and palm trees, seemed calm, but a crime analysis revealed a different story. The courtyard's ATM was prone to robberies; its secluded location made early-morning users easy targets. Over four months of data revealed a staggering number of incidents that surprised even the bank officials.

I proposed a simple but unconventional solution: close the ATM during high-risk hours. It wasn't a sexy tactic, nor did it yield dramatic arrests, but it worked. Robberies dropped by 65 percent, and the success led officials to consider similar measures citywide. This wasn't the kind of policing that resulted in headline-grabbing arrests, but it worked, a testament to the power of prevention over reaction.

I also emphasized tactical superiority among the unit's officers. Law enforcement is an unpredictable and dangerous profession that demands calm, clear decision making under pressure. I expected the officers to excel in assessing complex situations and responding with poise, even in the face of extreme stress. Policing isn't just about being tough. It's about being smart, deliberate, and ethically intentional. Letting emotions dictate decisions and actions wasn't an option.

To illustrate this, the officers would detain groups of gang members during routine investigations. Outnumbered, they faced the challenge of controlling those who remained behind while others fled. This was a test of composure under pressure that demanded they manage those who complied and establish a containment perimeter to direct backup units to apprehend those who fled. It was more than just keeping the peace; it was about protecting the officers while ensuring enforcement actions were effective and grounded in legal precedent.

Understanding the unintended consequences of prioritizing arrest numbers, I shifted the focus to the quality of arrests, targeting violent gang crimes and building strong, prosecutable cases. My approach wasn't glamorous, but it built credibility with prosecutors and marked a shift in how success was measured. Instead of the sheer volume of arrests, officers were now evaluated on case filings and conviction rates. Despite resistance, I knew the status quo needed to change.

Every arrest had to be justified, so legal knowledge was central to the unit's approach. To ensure the integrity of our operations I instructed the officers to base their actions on legal precedent and to explicitly reference case law in their reports to justify the decisions they made in the field. For instance, *Illinois v. Wardlow*, a landmark case establishing the authority to detain individuals fleeing in high-crime areas, became a key reference point. Citing precedent strengthened our cases and fostered a culture of accountability and professionalism.

Citing precedent also elevated the quality of our overall operations and even inspired other police managers to adopt the same practice. By embedding legal knowledge into every aspect of our work, we emphasized enforcement rooted in a measured legal approach rather than relying on force.

Training played a critical role. I prioritized specialized instruction on gang dynamics, behaviors, and traditions, combining classroom learning with field experience. That investment turned my officers into experts in both enforcement and gang culture.

Reducing gang crime required a clear strategy: increase officer presence, enhance intelligence, and target the most violent offenders. Yet, even with those measures, the realities of big-city policing never faded. Loss and death were constants, underscoring the stakes of our work and the importance of every decision we made.

* * *

Gangs in Los Angeles typically form along neighborhood and ethnic lines. One prominent example was a gang named after its hillside neighborhood overlooking Echo Park Lake and the downtown Los Angeles skyline, Varrio Vista Rifa. Established in the 1980s, the gang was an intimidating presence for decades. But as gentrification brought higher housing prices, many gang members were displaced, and their influence waned.

Even so, Varrio Vista Rifa experienced a resurgence in the vicinity of 3rd Street and Alvarado Boulevard, where the parents of one of the gang's original members lived. Their son, leveraging the opening of a tattoo shop, built a base to recruit neighborhood youth. Soon, the gang's graffiti marked the area once again, reasserting their claim to the territory.

The LAPD's CompStat system, introduced by former NYPD Commissioner William Bratton during his tenure as LAPD's fifty-fourth chief, was a valuable tool for addressing spikes in crime. Its use of comparative statistics allowed commanders to analyze trends and deploy resources strategically. Often, that meant temporarily assigning gang units to divisions experiencing increases in violent crime. While effective in theory, the task force deployments carried the risk of unintended consequences.

On October 1, 2004, our unit was temporarily assigned to a neighboring division as part of such a task force. During our absence, an incident in Rampart underscored the importance of localized intelligence and presence. A resident, frustrated by Varrio Vista Rifa gang graffiti on his apartment, confronted a gang member. The confrontation escalated into a physical altercation, and though the gang member retreated after the fight, he made a chilling promise to return.

That evening the resident sat outside his apartment with some friends, seemingly unconcerned by the gang threat. Later, he stepped into the street to speak with a female acquaintance who had pulled up in her car. A van arrived moments later, and a gang member, likely uninvolved in the earlier altercation, stepped out with a handgun.

After asking, "Who is it?" and being directed by someone in the van to the resident, the gang member shot and killed him in cold blood and fled the scene.

It's impossible to know what might have happened had our unit been working in Rampart that day. Based on our extensive local knowledge and relationships, I believe our presence could have de-escalated tensions after the initial encounter and prevented the violence from spiraling. Ultimately, our intelligence work proved instrumental in identifying and apprehending those responsible, bringing some measure of justice for this senseless crime.

The scale of our unit, particularly in the context of national law enforcement standards, reflected the unique challenges of policing Rampart. With twenty-four officers under my supervision, our gang unit alone was larger than half the law enforcement agencies in the United States. The average department consists of ten officers who serve small towns. In fact, 70 percent of departments serve populations of 10,000 or less, according to the National Police Foundation.

Later in my career I was the officer-in-charge of two teams as part of the Force Investigation Division that included a portion of over sixty detectives. Working with such a diverse group presented challenges, but it also provided an unprecedented opportunity to cultivate a team of talented and committed professionals. I focused on nurturing team members' unique skills and perspectives, ensuring they had the support and clarity needed to succeed.

* * *

One particular instance highlighted the importance of building strong relationships within our team and reinforced the synergistic nature of our work. It was near the end of our watch, and I had arrived at the station to see which officers had made arrests and to determine what personnel would be working overtime. I never ended my shift until all arrestees had been processed and the related reports completed. I reviewed every report and initialed the bottom right corner of each page in an informal audit to ensure the reports were thorough, accurate, and complete. But this night would prove to be different.

As I walked into my office I heard over the radio that officers in my unit were in a foot pursuit of a man with a gun who was running southbound on Union Avenue. My officers requested backup and a police helicopter, known in police jargon as an "airship." I dropped everything and ran to my police car, my mind transitioning to my tactical training. Those were my officers, and if I could help them, I had to try.

I was about halfway to where the foot pursuit had begun when I heard this chilling broadcast over the radio: "Officer needs help; shots fired." When you hear those words, your senses go into overdrive. With heart pounding and mind racing, I took a deep breath and consciously tried to remain calm. My focus had to be deliberate if I was going to assist my officers effectively. All I could do as I raced to the scene was trust that my emphasis on sound tactics and decision making under stress would guide them through the life-threatening situation.

Earlier in my career I had been skeptical of forming deep emotional connections with colleagues. Police management classes often spoke about "loving your personnel," and I would scoff at the idea. How could I feel that strongly about unrelated grown adults just because we wore the same uniform? It seemed unnecessary, even naïve. Perhaps it was my own emotional armor against grief after the loss of my mother that kept me at a distance. I chose to lead with impartiality while reserving trust and affection for those who earned it.

Eventually, I understood that my deep concern for my officers wasn't about their personal attributes but about our shared sacrifice. Each officer was unique, and despite any flaws or disagreements, they were part of a shared purpose. I felt a responsibility not only to them but also to their families. Any failure to protect them was like failing my own family. That was the emotion that seized me in that moment.

The chase had continued on Olympic Boulevard and reached a set of steps leading to a landing and a bank ATM. The suspect dashed up the steps, momentarily out of sight as the building obscured the officers' view. Effective tactics demand a balance between self-protection and risk mitigation. In a decision influenced by the potential risk of negligent discharge, the lead officer chose to holster his weapon during the foot pursuit. While that choice could have cost him his life, it also demonstrated his commitment to calculated decision making under extreme stress.

As the officer approached the steps, the suspect suddenly turned. My officer found himself staring down the barrel of the suspect's gun. The trigger was pulled…click. The weapon malfunctioned. In those split seconds, my officer drew his service pistol and charged up the steps, firing as he advanced. His shots struck the steps and the landing before hitting the suspect, who ran a short distance before collapsing and succumbing to his injuries.

When I arrived my officer was visibly shaken. He asked me to check him for wounds, unsure if he'd been shot. He was a young officer I had personally selected, a dedicated professional recently married with two young children. His actions were entirely justified, and had the suspect's weapon not malfunctioned, the situation could have ended tragically for everyone who would have been impacted by his loss.

That incident only deepened my confidence in the officers under my command and underscored the immense responsibility I carried for their preparedness and well-being. The psychological impact of such encounters extends beyond the officers directly involved to their colleagues and families. Even as a supervisor who wasn't present when the shooting occurred that night, the experience had a deep emotional impact on me.

* * *

The department's Behavioral Science Services provided debriefs after incidents involving significant use of force, but much work remained to destigmatize seeking mental health support. Today, there's a greater appreciation for psychological care within police departments, including mandatory sessions after deadly force incidents in some jurisdictions. But cultural barriers still exist, so some officers hesitate to seek help until it's too late.

I had an officer who worked for me when I was a patrol sergeant at Rampart. We worked morning watch, and his partner was scheduled to take the sergeant's exam the following morning. I let the partner go home early to get some sleep before taking the exam. Because Rampart was so violent, we never deployed single-officer cars during nighttime hours, so I told the other officer he could work the front desk or go home early as well. He elected to go home.

When he arrived, his two young daughters were asleep, but his wife was nowhere to be found. It turned out she was having an extramarital affair. As a result, the officer moved in with his partner and stayed in the guest room. One weekend while his partner was out of town, the officer got into an argument over the phone with his estranged wife. He learned she was in Las Vegas with her boyfriend, not on business travel as she had told him.

While sitting on the edge of his bed and still on the phone with his estranged wife, he took his handgun and shot himself in the head, killing himself instantly. I was shocked because, just two days earlier, I had spoken to him privately to see how he was doing. He looked great. He'd been eating well and working out regularly, and he said he had support from his father and church members. He had such a bright future and so much to look forward to with his daughters. His tragic death was a painful lesson in the silent struggles many officers face, and it deepened my resolve to make mental health support a priority by fostering an environment in which seeking help is seen as a strength, not a weakness.

* * *

Music has an uncanny ability to transport us to specific moments in time, acting as both a mirror and a messenger. For me, the soundtrack to my early years in law enforcement includes tracks like Tupac Shakur's "Changes." The song's poignant lyrics speak to racial inequality, systemic failures, and the yearning for something better. The line, "We gotta start makin' changes; learn to see me as a brother instead of two distant strangers," resonated deeply as a call for understanding and unity in a world divided by fear and mistrust.

At the time, hip-hop reflected the frustrations and struggles of the communities I was working in. It gave voice to truths that needed to be acknowledged, even if they were uncomfortable to hear. Yet, within LAPD ranks such songs were often dismissed as anti-police noise, their messages overlooked or misunderstood.

Public Enemy's "Fight the Power," famously featured in Spike Lee's *Do the Right Thing*, was another anthem that captured the unfiltered frustration of marginalized communities. Those songs, raw and unapologetic, served as a lens through which I could better understand the lived experiences of the people I had sworn to serve. The music challenged me to listen, to reflect, and to grow, not just as an officer but as a human being.

But some LAPD officers adopted a troubling culture, wearing tattoos that glorified killing, including symbols like the infamous "dead man's hand" of aces and eights. That symbol has its roots in a dark piece of American history. On August 2, 1876, lawman Wild Bill Hickok was playing a game of five-card stud at Nuttall and Mann's Saloon in the Dakota Territory. A gambler named Jack McCall approached Hickok from behind and shot him in the back of the head. At the time of his death, Hickok was holding two black aces and two black eights, and that's why those cards are known as the dead man's hand.

Officers in that culture represented the antithesis of the values I sought to uphold. Early in my career I resisted the accusations of police brutality prevalent in the lyrics of many hip-hop songs. My instinct was to defend the profession, believing those experiences didn't align with how I conducted myself, but my perspective evolved. I came to understand the lyrics as calls for racial equality and reflections of the socioeconomic realities faced by Black men, realities I could no longer ignore.

The turning point came during an officer-involved shooting that would be hard to believe if it weren't true. It confirmed the issues hip-hop artists had been voicing for years and forced me to confront the unchecked violence that could erode public trust.

By 2006 I was well beyond the five-year tenure I had initially envisioned for my career in policing. The consent decree, which mandated overhauls in LAPD practices, also introduced term limits for specialized assignments. After serving the maximum of three years with the gang unit, I was recruited for a coveted position within the Use of Force Review Division. The effectiveness of my work in the gang unit had not gone unnoticed, and this opportunity opened doors to influence policy and accountability on a broader scale.

My new role involved overseeing the adjudication of officer-involved shootings and other critical use of force cases. That's how I encountered a case involving an officer I had previously flagged during his interview for the gang unit—a man whose troubling motivations had raised red flags. He and his partner, both in plain clothes, had driven into a gang neighborhood in an undercover vehicle. Eventually, a shooting occurred that seemed like an ambush by gang members. But as I dug deeper, inconsistencies emerged.

During my review I meticulously examined officer statements, witness testimonies, physical evidence, and video footage. Everything needed to align, but it didn't. A witness reported hearing someone shout the name of a rival gang moments before the confrontation. That provocative act led armed gang members to emerge, ready to defend their turf. The situation soon spiraled into violence.

The statement from the witness brought back a troubling memory from my time at Rampart. In the shared locker room, I had overheard the officer in question boasting about how someone could orchestrate an officer-involved shooting. He described the very scenario I saw unfolding in this case: wear plain clothes, drive an unmarked car into gang territory, and call out a rival gang's name to provoke a response. At the time his remarks had struck me as disturbing bravado. Now they felt like a blueprint for what had just transpired.

I faced an ethical dilemma. While the evidence strongly suggested the officer's actions were premeditated, my recollection of his locker-room remarks wasn't part of the official record. Without corroboration, my hands were tied in proving intent. Still, I couldn't remain silent. I brought my concerns directly to Chief William Bratton, a leader known for his integrity and commitment to accountability.

"We're fixing this," Bratton said without hesitation. His response was a testament to his character. Where other leaders might have buried such a controversial issue, Bratton chose accountability over convenience. This marked the first of a number of self-imposed incidents involving this officer, which would predictably result in his termination. Bratton's handling of the situation marked a significant moment in my career and reinforced my belief in the power of ethical leadership. Bratton's decisive action didn't just resolve one case; it symbolized a broader cultural shift within the LAPD.

The evolution from skepticism to accountability wasn't an easy one. It required confronting uncomfortable truths and recognizing the complex interplay of organizational dysfunctions and individual actions. This journey solidified my resolve to reimagine policing and highlighted the critical role of integrity in doing so.

That pivotal moment was more than just a personal milestone. That moment set the stage for a broader exploration of leadership and accountability within law enforcement. Bratton's unwavering commitment to integrity marked the beginning of a cultural shift in the LAPD, one that would shape the department's future and my own perspective on leadership.

Chapter 5:
Chief Bratton

*A leader is one who knows the way, goes the way,
and shows the way.*

—John C. Maxwell

My life changed again, for the better, in 2002 when William Bratton was appointed LAPD chief. Bratton was all business. As an outsider coming from the New York Police Department (NYPD), he had no allegiance to other command officers. He surrounded himself with people he trusted, and he kept them accountable.

I began working directly for him in 2006 and often worked out alongside him during the morning in the gym at police headquarters, but I only engaged in a cordial hello, not in conversation of any substance. He kept a tight schedule and was a true professional, dressing appropriately for every occasion. His appearance was always impeccable, whether in uniform or in business attire. Like my father, when the chief spoke he shared something worthwhile in his stern and direct manner.

Bratton hails from the Dorchester neighborhood of Boston, Massachusetts, and he served in the Military Police Corps of the U.S. Army during the Vietnam War. After his service, he returned to Boston and joined the Boston Police Department (BPD) in 1970. By 1978 he had been promoted to lieutenant and had earned a Bachelor of Arts degree in Public Service/Public Administration. Two years later he was appointed executive superintendent of the BPD at the age of thirty-two, making him the youngest ever to serve in that position. He lost the position due to a mix of ambition and honesty after telling a journalist that his ultimate goal was to become the Boston police commissioner.

By the time he reached Los Angeles he had achieved that goal, having served as the Boston police commissioner and, later, chief of the New York City Transit Police in 1990. Four years later, Mayor Rudy Giuliani named him commissioner of the NYPD, and that's where he rose to national prominence by putting his "broken windows" theory of policing into practice.

To understand Bratton's rise to national prominence and his influence on modern policing, it's crucial to explore the ideas and historical forces that shaped his approach. Central to his philosophy was the previously mentioned broken windows theory, a concept founded in the belief that small but visible signs of disorder could spiral into more significant crime if left unchecked. But where did this theory come from, and how did it evolve into a cornerstone of American law enforcement?

The origins of the broken windows theory trace back to a 1969 experiment by Stanford psychologist Philip Zimbardo who demonstrated how neglect could breed disorder. Over a decade later, criminologists George L. Kelling and James Q. Wilson expanded on Zimbardo's findings, proposing that maintaining order in public spaces could empower communities and prevent crime. By the time Bratton took the reins as NYPD commissioner in 1994, he had turned that academic theory into actionable policy that would redefine the role of policing in New York City and, later, Los Angeles.

The central theory behind broken windows policing is that low-level crime and disorder create an environment that encourages more serious crimes. Bratton championed a balance between firm enforcement and measured leniency for minor crimes. He used the NYC subway system as an example, saying that the police should attempt to catch fare evaders, and the vast majority should be summoned to court rather than arrested and given a punishment other than jail. The goal was to deter minor offenders from committing more serious crimes later and to reduce the prison population by not jailing people for low-level crimes.

Broken windows focuses on panhandling, disorderly behavior, public consumption of alcohol, prostitution, and other quality-of-life violations. The premise is that disorder within the community causes subsequent occurrences of serious crime. As the NYPD increased misdemeanor arrests, the overall crime rate dropped.

When Bratton became NYPD commissioner, misdemeanors and overall crime in New York City were on par with other major cities in the state on a per capita basis. But by 1996 misdemeanor arrests were up nearly 15 percent while the overall crime rate was down 30 percent compared to other cities. Most notably, when Bratton left in 1996 felony crimes were down 40 percent and homicide rates had been cut in half.

Bratton resigned from the NYPD in 1996, partly because he was being investigated for signing a book deal and taking too many unauthorized trips, but I think it was mainly because Giuliani was annoyed that Bratton was getting credit for the huge reductions in crime instead of the mayor. So when I heard that Bratton would lead the LAPD, I picked up a copy of his book, *Turnaround: How America's Top Cop Reversed the Crime Epidemic* (1998), coauthored by Peter Knobler. It was named a *New York Times* Notable Book of the Year. In it Bratton lays out his philosophy of life and of policing.

A short section of Bratton's book beautifully sums up the man and his method. In that key passage he addresses the officers of New York City's 103rd Precinct in Jamaica, Queens. But before we get to that passage, a little background: The 103rd was a microcosm of New York City, multiethnic and multiracial with good neighborhoods, bad neighborhoods, and some in-between. It was New York Governor Mario Cuomo's home precinct, but it was not safer because Cuomo lived there. In fact, the 103rd struggled with many types of crime.

In 1988, six years before Bratton took over, NYPD Officer Ed Byrne was sitting in his patrol car in the 103rd, guarding the home of a man who had informed on a drug dealer, when Byrne was shot to death by drug dealers. It was a vicious, cold-blooded murder committed to send a message to the city: This turf is ours. But when Bratton arrived, he said he was going to take that turf back and make it safe for everyone…except criminals, especially drug dealers.

"This is my first official act as police commissioner," he told the officers of the 103rd. "I came a long way to get here. I know you're thinking, *Who's this guy who talks funny, this guy from Boston who's the new commissioner?*"

He was addressing the 103rd Precinct in NYC in this key passage from his book that I mentioned earlier, but he could have been speaking to us, his future officers in the LAPD:

> *I said when I took this job that we would take this city back for the good people who live here,*

neighborhood by neighborhood, block by block, house by house. But I'm going to need your help in doing that. I'm going to need all of you in the game.

I want my cops to be cops. I want them to be assertive. I don't want them walking by or looking the other way when they see something. No matter what the old rules were, I expect you to see something and take proper police action.

I expect you to be honest. I expect you to uphold the oath that you took on the first day. If you get into problems doing your job, and you're doing it right, I'll back you up. If you're wrong, I'll get you retrained and back to work. If you're dirty or brutal, I'll see to it that you're arrested, you're fired, and you're put in jail.

I like cops. I've been with cops most of my adult life. I want to bring three things to this department: pride, commitment, and respect. I want you to be proud of your city, of your department, and of yourselves. Proud that you're cops in the greatest police department in the world. I also want you to take pride in your appearance, in your uniforms, and in how you wear them.

When Bratton arrived in Los Angeles in 2002, I soon saw his theory in action. After the usual formalities, the first thing he did was to require every command staff officer to submit their resume and justify why they had their position. Some assistant chiefs were demoted to commander. If he didn't see them as effective leaders, he'd relegate them to managing a broom closet. Some accepted the demotion, but many chose to retire instead.

Following his NYPD blueprint to replicate his success in LA, Bratton searched for talented leaders within the command staff. He set his sights on Jim McDonnell, whom he promoted to his first assistant chief. Like Bratton, McDonnell is a Boston native. He was well revered by the rank and file as he had held a variety of assignments in patrol, detectives, vice, organized crime, and homicide. It was McDonnell's plan for community-based policing that Chief Bratton implemented as the foundation to improve the department.

Another brilliant move Bratton made for the LAPD involved Captain Michael Hillman, a long-term lieutenant in the Metropolitan Division with an unparalleled reputation as a police tactician and dynamic leader. Bratton knew talent when he saw it, and he promoted Hillman to deputy chief, skipping him over the rank of commander for the first time in the modern era of the LAPD.

Bratton was brilliant in assessing the skills of his command staff and had a knack for putting people in the right places. He appointed civilians to executive-level positions traditionally held by sworn personnel. Gerry Chaleff became the commanding officer of the Consent Decree Bureau where he oversaw the implementation of the 2001 mandates. In 2009 Chaleff became the special assistant for constitutional policing under Chief Charlie Beck.

John Miller became the bureau chief for Counter Terrorism and Criminal Intelligence at the LAPD. He had served under NYPD Commissioner Bratton as deputy commissioner of public information from 1994 to 1995. Following his time with the NYPD, Miller transitioned back to journalism, working as an ABC News correspondent and gaining widespread recognition for his 1998 interview with Osama bin Laden. He later co-anchored ABC's *20/20* alongside Barbara Walters. In 2003 Miller reunited with Bratton at the LAPD, bringing his unique blend of media expertise and law enforcement experience to the department.

Mary Grady became the LAPD public information director. Before that appointment she had worked for thirteen years as a TV reporter for Los Angeles stations KCAL, KCBS, and KCOP. She won three Emmys and four Golden Mike Awards and was named Associated Press Reporter of the Year. Her responsibilities at the LAPD included being the department's spokesperson, advising the chief on the effects of LAPD policies and procedures with the public, developing long-term strategies to partner with the media, and promoting the LAPD while navigating media and community concerns.

Luann Pannell had served as an LAPD police psychologist prior to Bratton appointing her as director of police training and education. She brought a fresh, outsider's perspective. In this role, she was responsible for designing, developing, and overseeing LAPD sworn personnel training. Bratton didn't care that he was going against the LAPD's organizational design that requires a specific number of each rank to work in particular assignments throughout the department. His attitude was, "I'll put the right people in the right places. I don't care about any of those numbers." That's how he ran the organization, and it worked.

While still a sergeant, I was chosen to fill a coveted position in the Use of Force Review Division. My job was to brief Chief Bratton and write reports on his adjudication recommendations for all officer-involved shootings and other deadly force incidents submitted to the Honorable Board of Police Commissions, the final adjudicators in such cases. I attended meetings about what the LAPD was doing and how we could do it better. I admired the people Bratton appointed and learned about commanding a world-class police department from the best, Chief William Bratton himself.

Bratton had a knack for breaking down his decisions, ensuring that I understood not just what actions were taken but why. His approach was rooted in meticulous planning, clear communication, and a willingness to take responsibility for both successes and failures.

Nothing escaped Bratton's attention. For instance, his masterful understanding of the power dynamic was on full display during the closed-session meetings with the Honorable Board of Police Commissioners. The board is comprised of five civilian members appointed by the mayor to serve as the head of the LAPD. They set department policies and oversee its operations. The board works in conjunction with the chief, who reports to the board. Bratton would deliberately sit at the far end of the table, opposite the commissioners, so all eyes would have to be on him when he spoke. This was in contrast with his successor, Chief Charlie Beck, who sat among the commissioners and, as a result, saw his power diffused.

Just like Bratton, Chief Beck was a thoughtful and insightful leader who didn't shy away from challenging established practices. For example, when officer-involved shooting incidents showed a steady rise in the number of rounds fired, Beck tasked me with conducting a study to examine whether department training practices had contributed to that trend.

Officers are accountable for every round they fire, but with an average "hit rate" of only 30 percent, many rounds miss their intended target. Those misses not only pose safety concerns, but they also fuel public criticism. Reducing the number of rounds fired during an incident improves officer performance, minimizes liability, and helps maintain public trust.

My study revealed key insights that resulted in adding an assessment component to our department's firearms qualification course and implementing targeted training to enhance officer performance under stress. Those measures ultimately reduced the average number of rounds fired in officer-involved shooting incidents. Chief Beck's willingness to challenge the status quo and embrace those findings was rare in the traditionally rigid culture of law enforcement.

Bratton's transformative leadership brought significant changes to the LAPD, not just in policy but in the department's overall culture. His ability to implement innovative strategies while demanding accountability set a new standard for his successors to maintain. But with progress came challenges, as deeply ingrained practices and systemic issues often clashed with the evolving standards of policing. One of the contentious issues was the phenomenon of "contagious fire," a critical area where training and culture collided, exposing the complexities of decision making under extreme stress, an aspect addressed in the study I conducted for Chief Beck.

Contagious fire is when officers fire their weapons simply because others are shooting. This behavior is particularly troubling, as each officer is trained to make an independent decision about when to use deadly force. Acknowledging the existence of contagious fire is essential to addressing whether certain training practices inadvertently reinforce this reflexive behavior. For example, traditional police shooting ranges often have officers firing in unison when targets appear, potentially conditioning them to react without independent judgment in real-world situations. The reality is, "I shot because my partner shot" will never justify the use of deadly force.

John Timoney, a respected expert on the use of deadly force and former first deputy commissioner of the NYPD under Bratton, shared his expertise with me while working for the Ministry of Interior in Bahrain. When I mentioned that an LAPD assistant chief overseeing our study denied the existence of contagious fire, Timoney's spirited response delivered in his unmistakable Irish-Bronx accent was unforgettable: "That's absolute nonsense!"

Timoney's insights were later confirmed during a shooting study I conducted with the LA Sheriff's Department in which we successfully induced and documented contagious fire. We randomly selected officers from the field and issued them handguns that fired "marking" chalk rounds, allowing us to track the number and rate of rounds fired. Each officer was unknowingly paired with a study team member during tactical scenarios, allowing us to control key variables such as the suspect's behavior and the partner officer's response. This control served as a benchmark to assess contagious fire.

Multiple officers firing multiple rounds doesn't, in itself, indicate contagious fire, provided each officer independently identifies a deadly threat. To differentiate, we conducted post-scenario interviews and collected written questionnaires. Predictably, the majority of officers admitted to firing only after a partner shot, specifically in the absence of a clear threat. This behavior was even more pronounced as the number of officers firing increased. Common justifications included "I don't know" or "I thought there was a deadly threat because others were shooting."

Despite widespread recognition of contagious fire within law enforcement and the clear findings of our study, the assistant chief overseeing the project refused to acknowledge the existence of contagious fire. Instead, our data was replaced with an academic study that claimed no empirical evidence of the phenomenon. The stance reflected an insular belief that officers could consistently articulate sound justification for every round fired, which dismissed contagious fire's tangible and measurable impact on officer behavior. In the assistant chief's view, "Cops can do no wrong."

The issue with the academic studies is that they rely on shooting data and the officers' justifications at the time of an actual shooting incident. It's unrealistic to expect any officer to openly admit, at the risk of civil or criminal liability, that they fired simply because others were shooting and without personally identifying a threat. As a result, those studies fail to provide a credible assessment of contagious fire.

Contagious fire is a real phenomenon with serious implications for police training, policy, and accountability. But the assistant chief's reluctance to acknowledge it, stemming from a desire to "protect law enforcement," stood in the way of meaningful progress. That resistance prioritized outdated practices over public safety, leading to preventable harm. Once again, I witnessed the system's tendency to shield itself at the expense of real change which, in the end, doesn't protect anyone.

While working for Chief Bratton, I developed new adjudication standards for officer-involved shooting cases, standards still in use today. I also created a debrief model that required all involved officers to participate shortly after an incident. This approach allowed us to promptly identify successes and areas for improvement, addressing deficiencies before memories faded or important details were lost. It was a significant upgrade from the previous process that delayed the critical debrief discussions until a case was fully adjudicated, up to a year later.

We had an officer involved in a use-of-force incident that resulted in the tragic death of the individual who had been arrested. The arrestee died after being handcuffed and left in a prone position on the ground for an extended period. It was likely a case of positional asphyxia, a phenomenon in which body positioning interferes with the ability to breathe.

What made this incident even more troubling was that it directly violated department policy. According to the guidelines at the time, individuals who are handcuffed must be seated upright or placed in a left lateral lying position as soon as practicable. The failure to follow procedure may have contributed to the loss of life, but it also highlighted critical gaps in adherence to training and policy.

Prior to the adjudication of the case, the same officer was involved in a similar incident that caused another person he had arrested to die. There had been no department intervention to correct the violation of department policy, tragically culminating in another death. That's the kind of thing I was working to change for the benefit of both the LAPD and the public we aim to serve and protect.

* * *

By 2004 Los Angeles was still reeling from the previous year's challenges marked by earthquakes, wildfires, and the broader Iraq War. It was also in 2004 that an incident in the LAPD's Southeast Division drew national attention. Known as one of the city's most dangerous areas, the Southeast Division was beset by widespread unemployment, poverty, the crack cocaine epidemic, and violent crime. Gangs like the Crips and Bloods, well-funded by the drug trade, wielded significant influence. The Southeast Division also had been central to the 1992 riots sparked by the acquittal of the officers involved in the Rodney King beating. LAPD data underscored the danger: Suspects fleeing police in Southeast Los Angeles were nearly twice as likely to be armed compared to suspects citywide.

On June 23, 2004, at approximately 5:25 a.m., officers spotted a Black man suspected of stealing a Toyota Camry driving north on the Harbor Freeway. A thirty-minute pursuit ensued on surface streets before concluding in Compton. Television news helicopters captured the chase in real time, and their footage would soon dominate the news cycle. Shortly before 6 a.m., about half a dozen LAPD officers pursued the suspect on foot after he fled from the stolen car. The chase ended in the concrete-lined Compton Creek channel where the suspect stopped, raised his arms, and crouched in apparent surrender.

Despite his compliance, the situation quickly escalated. Two officers restrained the man on the ground, but a third officer delivered a kick and then struck the suspect eleven times in the upper body with a metal flashlight. Moments later, with the suspect handcuffed and in custody, three officers were seen exchanging handshakes. All the officers involved were White.

The news helicopter footage aired repeatedly throughout the day on local stations and soon gained national attention. The imagery was damning and drew immediate comparisons to the infamous 1991 beating of Rodney King. South Bureau Deputy Chief Earl Paysinger, the highest-ranking African American officer in the LAPD at the time, described the scene as "Rodney King-esque." For those of us who had lived through the fallout of the Rodney King beating, the resemblance was clear and troubling.

Chief Bill Bratton was in Hartford, Connecticut, when the incident occurred, but he wasted no time in addressing the issue: "There is no denying that it looks very bad from what is seen on the video," he told the *Los Angeles Times*. "But there should be no rush to judgment before the investigations are completed." Bratton immediately initiated both criminal and internal investigations.

This event was a significant setback for the LAPD, particularly for Bratton's efforts to rebuild trust with South Los Angeles communities. Over the previous two years Bratton had made notable strides in improving relations, particularly with African Americans who had endured decades of police abuse. "Chief Bratton, to his credit, has been aggressive in reaching out," John Mack of the Urban League told the *Los Angeles Times*. "Back during Rodney King, it was an all-out war; it was very antagonistic. But there has been general improvement."

Still, this incident tested that progress. California law at the time permitted the use of force that was "objectively reasonable" to make an arrest, overcome resistance, or prevent escape. Metal flashlights were an approved tool, but they were to be used only when necessary to subdue resistance. But the footage of the incident showed there had been no resistance, so the fallout was swift.

As soon as he returned to Los Angeles, Bratton met with community leaders in South LA and took immediate action. Recognizing the potential for metal flashlights to be misused, he implemented a department-wide policy change: "Flashlights are for illumination purposes," he declared, and he ordered the replacement of all metal flashlights with plastic ones, a practical solution that maintained the utility of flashlights while removing a tool that had become a symbol of excessive force.

Bratton's straightforward yet impactful decision sent a clear message: The LAPD was committed to making changes that would prevent similar incidents and address community concerns. It was one less source of contention between the department and the communities it served, a necessary step in the ongoing effort to rebuild trust.

* * *

On May 1, 2007, Chief William Bratton faced another critical challenge as the LAPD's handling of a rally in MacArthur Park spiraled into chaos. The May Day rally, organized to demand amnesty for undocumented immigrants, began with about 25,000 participants peacefully marching. The organizers had secured permits to hold the event until 9 p.m., and the day started without incident.

But by 5 p.m. a small group of protesters began blocking the street, violating the permit conditions. LAPD officers repeatedly asked the protesters to clear the road, but instead of dispersing, the crowd grew larger. Unable to manage the increasing numbers, LAPD commanders declared the event an "unlawful assembly," effectively revoking the rally's permit.

Despite the overwhelming presence of Spanish-speaking rally participants, the order to disperse was communicated solely in English. Announcements were made from a police helicopter, squad cars, and officers with megaphones, but for many in the crowd the language barrier rendered those directives meaningless.

As confusion grew, LAPD officers formed a line and advanced about fifty feet at a time to give those complying with the dispersal order time and space to get out of the way. Most protesters left the area, but those who remained began to throw rocks and bottles at the advancing police. Officers then used batons and rubber bullets on the crowd.

Altogether, the estimated 600 police officers fired 146 foam-rubber projectiles. It was bad enough that the LAPD had injured marchers advocating for immigration rights, but the force with which they went after the media who were covering the event once again put Bratton's challenge in a very public light. Several TV reporters were beaten with LAPD batons, and a rubber bullet hit one. TV news caught it all, and once again, LAPD brutality was on television for all to see. The melee injured 246 journalists and protesters as well as 18 officers, and more than 250 legal claims were filed against the city. Bratton once again acted swiftly. The day after the violence Bratton called it the "worst incident of this type I have ever encountered in thirty-seven years" in law enforcement.

He also asked the FBI to open a civil rights inquiry into the incident, and two internal investigations were begun by the police department. Five months later the LAPD released a report, and unlike days of yore when blame was routinely placed on the victims, this time the blame landed squarely on the department itself. Bratton, in a news conference, repeatedly apologized for "significant senior management failures, myself on down. I, as chief of police, regret deeply that this occurred on my watch. I accept full responsibility."

It was classic Bratton. The accountability didn't end there. Deputy Chief Lee Carter, who was in charge of policing the event, "underestimated the size and significance" of the demonstration, even though a May Day gathering a year before had drawn hundreds of thousands.

The department's report said that when a Rampart-area captain suggested additional planning before the march, Carter "verbally reprimanded" him. Additionally, the officers who ultimately confronted the protesters, including those from the elite Metropolitan Division, played no role in the planning phase.

Three hours before the march turned violent, Carter, Assistant Chief Earl Paysinger, and Deputy Chief Richard Roupoli decided to reduce the police presence at the park. The commands released three of four platoons ordered to stand by. As the crowds grew that afternoon, Carter and the other commands didn't take advantage of the more than 450 officers available to handle the large numbers, relying instead on a smaller group of Metro officers who quickly became overwhelmed. Even the 450 officers were only about half what several local police captains had told superiors were needed to handle the crowds.

As tensions grew in the park, officers and their supervisors grew confused over who was in charge. The resulting mix-up left no single "incident commander" in control, so line officers were uncertain about who was directing the operation. In one radio transmission a lieutenant referred to the person in charge as "they," underscoring the absence of the single leader LAPD policy requires. The report said officers noticed "obvious tension" among the three command officers and that numerous requests over the radio for information and resources went unanswered, leaving lieutenants in the field to formulate their own plans to control the crowd.

When clashes with protesters and journalists began, officers used more force than LAPD policies allow, the report found.

"Had a higher degree of leadership been exhibited that afternoon, the events of May 1, 2007, may have never occurred," the report concluded. Bratton acted immediately and demoted the highest-ranking officer at the scene, Deputy Chief Carter, and removed approximately sixty officers from field-related duties, pending the outcome of the investigation. In the end, seventeen officers and two sergeants were disciplined. Bratton held people accountable, regardless of rank.

To ensure such an incident didn't happen again, Chief Bratton directed Deputy Chief Michael Hillman to comprise a critical incident management team to handle all planned demonstrations. I had been the assistant platoon leader for the 2000 Democratic National Convention held in downtown LA, so I was added to the team and placed in charge of enhancing communications with demonstrators. I implemented a state-of-the-art crowd management vehicle, which we proudly named the Critical Incident Utility Vehicle. It was equipped with a speaker system that could be heard at a quarter-mile distance and an interactive signage board that could provide messaging in countless languages. Those changes made the LAPD a nationally recognized leader in crowd management and control techniques, which were reflective of the ideas I took with me into the next level of my career.

* * *

In 2008 I received a promotion to lieutenant. I was keen to become a watch commander and get back into the mix of overseeing the field operations of patrol officers, but Chief Bratton had a different plan.

"The way I look at it," Bratton said, "you can go out and learn how to run a watch at a patrol division, or you can continue to work directly for me and learn how to run a department." There was no greater honor, so there was nothing further to consider. I stayed and continued to learn under the guidance of the astute Chief William Bratton.

I was lucky enough to receive an elite education in police management from a front-row seat. For seven years I saw how Bratton ran the LAPD. I sat in on meetings with Bratton, Assistant Chief Jim McDonnell, who later served as chief of police of Long Beach and sheriff of LA County before becoming the fifty-seventh chief of the LAPD in 2024, and Gerald Chaleff, the civilian commanding officer of the Consent Decree Bureau. I saw firsthand the issues they had to manage and how Bratton took command of situations quickly and with integrity and accountability. Through that experience, I developed a deep understanding of what it takes to lead a world-class police department.

Despite my exposure to those influential leaders, some have questioned why I didn't advance beyond the rank of lieutenant. The captain promotional assessment process at the time was straightforward. There were three graded essays and an interview score that reflects the average score from a three-person panel of two command-level officers and a civilian. Those combined scores determine your overall rank for promotion to captain. I took the test after Bratton's departure and scored high enough to be promoted.

Months later, as I walked through the locker room at police headquarters, I was approached by a commander who extended his hand in a congratulatory greeting. He had attended the promotion selection meeting earlier that morning and knew I had been chosen for promotion. A sense of confusion must have been apparent in my expression, as I had no idea what he was referring to. After a short pause he said, "Have you not been notified? You were selected to promote to captain." When chosen for promotion to captain, the police chief personally summons you to his office on the tenth floor of police headquarters. In anticipation of that call I returned to my office, placed my phone on my desk, and waited.

But the call never came. Instead, I received a call from a lieutenant friend of mine who asked that our conversation remain confidential because he was not authorized to contact me. He informed me that I was selected to be promoted to captain, but the Medical Liaison Division had listed me as having a restricted duty status, prohibiting me from promoting. The condition of exertion-induced asthma I had sustained while evacuating people from the burning convalescent home was erroneously input into their system, categorizing me as permanently light duty. Since becoming inflicted with asthma,

I had been promoted twice, to sergeant and then to lieutenant. But this time was inexplicably different.

The following morning I made an appointment with my physician to obtain documentation that my asthma didn't limit me from working full-duty assignments, the type of assignments I had worked throughout my career, but the department selected another candidate to fill the captain's vacancy without officially notifying me of my selection or the light-duty status that prohibited my promotion.

I had the professional aspiration and drive to promote as high as possible within the organization. Still, despite having grounds for reinstating my promotion, I chose not to pursue it. I had recently been granted sole legal and physical custody of my five-year-old son, so after significant contemplation, I decided to forgo my career aspirations because my child was—and is—my priority, and promotion to captain would have significantly impeded the flexibility required in my schedule to best parent him.

But Bratton's leadership provided me with far more than a career trajectory; it offered a framework for how policing could and should evolve. His lessons, and my own experiences, shaped a vision for reimagining law enforcement, not just in Los Angeles but across the country. Bratton often referenced Sir Robert Peel's foundational principles of policing: "The basic mission for which the police exist is to prevent crime and disorder." Bratton believed these words were the most important in the history of Western policing, and I came to share his belief.

I also was struck by something Bratton had written in a recent article: "The top cop can no longer be judged simply on the basis of whether the major crime categories traditionally tracked by the organization rise or fall, but also on the public's perception of order and safety on the city streets." His words so eloquently capture the essence of what I've seen over decades of service. Trust is the bedrock of effective policing, trust within the organization and in the communities we serve. Without it, even the best strategies falter. Perception shapes reality and fostering public confidence in law enforcement is as vital as reducing crime itself.

Bratton's work and Peel's enduring philosophy have shaped my understanding of what needs to change for policing to better serve our communities and rebuild trust with citizens. To chart a path forward, it's essential to examine not only the foundational principles of law enforcement but also the historical forces that shaped it.

A Visual Companion to
On Thin Ice

NOV • 71

Here we are after a family trip to SeaWorld in 1971, sporting our souvenir hats and smiles. Growing up in Kent, Ohio, as part of a multiracial adoptive family shaped me in ways I couldn't fully understand at the time.

Though my family felt completely normal to me, even as a child, it wasn't lost on me that our story was different. My parents weren't just raising children; whether intentional or not, they were making a statement.

Growing up in a multiracial family in the 1960s and 1970s in Kent meant ignoring whispers and stares at the A&P grocery store, but my mother met every judgmental gaze with unwavering dignity, teaching us to value our uniqueness over others' ignorance.

Every race was a tribute to my parents, accomplished athletes themselves, who taught me to strive for excellence. Pushing toward the finish line here at fourteen years old wasn't about outrunning the competition; it was about a willingness to endure the pain in pursuit of my potential. Each stride beyond my perceived limit was a personal victory.

With my linemates in Kent, Ohio, where it all began. Long before the championships and scouting reports, these friendships taught me what hockey—and life—was really about: teamwork and discipline. All three of us went on to play Division I collegiate hockey with my teammate in the middle going on to play for the NHL's Vancouver Canucks.

DUBUQUE FIGHTING SAINTS
1984-85

Back Row: Trainer Pat McCormick, Mike Budlove, Kord Cernich, Greg Poss, Dale Calcamuggio, Ken Rowe, Mike Cusack, Jeff Wenninger, Darrin Semeniuk, Kurt Kabat, Steve MacSwain and Coach Jack Barzee.

Front Row: Tim Cortes, Kent Middleton, George Stetson, Mark Nason, Mike Hess, Bill Cody, Steve Chartrand, Jim Cammarata and Dave DePinto.

Missing: Jeff Ingalls and Paul Erickson

The 1984–1985 Dubuque Fighting Saints team photo. Playing under Coach Jack Barzee taught me as much about handling life's pressures as it did about hockey. His humor, perspective, and leadership shaped not just my season but my outlook.

Reporters once described me as playing like "a man possessed" on the ice. The truth is, the motivation to win every on-ice battle was inspired by watching Mom confront her fight against cancer with the strength that propels my relentless spirit to this very day.

For me, hockey wasn't just a game; it was my refuge and training ground for life. It instilled a mindset of discipline and relentless drive for self-improvement, values I carried with me long after I hung up the skates and picked up the badge.

155

The academy was not about competence. It was about mastering knowledge, control, and discipline. Skills learned here weren't just about passing a test: they were about surviving on the streets.

In the ring, as in hockey, I learned that strength wasn't about landing punches, but about anticipating, adapting, and staying calm under pressure, lessons that defined my entire law enforcement career.

Being chosen by my academy drill instructors and classmates to serve as class guidon was a highlight in my early career. It was my first realization that I was representing not just myself, but also my peers and the entire law enforcement community.

Receiving the Certificate of Merit as the top recruit in my academy class. This honor motivated me to further push my limits and pursue excellence in everything I set out to achieve.

As a fellow deputy sheriff, Teri's insight not only taught me about the realities of our relationship within the police culture but also how to navigate policing diverse communities with understanding. Her strength, intelligence, and friendship remain invaluable to me today.

The LAPD became a proving ground that pushed me physically, mentally, and emotionally, shaping not just the officer I'd become but also reinforcing the importance of the values instilled in me from childhood.

Pictured with Sergeant Mike Patriquin, who would be my successor in leading the gang unit. Rampart Division was ground zero for some of American policing's toughest lessons. I helped lead it through one of the worst scandals in modern policing. But as a nation, these lessons have not been learned. Two decades later, I watch the same culture of brutality resurface time and time again.

Some colleagues leave a lasting mark on us. Sergeant Curtis Woodle, pictured here, profoundly influenced my understanding of what service truly means. He modeled not just exceptional leadership within the LAPD but also reminded me of the deep responsibility we hold to the communities we serve.

Standing beside Chief Bratton at the Medal of Valor ceremony reminded me how thin the line is between courage and casualty. Receiving the department's highest honor was a humbling recognition of the daily risks officers face, often in the most unexpected moments.

My father and I pose for a photo prior to the Medal of Valor ceremony. My father instilled the courage to speak out when it matters most. He developed my critical thinking and moral reasoning, which was reflected in my 30-plus-year law enforcement career.

Recognized alongside fellow officers for the Medal of Valor prior to a game at Dodger Stadium. Despite the sheer size of LA, the dedication and passion for the city's professional sports teams make it feel like a close-knit community.

Taking home the gold medal at the Nevada Police and Fire Games in CrossFit. Strength, discipline, and dedication pay off—on and off duty.

Outside my CrossFit gym with my "City of Angels" wings—just a block from LAPD headquarters. Every morning started right here, a daily commitment to fitness and discipline that carried me through my entire law enforcement career.

International Police Winter Games gold medal team. Athletics built more than camaraderie; it also gave us an opportunity to support meaningful community charities like the Make-A-Wish Foundation.

Running my leg of the 120-mile Baker to Vegas relay race. I was a member of three winning teams over the years. The honor of winning the open portion of the competition came with significant bragging rights for the department and respect from all who competed. *Truly* a team effort.

A lighter moment with colleagues from the LAPD Force Investigation Division leadership team.

Section II.
Forgotten Past, Misguided Present

Chapter 6:
The History of Modern Policing

The measure of a society is how it treats its most vulnerable members.

—Mahatma Gandhi

Law enforcement, as an institution, sits at the intersection of power, trust, and accountability, a role as complex as the communities it seeks to protect. The story of modern policing is one of aspiration and contradiction, where lofty ideals coexist with troubling realities. To understand how we arrived at this moment of reckoning, we must look backward, not only to the origins of American policing but also to the primeval frameworks of law and order that shaped its foundation.

At its core, policing reflects the values of the society it serves. Yet, in the United States the journey from its troubling origins to what many perceive as today's militarized police forces reveals a deep disconnect. This chapter examines the historical evolution of policing, juxtaposing Sir Robert Peel's vision for ethical law enforcement with the harsh realities of racial injustice, militarization, and eroded public trust.

Before we delve into Peel's principles and their influence on modern policing, let's step even further back to the ancient roots of justice systems that first grappled with the balance between power and fairness. Those origins provide a lens through which we can understand not just where law enforcement has been but also where it must go to meet today's challenges.

The concept of policing is as old as civilization itself, rooted in humanity's enduring struggle to maintain order and justice while living in groups. King Hammurabi's Code, carved into stone around 1792 BCE, stood as one of the earliest recorded legal systems in ancient Babylon. That code introduced the notion of justice as a tool to govern society. Yet, its principles of retribution, captured in the phrase "an eye for an eye," laid the groundwork for punitive enforcement practices that still reverberate through modern systems of law and order.

Centuries later in ancient Rome, Emperor Augustus established the Vigiles, a group of free Roman citizens tasked with maintaining public safety and fighting fires. The Vigiles were intentionally designed to avoid the militaristic image of Roman legions, donning civilian clothing to embody a more community-focused role. Over time, under the reign of Emperor Justinian, those efforts evolved into a system of codified laws that emphasized state responsibility in proving guilt and ensuring fair trials. Those developments advanced the concept of justice and highlighted the crucial role of law enforcement in maintaining social order.

But those early systems also revealed a persistent tension: the delicate balance between upholding order and wielding power. That tension between authority and accountability, fairness and force, has shaped the evolution of policing for millennia. As we explore the development of modern law enforcement, those ancient origins remind us that the challenges we face today are part of a far longer story, one that continues to wrestle with the question of how to use power responsibly in service of the public good.

* * *

When English settlers established colonies in North America, they brought with them the influence of England's constabulary and night watches. Yet, the origins of policing in America are undeniably tied to the nation's embarrassing transgressions, particularly the institution of slavery. Early enforcement groups, though not officially referred to as "police," were designed to maintain a brutal economic hierarchy. Those patrols emerged in South Carolina in the early 1700s and operated in other slaveholding territories, enforcing laws that upheld the forced labor system. Their mission was to maintain control over enslaved individuals, monitor their movements, and suppress any hint of rebellion.

An oath from a North Carolina patrolman reflects the grim purpose of these groups:

> *I (patroller's name), do swear, that I will as searcher for guns, swords, and other weapons among the slaves in my district, faithfully, and as privately as I can, discharge the trust reposed in me as the law directs, to the best of my power. So help me, God.*

That pledge illustrates the inherent violence embedded in early enforcement practices. Those patrols were not about justice but about preserving an oppressive social and economic order. White men, often cloaking their actions in divine justification, carried out those duties with unchecked brutality. While women occasionally participated, their roles were primarily tied to their association with powerful plantation owners.

In cities like New Orleans, those patrols evolved into more formalized entities. Armed city guards in military-style uniforms were employed to enforce the same oppressive order. After the Civil War, the structure of policing began to shift, but not uniformly. In the Reconstruction-era South, many former patrols were rebranded as police forces responsible for enforcing Black Codes, laws designed to control the movements, labor, and rights of newly freed Black individuals. In the North, law enforcement often targeted immigrant communities and labor unions, revealing a similar focus on maintaining control over marginalized groups. These regional variations contributed to a national culture of policing that prioritized social and economic hierarchies over justice. This brutal system prioritized property over humanity, embedding racial inequities into the foundation of American policing, a legacy that many believe persists today.

Urbanization during the Industrial Revolution necessitated organized policing, leading to the establishment of paid departments like Boston's in 1838. Yet even those early institutions disproportionately targeted immigrants, labor activists, and marginalized communities, mirroring the social biases of the time by protecting the interests of wealthy landowners and merchants. Though these groups adopted the characteristics of early civic police forces, their mission was still rooted in controlling marginalized populations rather than ensuring equity or public safety.

* * *

In 1829 Sir Robert Peel, a two-time prime minister of the United Kingdom, introduced a revolutionary framework for law enforcement that continues to inspire those seeking to reimagine policing today. Peel's Nine Principles aimed to create a system that served the public equitably, emphasizing crime prevention over punishment and relying on the willing cooperation of the community. Those principles, grounded in trust and accountability, represented an alternative to the fear-driven, militaristic approaches that often defined law enforcement in Peel's time.

Peel's vision materialized with the creation of the London Metropolitan Police where his "Bobbies" patrolled communities as visible guardians of order, not as instruments of oppression. It was a radical idea, a police force that succeeded not through brute force but through the approval and cooperation of the people it served. Peel's principles remain a benchmark for ethical policing, offering a blueprint for how law enforcement can uphold justice while maintaining public trust:

1. The basic mission of the police is to prevent crime and disorder.

2. The ability of the police to perform their duties depends on public approval of their actions.

3. Police must secure the willing cooperation of the public in voluntarily obeying the law.

4. The greater degree of respect that can be gained reduces the amount of force that needs to be used.

5. Police must demonstrate constant and absolute impartiality in service to the law.

6. Police use physical force only once persuasion, advice, and warning have been insufficient.

7. The police are the public, and the public are the police.

8. Police should never appear to be punishing wrongdoers themselves.

9. The test of police efficiency is the absence of crime, not a visible response to crime that has already happened.

Despite Peel's principles offering an aspirational foundation, their influence in the United States has been complicated. While his model inspired early American policing, it coexisted with systems born in violence and racial supremacy. Reconciling those two legacies—one that seeks neutrality and trust and the other that perpetuates control and inequity—is essential to understanding the dual narratives that define modern law enforcement in the United States.

Even the language we use to describe law enforcement reflects this complex legacy. Words carry weight, and the term "cop" offers a small but telling window into how the public has perceived and engaged with the profession over time.

The term "cop," the everyday nickname for police officers, carries an interesting history. One theory traces its origin to the word "copper," a reference to the distinctive copper buttons on the uniforms of nineteenth-century English officers, making them easily identifiable as law enforcers. Another explanation links it to the verb "cop," meaning "to seize" or "to capture," derived from the Latin "caper," meaning "to take." Officers who apprehended criminals were colloquially called "coppers," a term of function and recognition that eventually was shortened to cop.

As this nickname crossed the Atlantic, it became a casual, familiar way to refer to police officers in the US. Cop isn't the only moniker the profession has garnered. Over the years slang like "the fuzz," "the heat," and "the boys in blue" emerged, reflecting different cultural attitudes toward law enforcement, sometimes reverent, sometimes critical. Whether included in a noir detective story or muttered under their breath on a city street, these nicknames remind us of the deep, complex imprint police officers have left on our language and society.

These evolving terms also mirror the shifting dynamics between law enforcement and the public. They reflect how officers have been viewed, sometimes as protectors, other times as oppressors, often depending on the historical moment and the community being served. In this way, the language surrounding policing offers insight into the broader challenges of reconciling Peel's vision with the realities of American law enforcement.

Peel's revolutionary framework sought to elevate policing as a profession grounded in trust, prevention, and community partnership, values that have profoundly influenced modern law enforcement, even as their application has diverged in significant ways. His principles offered a pathway to foster cooperation and mutual respect between officers and the public. To understand how Peel's ideals took root, and where they strayed, we must examine the direct influence his model had on the development of American policing.

Peel's revolutionary vision shaped British policing and influenced the development of municipal police forces in cities including Boston, New York, and Philadelphia during the mid-nineteenth century. Those early departments adopted some elements of Peel's model, such as uniformed officers patrolling their beats to prevent crime and maintain order. But American policing quickly devolved in significant ways.

Unlike Peel's constables who carried only batons to emphasize community trust, American police were armed from the outset. This choice was informed by the entrenched culture of violence that shaped early American law enforcement. In the US, Peel's emphasis on public cooperation often gave way to coercion, particularly in marginalized communities where the police were viewed as oppressors rather than protectors.

At the same time, anti-immigrant fervor drove U.S. law enforcement practices that prioritized controlling dis-enfranchised populations over fostering public trust. Those policies, fueled by racial and class-based inequalities, highlight the challenges of applying Peel's principles in the uniquely fractured and contentious landscape of American society. The result was a policing system that often strayed far from Peel's original vision of prevention and partnership.

Peel's seventh principle, "The police are the public, and the public are the police," captures the ideal relationship between law enforcement and the people they are entrusted to protect and serve. But in the United States this principle has often been undermined. Even today, echoes of those patrols persist in the over-policing of Black and Brown communities and the systemic inequities embedded in the criminal justice system.

But Peel's principles remain a powerful blueprint for reimagining policing. They challenge us to ask questions like these:

What would it take to build a system where public trust is earned through fairness, impartiality, and prevention rather than through fear or force?

How can we ensure officers are seen as part of the community rather than as an occupying force?

* * *

Modern American policing began in 1909 when August Vollmer became the chief of police in Berkeley, California, and remade it after an organization he knew well, the American military. Since 1789, the United States had been isolationist, viewing the main threats to its security as coming from within. The domestic wars fought by the United States against Native Americans and the Civil War fought between the Union and Confederacy roiled American society.

Not until the late nineteenth century did the United States step away from isolationism to fight in the Spanish-American War of 1898. That war featured battles on the other side of the world, in the Philippines where Vollmer served with the Eighth Army Corps. "For years, ever since the Spanish-American War days, I've studied military tactics and used them to good effect in rounding up crooks," he said. "After all, we're conducting a war, a war against the enemies of society." Those enemies of which Vollmer spoke were, by and large, criminals, labor organizers, immigrants, and nonwhites.

By the early twentieth century, Vollmer and others ushered in significant changes to policing: police academies, forensic science, and military-style hierarchies. Those innovations brought professionalism and structure, but they also embedded a culture of force and authority. Vollmer's advocacy for higher education in policing was progressive for its time, but it reinforced a warrior-like mentality in law enforcement that prioritized tactical readiness over community engagement.

The consequences of this history are still visible today. From the militarization of police forces with their armored vehicles and tactical combat gear to modern racial profiling and disparities in the use of force, many practices can be traced back to these origins. The emphasis on control and suppression remains deeply ingrained in U.S. law enforcement.

Resistance to such practices has a long and storied history. Abolitionists in the nineteenth century, civil rights leaders in the twentieth, and modern-day advocates for accountability and transparency have pushed back against oppressive enforcement. Today, the call for systemic change continues, championing equitable practices that prioritize justice and community trust.

Acknowledging this history is not an indictment of individual officers but a necessary reckoning of the choices that shaped our systems of law enforcement. But because these systems were created through conscious decisions, they can be reshaped through better ones.

* * *

Policing in America has always been shaped by the people in charge. Every shift in law enforcement has reflected the values of the time, sometimes for the best, but too often for the worst. The result is a system that claims to serve the public while, in many cases, it's used to control it.

History isn't just something to acknowledge, it's something to learn from. Ignoring failures doesn't erase them; it just ensures they'll continue. If law enforcement is to move forward, it must reckon with its origins, confront the inequities embedded in its structure, and embrace a model that prioritizes accountability, fairness, and community trust.

The question isn't whether change is necessary—it is. Instead, the question is whether leaders within policing are willing to recognize that a broken system cannot be defended, only rebuilt. Peel's vision of ethical policing, centered on public cooperation rather than fear, offers a roadmap, but turning that vision into reality requires more than rhetoric. It demands officers trained to de-escalate rather than dominate, policies that reward transparency over aggression, and leadership that prioritizes justice over politics.

The next chapter examines one of the greatest barriers to achieving this vision: the increasing militarization of American law enforcement. Over the years police departments have stocked up on military-grade gear, adopted combat tactics, and trained officers to see everyday people, their neighbors, as potential threats instead of partners in society. This approach isn't making communities safer. Instead, it's deepening distrust and escalating tensions. To rebuild trust we must first understand how policing became so militarized and, more importantly, what it will take to reverse course before that trust is irretrievably lost.

Chapter 7:
The Militarization of Policing

On either side of a potentially violent conflict, an opportunity exists to exercise compassion and diminish fear based on recognition of each other's humanity.

— Aberjhani, *Splendid Literarium*

Modern policing in the United States has evolved into something that would be unrecognizable to its early architects. What began as a patchwork of community watches, constables, and night patrols has transformed into a force that, in many ways, resembles the military more than a civilian institution. From armored vehicles rolling through suburban streets to officers outfitted in tactical gear reminiscent of war zones, policing has steadily moved toward a combat-ready approach.

Some of these tactics are justified in extreme circumstances: active shooter incidents, hostage situations, or large-scale emergencies. But their widespread use in everyday policing has changed the nature of law enforcement itself. It fosters a them versus us mindset, escalating routine encounters into confrontations, replacing trust with fear, and turning neighborhoods into what some perceive as war zones.

To understand how we got here, we must examine the history that shaped policing's descent into militarization. Law enforcement in America has always prioritized control over accountability, reflecting the power structures of the time. The shift toward militarization wasn't the result of a single policy or decision but a series of reactions to crises, each one reinforcing the exact problems it aimed to solve.

The examples that follow aren't isolated incidents. They are the predictable outcomes of decades of policy decisions and leadership failures that have blurred the line between policing and warfare. If we want to restore public trust and reshape law enforcement for the better, we need to start by understanding how policing became so militarized in the first place.

* * *

Not only do many police departments actively recruit officers with military combat experience, they also equip their personnel with weapons and vehicles initially designed for war. And that equipment is being supplied directly by the U.S. government through the 1033 Program, named after the section of law that established it, and born from the country's ongoing War on Drugs.

In 1989 Congress gave the Pentagon temporary authority to give equipment no longer in use by the military to local police and sheriff's departments. Since the actual transfer of equipment began in 1996, nearly 10,000 American policing jurisdictions have received more than $7 billion of military equipment, including combat vehicles, rifles, armored personnel carriers, and grenade launchers.

Since 2011 the military has transferred an average of $390 million worth of military equipment annually to all fifty states and several U.S. territories. I saw evidence of this firsthand during my time with the LAPD. For several months I was part of a military acquisition team tasked with visiting military bases throughout California to find equipment we could use.

Helicopters, tactical weapons, and even armored vehicles were made available with shocking ease. And it was all free. We just had to complete the paperwork. Our marching orders were basic: "Go find some good shit."

Although I appreciate the role specialized equipment plays in critical tactical scenarios, it's been my experience that patrol officers' access to military equipment is counterproductive to nurturing community relationships. Today, the shift toward militarization is evident in even the smallest communities where patrol officers routinely wear external ballistic vests, once reserved for situations like high-risk search warrants and critical tactical incidents.

The weapons, military equipment and, indeed, military outfitting of the police force prompts a militaristic mindset. When officers are outfitted like soldiers, it shifts the perception of their role. Civilians are no longer community members but potential threats, and the streets are seen as battlefields rather than neighborhoods. This militarized approach risks alienating the very communities law enforcement is sworn to protect, particularly those already grappling with historical grievances against policing.

* * *

On August 10, 2014, just one day after a police officer fatally shot Michael Brown, an unarmed Black teenager, Ferguson, Missouri, descended into chaos. The streets erupted, not only with grief and outrage but in a battle for the soul of American policing. What began as a demand for justice for Michael Brown quickly escalated into a national reckoning, forcing Americans to confront uncomfortable truths about race, law enforcement, and the unchecked armament of police forces.

The unrest sparked fierce debates, initially centered on the fractured relationship between law enforcement and Black Americans. But the conversation soon widened, encompassing the militarization of police, Missouri's use of force laws, and systemic inequities in the criminal justice system. Activists pointed to broader injustices, from for-profit policing and the criminalization of poverty to the enduring segregation of American schools, each point revealing how deeply entrenched disparities shaped Ferguson's tragic reality.

One of the most glaring examples was Ferguson's debtors' prison system, a practice that disproportionately punished the city's poorest residents. The calculation for this injustice came nearly a decade after the riots, but the foundations of the system had been in place long before protests filled the streets. For years, Ferguson had relied on jailing people for unpaid fines, often for minor infractions, as a revenue stream, prioritizing profit over justice. In 2024 the city agreed to a $4.5 million settlement after a federal lawsuit revealed that thousands of residents had been detained in squalid conditions until they could pay for their release. The lawsuit exposed how Ferguson and surrounding municipalities had turned their courts into financial traps, disproportionately targeting Black residents and low-income individuals. This wasn't just a policing failure; it was a systemic exploitation of the most vulnerable, reinforcing cycles of financial instability and further eroding trust between the community and law enforcement.

The images from Ferguson remain seared into the nation's consciousness. Unarmed protesters filled the streets, demanding accountability for Michael Brown's death, only to face an overwhelming show of force. Officers in riot gear, tactical rifles slung across their chests, advanced behind ballistic vehicles that looked like they belonged on a battlefield. Tear gas and rubber bullets were deployed with alarming regularity while smoke hung heavy in the air. Even journalists weren't spared: Some were arrested, and a SWAT team dismantled the equipment of an Al Jazeera news crew that was broadcasting live from the scene.

At the time, Ferguson's population was overwhelmingly Black, yet only four of its fifty-three police officers were. This stark imbalance wasn't just a statistic; it symbolized a long-standing divide between the people and those sworn to protect them. Instead of addressing this disconnect, the militarized response further inflamed tensions that had been simmering for years.

By 2015 the U.S. Department of Justice released a scathing report that laid bare the structural failures in Ferguson's criminal justice system. Officers routinely violated constitutional rights by detaining people without reasonable suspicion and using stun guns after little provocation. Black residents were disproportionately targeted with traffic stops, fines, and arrests while the justice system operated more like a revenue machine than a guardian of public safety. The DOJ didn't mince words: Ferguson's entire system needed an overhaul.

Some changes followed, but progress was uneven. The police chief resigned, and the city prosecutor who declined to indict the officer who shot Michael Brown was voted out of office. The department increased its number of Black officers from four to twenty-one, a significant shift but far from a comprehensive solution.

Yet by 2019 a *New York Times* investigation revealed a troubling trend. Black drivers in St. Louis County, where Ferguson is located, were being stopped at even higher rates than before the protests, while White drivers were being stopped even less than before. The disparities that had fueled the unrest remained deeply entrenched, showing how difficult it is to dismantle systemic inequities.

Ferguson wasn't an anomaly. Ferguson was a flashpoint. The images of armored vehicles rolling through suburban streets and officers wielding military-grade weapons against unarmed civilians forced the nation to grapple with the consequences of police militarization. Far from restoring order, those tools of war escalated tensions, fractured trust, and deepened the wounds they were meant to heal.

What happened in Ferguson revealed a hard truth: When law enforcement views the communities it serves as adversaries, the consequences are devastating. Militarization shifts the focus from collaboration to control, fostering fear instead of trust. It's a mindset that's not just harmful but also incompatible with the fundamental purpose of policing.

Reflecting on Ferguson and its lasting impact, I see a path forward, not just for Ferguson but for all of us. Policing must return to its roots, guided by the principles Sir Robert Peel envisioned nearly two centuries ago. The measure of a successful police force isn't the number of arrests it makes or how forcefully it asserts control; it's how well it fosters safety, trust, and mutual respect in the communities it serves.

Ferguson showed us how far we've strayed from that vision. The question now is whether we have the courage to find our way back. The excessive militarization on display in Ferguson fractured trust. It underscored a culture of aggression that had been embedded in the profession for decades, one that had already taken root in some of the most elite units in law enforcement.

* * *

The police response to demonstrations at UCLA in the spring of 2024 served as yet another reminder of how far law enforcement still had to go in addressing excessive force. The incident also highlighted a glaring contradiction: despite legislative efforts to limit the militarized use of less-lethal munitions after past abuses, officers continued to deploy them in ways that directly conflicted with the law's intent.

Following the 2020 protests in response to George Floyd's death, California enacted Assembly Bill 48, designed to restrict law enforcement's use of rubber bullets, beanbag rounds, and tear gas against protesters. The legislation specifically required that such force should be used only when individuals posed an immediate threat to life or serious bodily injury or when necessary to bring an objectively dangerous and unlawful situation safely and effectively under control.

And yet, during the UCLA demonstrations officers with the California Highway Patrol (CHP) fired indiscriminately into crowds in clear violation of those legal standards. I watched as an officer fired a single beanbag round, paused, and then fired three more in rapid succession, not at an identifiable threat but into a sea of protesters.

Beanbag rounds are meant for single-target acquisition, not to be fired at will into a crowd. They should be used only when an individual is actively engaging in violence, and no other options are viable. If there was such a threat at UCLA that day, it wasn't apparent in the footage. There was no evidence of a threat to life or serious bodily injury to anyone. More importantly, if there truly was a need for this level of force, where was the effort to make an arrest? When no attempts to make arrests were made in conjunction with the force used, it calls into question whether the force was justified at all.

California's legislation was intended to hold law enforcement accountable. The law mandates that agencies be required to publicly justify via report their use of kinetic energy projectiles within sixty days of deployment. But in the UCLA case, the CHP report was glaringly deficient. There was no evidence to support the claim that the use of force complied with the legislative statute. The lack of compliance surrounding the intended legal safeguards made it clear that passing laws alone isn't enough. Real cultural change within policing still had not taken hold.

This isn't a new problem. We've seen it time and time again, from the LAPD's response to the 2007 MacArthur Park immigration protests to the violent dispersal of demonstrators during the Ferguson unrest in 2014 to the excessive force used against LA protesters in the wake of George Floyd's murder. The failure at UCLA wasn't just about one officer's actions; it was about a broader culture within law enforcement that continues to default to force, even when the law says otherwise. Most recently, this is evident in the force displayed during the anti-ICE demonstrations in Los Angeles.

Policing demonstrations requires skill, restraint, and a deep understanding of how law enforcement actions shape public perception. Too many officers are unequipped for these high-pressure situations, lacking both the training and self-awareness needed to control crowds effectively. As long as agencies continue to skirt legislative improvements and default to old habits, public trust will remain fractured.

Laws may set the standard, but until officers internalize those expectations, and are held accountable when they fail to do so, the cycle will repeat.

* * *

The influence of militarization reaches beyond public perception to fundamentally shape law enforcement's internal culture. Nowhere is this clearer than in the LAPD's elite SWAT unit, which was once regarded as a model of discipline and professionalism. But it evolved into an entity where aggression outweighed accountability, and one that was protected by a culture resistant to oversight.

Former SWAT Sergeant Timothy Colomey exposed these issues in a lawsuit alleging the existence of a "SWAT mafia" within the department, a tight-knit group of senior officers who fostered a culture of violence, glorified deadly force, and retaliated against anyone who questioned their methods. Colomey's lawsuit detailed hazing rituals, cover-ups of friendly fire incidents, and unlawful killings, all shielded by a system designed to silence those who spoke out. One lieutenant reportedly labeled Colomey and others as "enemies within the platoon," sending a clear message that dissent had consequences.

A jury awarded Colomey slightly over $3.5 million in damages, a major defeat for the LAPD. The ruling exposed deep leadership failures, reinforcing the need for greater scrutiny of elite law enforcement units. Colomey's trial made clear what many had long suspected: a lack of oversight, an obsession with force, and an ingrained resistance to change within the LAPD.

What was once an elite tactical team had become a case study in unchecked power where internal loyalty was valued more than ethical leadership.

* * *

The story of Adair, Iowa, a town of less than 800, highlights another disturbing trend in law enforcement: the misuse of authority to profit from illegal arms sales. When the town's three-person police department requested ninety machine guns, including an M134 Gatling-style minigun capable of firing 6,000 rounds per minute, eyebrows were raised. Federal investigators discovered the Adair police chief had turned his badge into a business, acquiring weapons meant for public safety and selling them for personal gain. Even after being convicted and sentenced, the chief maintained an unapologetic stance, claiming that "every cop in the nation" could face similar charges, a stance that revealed an alarming cultural rot within law enforcement. Unfortunately, Adair isn't an isolated case.

According to a 2012 LAPD investigation, SWAT officers purchased specially branded Kimber pistols at a steep discount, $600 each, only to resell them for thousands, earning profits of $3,000 or more per gun.

Those firearms, embossed with the "LAPD SWAT" insignia, were intended to bolster the prestige of the unit, not pad the wallets of officers. Yet an inadequate internal investigation left many questions unanswered: How many officers were involved? How many guns were sold? And why did the LAPD lack policies to prevent such profiteering?

Even more troubling was the revelation that these officers were effectively operating as unlicensed firearms dealers, selling weapons for personal profit without the required federal authorization. Law enforcement officers, by virtue of their position, are granted access to firearms and equipment unavailable to the general public. The idea that they could exploit that access for financial gain, circumventing regulations designed to prevent illegal gun trafficking, raised concerns about accountability, oversight, and the potential for these weapons to fall into the wrong hands.

For young officers who look up to these units as role models, the message is clear and dangerous. When those who should be held to the highest standards of the profession engage in unethical practices, they set a toxic example, perpetuating a culture of entitlement and exploitation.

This misuse of authority raises broader questions about accountability and oversight within law enforcement. A CBS News investigation found that over fifty officers across twenty-three states have been criminally charged in the past two decades for illegally selling firearms, including military-grade weapons. Alarmingly, nearly 26,000 guns traced to American crime scenes between 2017 and 2021 originated from government agencies, law enforcement, or the military. Such betrayals of public trust tarnish the badge.

The examples in this chapter are just the tip of the iceberg when it comes to exposing the level of corruption that seeps into law enforcement and undermines the entire system. A police chief turning his department into a black-market weapons supplier or a SWAT unit profiting off firearms intended for nostalgia isn't just misconduct; it's a betrayal of public trust. When officers see their peers engaging in unethical behavior without consequence, it signals that power outweighs accountability. Fixing this problem requires more than policy tweaks; it demands meaningful oversight, strict enforcement of ethical standards, and a shift in policing culture that prioritizes service over self-interest. Without that, legitimacy crumbles, and the communities law enforcement is meant to serve will continue to view it with skepticism if not outright distrust.

Beyond the gear, training and leadership play critical roles in shaping officer behavior. When law enforcement agencies model themselves after military units, officers are conditioned to see civilians as potential combatants rather than community members. This mindset has far-reaching consequences, from excessive use of force to the erosion of public confidence in police institutions. It's also no coincidence that many of the most high-profile cases of police violence in recent years have involved heavily militarized units acting with little oversight.

To move forward, policing must return to its original purpose, not as an occupying force but as a community-centered institution rooted in trust, accountability, and justice. This process requires more than just policy changes; it demands a fundamental shift in law enforcement culture. Departments must reconsider how they train officers, limit the unnecessary use of military equipment, and create stronger mechanisms for oversight and accountability.

True safety isn't created through intimidation or force. It's built through trust, transparency, and a commitment to serving the public.

Chapter 8:
The Day the Secret Service
Got Lucky

The tragedy of life is often not in our failure, but rather in our complacency; not in our doing too much, but rather in our doing too little; not in living above our ability, but rather in our living below our capabilities.

—Benjamin E. Mays

There are events in policing that redefine everything you've trained for, where everything you believe about security collapses in real time. The assassination attempt in Butler, Pennsylvania, was one such instance. It wasn't just a national crisis. This was a masterclass in failure, exposing gaps in preparation, response, and execution at the highest levels of security.

Presidential security has evolved through tragedy. The Secret Service, originally created to combat counterfeiting, didn't take on its protective role until after the assassination of William McKinley in 1901. More than a century later, history repeated itself in Butler, Pennsylvania, when an armed assailant attempted to assassinate then-candidate Donald Trump. It exposed a vulnerability that had been hiding in plain sight. Watching it unfold on live television, I wasn't processing it as a civilian or a political spectator. My instincts immediately took over, sharpened by years of working with and alongside the Secret Service to ensure the safety of those in power.

The imagery was unreal: Secret Service agents moving with urgency, shielding and whisking away a bleeding Trump as the crowd erupted into confusion and panic. It was a visceral reminder of how thin the line between order and chaos is, and how quickly that line can be breached.

That fateful moment in July 2024 exemplified the flaws and failings of our police across America and served as a lens to confront a critical truth: Policing in this country is on thin ice. The cracks aren't just forming, they're spreading and undermining the very foundation on which we stand.

By now you've probably noticed that this book doesn't shy away from those fractures. Instead, it challenges us to confront them as the difficult realities they are, not because I don't bleed blue but because I genuinely care about this profession and want cops to succeed. It's not enough to repair what's broken; we need to fundamentally reimagine what law enforcement should be in a society that's evolving faster than the institutions sworn to protect it.

To the untrained eye, the events of July 13, 2024, might appear as a chaotic series of missteps or even an elaborate conspiracy. But the reality is more complex but no less alarming. The layers of failure, spanning operational shortcomings and cultural stagnation, expose a dangerous complacency within the Secret Service. Those layers, in themselves, reflect the everyday challenges faced by law enforcement across America.

Thomas Matthew Crooks, a twenty-year-old from Pennsylvania with zero military or specialized training, managed to position himself on a rooftop and fire multiple rounds at a presidential candidate. According to the *New York*

Times, local law enforcement identified the shooter's presence nearly one hundred minutes before he fired. Yet Crooks remained undetected long enough to exploit a series of gaping security lapses. From using a drone to scout the rally site, something the Secret Service failed to anticipate, to slipping by dozens of police and Secret Service, the attack underscored an inexplicable breakdown in both planning and execution.

The question is not whether the agents on duty were aware of the required protocols—they undoubtedly were. The deeper issue lies in why those protocols weren't followed. This reflects a broader cultural problem within law enforcement: a growing overconfidence and an assumption that since tragedy had not occurred in recent times, the current security detail would be uneventful. But history has repeatedly shown us this kind of arrogance can be fatal.

It's tempting to search for a scapegoat when things go so incredibly wrong. In the aftermath of Butler, some commentators suggested that diversity, equity, and inclusion (DEI) hires were to blame, a narrative designed to inflame political tensions rather than solve real problems. This assertion not only misrepresents the purpose of DEI initiatives but also perpetuates harmful stereotypes that undermine the potential for meaningful progress.

In fact, DEI programs are often mischaracterized as compromising quality, but the reality is the opposite. Research consistently shows that diverse teams excel at decision making and problem solving by approaching challenges from multiple perspectives. In law enforcement, this diversity is especially critical: Officers with a variety of cultural, racial, linguistic, and socioeconomic backgrounds bring nuanced understanding to their communities, enabling better de-escalation and trust-building efforts. Blaming DEI for operational lapses not only distracts from the actual underlying issues but risks alienating talented individuals who are essential to modern policing.

As for mediocrity, it isn't tied to gender, race, or ethnicity; it exists in every group, including White males. Pointing to a few isolated examples of poor performance from women or minorities to discredit DEI initiatives ignores reality and misrepresents the goals of such programs. And when some criticize diversity, they promote a culture that tolerates complacency and that fails to address systemic challenges. Criticizing DEI also detracts from addressing the broader issue of the lack of progress, growth, and evolution within policing.

I'm unflinching in my view that what has been disclosed to the American people is a shocking, hollow, and purposefully deceptive view of what is known about the assassination attempt. The Secret Service has acknowledged the shortcomings in its public response, but what is absent is a discussion about the underlying cause.

The Secret Service, tasked with safeguarding our nation's leaders, appeared aimlessly adrift, much like a rudderless boat during a storm at sea. This wasn't just about being present at the scene and implementing security measures as trained. Had these measures been properly implemented, any one of them could have thwarted Crooks from gaining access to the roof.

Less than two weeks after Butler, Secret Service Director Kimberly Cheatle resigned under mounting pressure, acknowledging the agency's security lapses but offering little in terms of real answers. Her departure was largely a symbolic move that attempted to shift accountability to a single individual rather than addressing the systemic breakdowns that enabled the attack.

Despite widespread demands for transparency, critical questions remain unanswered: How did a known threat manage to infiltrate a supposedly secure perimeter? Why weren't protective measures, drilled into agents through years of training, properly executed? The resignation of one leader does not solve a problem that is fundamentally cultural, a persistent belief that the worst will not happen, even when the warning signs are glaring.

If Butler was a wake-up call, the alarm bells didn't ring loud enough. Just two months later, on September 15, 2024, a second assassination attempt unfolded at Trump International Golf Club in West Palm Beach, Florida. A gunman, armed with a rifle, had concealed himself in dense foliage near the course. Despite the heightened security climate following Butler, he managed to position himself unnoticed. Investigators later determined that he had surveyed the location multiple times in the days leading up to the planned attack and remained on-site for hours before being detected, further evidence that security gaps persisted.

The breach went unnoticed until a Secret Service agent conducting a sweep spotted movement and fired, prompting the suspect's escape and later capture. For a second time in just two months, a would-be assassin had come alarmingly close to his target, a would-be president, underscoring how little had changed since Butler. Key vulnerabilities remained unaddressed, and law enforcement once again found itself reacting instead of preventing them. The debacle in Florida was not an isolated failure but part of a larger pattern, one that exposed systemic weaknesses in training, planning, leadership, and accountability. These issues had been flagged before, yet they continued to persist despite clear warnings.

The incidents in Pennsylvania and Florida underscore the dangers of a culture that deflects responsibility and operates on misplaced confidence rather than proven preparedness. Further evidence of the arrogance of complacency, these failures highlight a dangerous pattern where warnings go unheeded, and lessons remain unlearned. Until leadership acknowledges these failures and enacts real, enforceable change, the same deficiencies in standard security measures will continue to happen, each one further eroding public trust and the credibility of the institutions meant to protect us.

The stakes have never been higher. Following the recent bombings of Iran's nuclear facilities, global tensions have surged, significantly increasing security risks for President Trump. With the threat of retaliation mounting, the possibility of further assassination attempts cannot be ignored. This volatile climate demands heightened security measures and strategic caution.

* * *

Restoring trust in law enforcement demands more than acknowledging failures. Restoration requires a fundamental shift in how agencies balance operational confidentiality with public accountability. Transparency can no longer be relegated to a buzzword or a crisis management tool. It must become a foundational principle in modern policing. When silence takes precedence over openness, damaging speculation, rumor, and innuendo become the predominant influence, eroding the trust needed for law enforcement success.

According to a *New York Post* article, the Secret Service attempted to shift blame onto local law enforcement, claiming that securing the rooftop from which the shooter fired was not their responsibility. While cooperation between federal and local agencies is standard practice, ultimate responsibility for the entire security detail rests with the Secret Service. This deflection of accountability is a familiar pattern in law enforcement, an instinct to protect the institution rather than own up to critical failures. Instead of acknowledging their lapses, officials leaned on a bureaucratic excuse, reinforcing the public's skepticism about the agency's willingness to be fully transparent.

The need to maintain trust presents a unique challenge. Policing often involves decisions that demand discretion, but discretion should never come at the expense of confidence. Agencies must find innovative ways to inform and reassure the public without compromising operational security. When approached thoughtfully, transparency has the power to build bridges while silence deepens divides.

Following high-profile failures, especially those involving terrible human loss, transparency cannot end with damage control. Instead, transparency should be a proactive, ongoing effort embedded into the fabric of law enforcement agencies. Only by embracing honesty, even in difficult moments, can we move forward.

In my experience, law enforcement executives often hesitate to share information publicly for three key reasons: (1) to maintain investigative integrity, (2) to shield the organization from potential criticism, and (3) to withhold information that could cause public panic or paralysis.

The first reason exists to prevent exposing leads, causing interference, or tampering with evidence, which preserves the credibility of an investigation, a valid consideration. But not all withholding of information comes with a straightforward rationale.

The second reason is usually a calculated PR strategy designed to dodge public scrutiny and let criticism fade as the breakneck speed of our twenty-four-hour media cycle runs interference. For example, after the attempted Butler assassination, media attention quickly shifted to the Republican National Convention, President Biden's withdrawal from the presidential race, and escalating conflicts abroad. By the time Vice President Harris announced her running mate, the attack had faded from public focus, achieving exactly what some officials likely intended.

The third reason stems from the need to maintain public calm. During my career, especially after 9/11, I had access to classified intelligence about terrorist threats that never reached the public's ear. The reasoning was clear: Widespread panic could disrupt daily life, paralyze communities, and amplify fear.

The 2024 Taylor Swift concerts in Vienna were canceled due to unspecified security concerns. While Swifties took to the streets to sing in the absence of the concerts, police worked quickly behind the scenes to foil what would have been a horrific terrorist attack. Such decisions come with challenges because a balance must be struck between withholding information for the greater good and ensuring individuals can make informed decisions about their own safety.

Regardless of how powerful a tool it can be, secrecy creates a vacuum that conspiracy theories rush to fill. And if we know anything about our society's appetite for this kind of discourse, all it takes is a single ambiguous statement or a lack of clarity from officials to spark speculation.

For instance, following Jeffrey Epstein's death while in custody, the lack of transparency around the circumstances, paired with conflicting reports and missing security footage, fueled a cascade of conspiracy theories. The absence of clear, verified information allowed speculation to dominate the narrative, eroding public trust in the justice system and its accountability.

One tweet goes around the world in a second, which is great for informing the public, but it's also prime for starting conspiracies where conjecture without facts often does more harm than good.

Over the decades of my involvement in policing, I've learned the importance of untangling truth from fiction. I encourage the public to approach narratives critically by prioritizing facts, scrutinizing sources, and seeking verified information from every perspective. At the same time, law enforcement must balance its responsibility to protect operational security with its duty to be forthright. Without open communication, trust implodes and becomes as impossible to rebuild as the Twin Towers. We're not talking about superficial adjustments or temporary fixes, we're talking about a fundamental reimagining of what policing should be in a society as diverse and complex as ours.

Every issue exposed in Butler, complacency, leadership voids, failure to act, and the persistent lack of transparency in post-incident disclosures, can be fixed. And I'll explain how later in this book, because there's little point in identifying problems unless you have a plan to fix them, and I do.

Chapter 9:
Beyond Policy, Beyond Excuse

A man dies when he refuses to stand up for that which is right.
—Martin Luther King

Making progress in law enforcement requires more than ambition. Progress demands honesty, accountability, and the willingness to confront uncomfortable truths. Policing isn't just about enforcing laws; it's about protecting lives, serving communities, and earning public trust. Yet when systemic failures persist, those fundamental responsibilities are undermined. To move forward we must dissect the culture, leadership, and decisions that allow such failures to persist.

The tragic death of Tyre Nichols in Memphis, Tennessee, was not an isolated event. Nichols' death was another stark illustration of the gaps in training, leadership, and accountability that permeate law enforcement. Tyre's story forces us to face a painful but necessary question: What happens when those sworn to protect fail to uphold the basic tenets of humanity?

Tyre's case is a microcosm of larger issues that plague modern policing: breakdowns in communication, toxic cultural dynamics, and a troubling lack of oversight. The details of his death expose those weaknesses in excruciating clarity, offering a masterclass in what not to do if instilling community trust is a goal.

This chapter will explore what happened to Tyre Nichols and what it reveals about the state of policing today. From the cultural underpinnings of toxic loyalty to the systemic failures of accountability, we will uncover the hard truths that must be addressed to prevent such tragedies from occurring again. These stories I'm sharing are not just cautionary tales, they're calls to action that urge us to reimagine the principles that guide law enforcement so we will prioritize justice, empathy, and transparency.

Without meaningful change, the very systems designed to protect public safety risk becoming the source of its greatest harm. Through an honest examination of these failures we can chart a path forward, a path where accountability is not an afterthought but a foundation, where progress is measured not by promises but by tangible results.

* * *

During my decades of policing and thereafter, I've seen police brutality, corruption, and sheer incompetence in many forms, and I've had a hand in fixing some of those issues. But the work is only beginning.

Tyre Nichols, a loved and cherished twenty-nine-year-old Black man, was beaten by Memphis police officers for roughly three minutes on the evening of Jan. 7, 2023, after he was stopped for what the police initially said was reckless driving. The stop escalated into a violent confrontation that ended with Mr. Nichols being hospitalized in critical condition because of the police beating. Three days later, he died.

Five Black police officers were fired and later charged with various felonies, including second-degree murder. Additional law enforcement personnel from a variety of agencies were also let go or disciplined for failing to intervene, failing to report observed misconduct, and lying about being present on the scene during the incident.

This case undoubtedly includes a racial element, even if it isn't overt. It can't be ignored that those officers, despite being the same race as the victim, brought with them the experiences and biases shaped by the communities they policed. Whether consciously or subconsciously, bias played a role in dictating their actions during the encounter with Tyre.

In mid-March 2023, five weeks after Nichols was killed, a lieutenant in the Memphis Police Department (MPD), who had been with the department since 1998, chose to retire before a disciplinary hearing on the case was held that could have resulted in him being fired. It had not been previously publicly disclosed that a supervisor of rank was on scene. Indeed, the department claimed no supervisor had been present because of a personnel shortage, a manufactured explanation based on a lie to suggest the incident was an aberration.

In the hastily retired lieutenant's absence, a disciplinary hearing was held. It found that he would have been terminated for failing to obtain pertinent information from the officers after the substantial use of force, and for failing to suggest that Mr. Nichols receive immediate medical care. Also troubling, he failed to ask why Mr. Nichols was bleeding from the face when the force reported to have been used was pepper spray and a taser. The lieutenant also was found at the disciplinary hearing to have failed to direct officers to remove the handcuffs from Mr. Nichols when he was slumped over and saying, "I can't breathe." The lieutenant was also overheard on an officer's body camera telling a member of Mr. Nichols' family that he was under arrest for DUI, which was unsubstantiated.

Jim Strickland, Memphis mayor, announced that the DOJ and the International Association of Chiefs of Police would conduct an independent external review of the Memphis Police Department's specialized units and use-of-force policies.

While this may be standard policy for investigations of this nature, it underscores a deeper issue within police culture. The fact that outside entities must conduct such reviews in the first place confirms what many already suspect: law enforcement often struggles to remain objective when investigating its own. This lack of internal accountability erodes public trust and perpetuates the problematic dynamics that such investigations aim to address.

It took three long weeks for the Memphis Police Department to finally release the footage that shows officers punching, kicking, and using a baton to beat Mr. Nichols as he begs them to stop. This is notable because the incident was captured on more than one officer's body camera and recorded by a street camera linked to police communication headquarters.

The footage begins with a police officer driving up to the intersection where Mr. Nichols' car had been boxed in by two unmarked police vehicles. The officer jumps out with his firearm drawn and joins a pair of officers rushing to remove Nichols from the driver's seat. One officer pulls Mr. Nichols out of his car, and all three officers immediately start screaming, "On the ground!"

Mr. Nichols points out that he is sitting on the ground, as the officers instructed him to do. Still, multiple officers repeatedly shout the same command with intensifying frustration and physical threats. "Get on the ground!" one orders. "I'm gonna tase your ass."

This is wrong from the start. There are several officers shouting confusing commands. He's already sitting on the ground, and yet the officers are threatening him with being tased if he doesn't get on the ground. As a former police officer, I know the intent was likely to have Mr. Nichols lie prone, but he clearly does not understand that. He likely believes he has already complied with their commands to get on the ground, and their escalating threats only add to the confusion. This failure to communicate effectively, combined with the officers' aggressive posture, set the stage for the tragic events that followed.

The problem is that we don't train our officers to be in tune with the needs, challenges, or circumstances of the individuals they are engaging. The Tyre Nichols incident establishes that reality in the most brutal way.

This disconnect is often rooted in a hypervigilant mindset shaped by a toxic police culture, a systemic cycle of identifying citizens as either perpetrators or victims. This isolationist mentality leads officers to misinterpret actions that onlookers would consider reasonable, framing them instead as challenges to authority or manifest disrespect. When that happens, the reaction too often escalates from frustration to retributive violence.

When Mr. Nichols finally repositions himself, it appears to antagonize the officers further. Mr. Nichols tries to explain that he poses no threat: "You guys are really doing a lot right now. I'm just trying to go home."

With officers pinning down his arms, pressing a taser against his leg, and barking intensifying verbal threats, Mr. Nichols explodes: "I am on the ground!" It would be the kind of video you would use to teach how not to control a suspect, but it's so terribly hard to watch, as both a law enforcement officer and as a human being, because it personifies all that's wrong with law enforcement.

Finally, one of the officers yells a more specific command: "On your stomach!" But this command fails to capture the critical sequence of events that would follow.

We won't ever fully know why, perhaps out of fear of being hurt, but Tyre fled, running a few blocks toward his mother's house, only to be detained mere steps away. One of the officers proceeds to use pepper spray on Mr. Nichols. The other cops start punching Mr. Nichols's face. There, under the watchful lens of the pole camera, Mr. Nichols is about to endure one of the most brutal beatings imaginable.

Mr. Nichols responds by pulling his hands up to protect himself as anyone would. The punching intensifies, and the pepper spray is fired again. He wipes the pepper spray from his eyes and tries to tell the people assaulting him that he's going to comply. "Okay," he says. "All right, all right."

The horrible incident could have ended there, but the arrival of another cop makes it worse. Just as one of the officers gets hold of Nichols, a new officer arrives and demands that Mr. Nichols give him his hands. Again, Mr. Nichols is unable to follow the conflicting directions.

He flails about, which only multiplies the police officers' commands and the physical punishment they inflict. He is doused with pepper spray for a third time. Two officers stand above Mr. Nichols, who is lying on his side and rubbing his eyes. An officer kicks Mr. Nichols in the face. Mr. Nichols appears to be barely conscious or coherent, but officers treat him as if he is resisting orders. "Lay flat, goddamn it!" one officer commands.

Mr. Nichols moans and writhes on the ground. By this point he has been tased, kicked in the head, punched, and pepper-sprayed repeatedly. "Lay flat!" another officer shouts. Mr. Nichols is lying limp as an officer, with no apparent difficulty, snaps a pair of handcuffs to one of Mr. Nichols' wrists. Officers continue to issue commands while simultaneously constraining, controlling, and beating Mr. Nichols in ways that render it physically impossible for him to follow any command.

One officer uses his handcuffed arm to pull the victim's body from the ground and into a kneeling position. Then another officer strikes the victim with a baton three times, yelling, "Give us your hands!" Surrounded by four officers, Mr. Nichols tries to move away from the baton. "Give me your fucking hands!" one officer shouts.

At this point the pole camera footage captures a deeply unsettling moment: One officer quickly pulls the hood of his sweatshirt over his head, presumably to obscure his identity. With Mr. Nichols restrained, his arms pinned behind his back by one officer, his handcuffed wrist gripped by another, he is defenseless. Yet the officer takes advantage of this helplessness, delivering a vicious kick to Tyre's head as he lies on the ground.

The officer's decision to conceal his identity before delivering a violent blow is more than an individual act of cruelty. It's a textbook example of how anonymity enables misconduct. Psychological research has long shown that when individuals believe they cannot be identified, they are more likely to engage in behavior that violates social norms and ethical boundaries. This phenomenon, known as deindividuation, is precisely why protocols around identifiable uniforms exist.

I saw firsthand why these policies matter while running the Rampart gang unit under a federal consent decree. We were tasked with implementing strict oversight measures that reined in abuse, including prohibiting officers from wearing nondescript clothing unless explicitly authorized through a written operations plan. The reason was clear: When officers can't be easily identified, by name, badge number, or even department affiliation, it creates an environment where accountability breaks down. Without these safeguards, misconduct becomes easier to commit and harder to trace. In Memphis, those lessons were either ignored or never learned, allowing officers to operate under a dangerous illusion of impunity.

It's the same reason people behave differently online than they do in person. Everyone's seen them, keyboard warriors who suddenly find their courage behind a screen, slinging insults, picking fights, and saying things they'd never dare repeat face-to-face. Social media is a breeding ground for this kind of behavior because there's no immediate consequence, no accountability, just an avatar and a comment section to hide behind. This book is sure to send some of them my way, and that's fine, because that's the difference between standing behind what you say and lobbing attacks from the shadows. If you can't put your name on it, own it, and say it out loud, then maybe it's not worth saying at all. In policing, as in life, accountability is everything. When it disappears, so does integrity.

Pivoting back to the analysis of the pole camera footage, the cruelty doesn't end there. Restrained and unable to comply with the officers' commands, Mr. Nichols doubles over and, in the most heartbreaking moment of all, calls out "Mom!" at least three times. This desperate plea for help is met not with compassion but with more cold, hard violence. The officers respond by continuing to beat him, their actions devoid of restraint, empathy, or humanity.

An officer was heard saying, "I'ma baton the fuck out of you," before striking Tyre on the back three times. Nichols was then pulled to his feet, and officers appeared to punch and slap him. Following the incident, Nichols complained of shortness of breath and was transported to Memphis' St. Francis Hospital in critical condition. The Shelby County District Attorney's Office asked the Tennessee Bureau of Investigation to conduct a use-of-force investigation.

Nichols died three days later, on January 10, while the officers involved were relieved of duty pending the investigation's outcome.

The actions of the Memphis police in beating Tyre Nichols to death were not an excessive use of force because at no point was any force of this magnitude justified. What I observed was nothing short of a violent criminal act perpetrated on a defenseless individual. What these officers did to Tyre Nichols exposed the pervasive, corrosive police culture throughout the Memphis Police Department.

As I mentioned, four videos were released: three body-worn videos and a pole camera video. When reviewing the footage, I saw the pole camera scan from its original vantage point to where the second police interaction and most violent encounters occurred. That pole camera was monitored by department personnel at the Real Time Crimes Center. The police were watching the crime happen in real time, but they did nothing. What stopped them from contacting those in the field or escalating the situation to a commander? Their inaction suggests this kind of brutality was disturbingly routine, so much so that it failed to raise any alarm among those watching.

Despite the Memphis Police Chief Cerelyn Davis indicating that she was aware of the incident within hours, the initial department statement wasn't made until eight days after the incident, five days after Tyre Nichols died from his injuries. The department knew the truth the night it happened, but the chief delayed addressing it in a forthright fashion, which only compounded the sinister aura surrounding the case.

Interestingly, while watching the pole camera video in its entirety, I noticed an individual wearing a black uniform jacket with a white uniform shirt underneath, indicating he was an officer of rank.

My suspicions grew that this individual was of supervisory rank, as none of the officers on the scene acknowledged or interacted with him. I found this significant because, in my experience, personnel of supervisory rank are to be consulted on the scene in healthy police cultures and are often ostracized in the most toxic police cultures. I suspect the presence of this individual officer was withheld because his rank reflected even more negatively upon the MPD, namely because he did absolutely nothing to help Tyre Nichols.

When I watched the video, I knew a supervisor was on scene, a fact that took the department weeks to disclose. My suspicions were confirmed when this individual was proven to be the lieutenant I previously mentioned, who resigned in lieu of being fired at the disciplinary hearing.

I'm confident there's more footage we'll never see. With more than three officers at the scene, there should be additional body-worn videos available to the public. The fact that only three were released suggests the department is withholding footage, likely because it contains even more damning information.

Multiple police officers participated in the beating death of Tyre Nichols, either actively or passively. It is unfathomable that, as with George Floyd, not one of the officers tried to intervene and stop what was clearly madness. Even if they had been thinking in a totally self-protective way, knowing what they were doing was wrong and would be exposed and should be stopped, not one of them, on the ground or in the communication headquarters, commanded the crime to stop. It speaks to so many things wrong with the Memphis Police Department that I'm inclined to say, "Shut it down and start all over with competent leadership." This is to say, I believe the changes we need can be made.

Improving training and methods is critical, but what happened to Tyre Nichols goes beyond policy or procedural shortcomings. It was an unthinkable act of criminal brutality. The beating he took in Memphis was not poor policing; it was murder under the guise of law enforcement. While it may not have been premeditated, it was deliberate, unlawful, and an indictment of a broken system that allows unchecked violence to persist.

* * *

After the beating, the depravity of the Memphis officers' actions became even more apparent. Body-worn camera footage captured an officer describing the violence as "fun." In another disturbing revelation, an officer used his personal cell phone to take photographs of Mr. Nichols after the beating and sent those images to other members of the department as well as individuals outside law enforcement. Such a level of callousness and moral corruption is beyond reprehensible. It is evil and disgusting.

These embarrassing and distasteful failures once again highlight the insular and often out-of-touch culture within so many law enforcement organizations that resist looking outward for lessons learned. If the lessons of Rampart, learned decades prior, could be ignored, then what hope is there for real change without decisive, external intervention? It's time to break this cycle once and for all.

The Tyre Nichols video evokes memories of other incidents where law enforcement actions, caught on camera, defied any alignment with the principles of justice. Had Mr. Nichols' murder not been recorded, the official police narrative would likely have painted him as the aggressor, rationalized the excessive force, and downplayed the severity of his injuries. Without the undeniable evidence provided by the video, we can speculate that accountability for the criminal conduct that day would have been almost nonexistent. Notably, two of the five officers originally charged pleaded guilty to both state and federal offenses and testified against the remaining three. Those three chose to take their case to trial and were acquitted of all state charges. However, this outcome is far from an exoneration. They still face lengthy prison sentences following their federal convictions, further underscoring the gravity of their actions.

Despite the national outrage following Tyre Nichols' death and the damning conclusions of the Department of Justice's investigation, Chief Cerelyn C. J. Davis was not only allowed to remain in power, she was confirmed as the permanent chief of the Memphis Police Department in 2025. That decision defies logic. At best it signals a city leadership unwilling to hold its top law enforcement official accountable for systemic failures. At worst it confirms that political maneuvering outweighs genuine progress. Davis' tenure was already marred by claims of mismanagement, failed oversight, and a pattern of avoiding responsibility. Yet, in a move that blindsided many, the Memphis City Council voted 13-0 to keep her in charge, despite fierce opposition from activists and members of the community who saw her leadership as a continuation of the very problems that had led to Tyre Nichols' death. While city officials pointed to a reduction in violent crime as justification for their decision, the deeper issue remains unchanged: a culture of impunity within law enforcement where those at the top evade consequences even if the rank-and-file officers beneath them take the fall.

* * *

When I watched the August 2023 video of the Blendon Township Police shooting of Ta'Kiya Young, both the footage and the police chief's response were troubling.

A Kroger grocery store employee approached two police officers and alleged that Ms. Young, a pregnant, twenty-one-year-old Black woman and mother of two who was sitting in her car, had stolen some bottles of alcohol. The alleged crime constitutes petty theft, a misdemeanor not committed in the presence of an officer, which precludes a citizen's arrest. Whether known to the officers or not, the Kroger store policy is to request the return of the stolen property, not to prosecute the offender. Regardless, those circumstances should have influenced a more measured police response, but what occurred was abhorrent.

One of the officers approached the driver's side window and informed Ms. Young that she was being accused of shoplifting. The officer instructed her to exit her vehicle. But hard to reconcile were the actions of the other officer who purposely walked in front of Ms. Young's car and pointed his gun directly at her.

Officers are expected to act with intelligence, to exercise sound judgment, and not place themselves in unnecessary peril, as this officer did when he chose to stand in front of Ms. Young's car with his gun drawn. But the officer is unable to mitigate his responsibility for what occurred because there was nothing to support a reasonable belief that he needed to draw his gun to protect himself, let alone point it directly at Ms. Young. All he did was escalate the situation. Ms. Young can be heard in the video asking, "Are you going to shoot me?"

Another observation further exposes the inadequate training and poor judgment on display in that incident. The officer placed his finger on the trigger of his firearm the moment he drew his gun. Basic firearms safety requires that he keep his finger off the trigger until his sights are aligned on the target and he intends to shoot. This rule exists partly because we all have a squeeze reflex that we have little to no control over when distressed, angry, or experiencing an adrenaline rush. This universal safety standard is meant to prevent negligent discharges and a tragic outcome like the one we saw here.

Although it's reasonable to consider the officer had a negligent discharge, regardless of why the trigger was pulled, the result was the same—the death of the pregnant mother of two. Even if it were just a mistake, it's not likely that an officer would ever acknowledge an error of this magnitude because officers are inclined to articulate a justification for their actions. At this point, changing one's statement after the initial interview would be worse than the act itself.

Assuming the shooting was intentional, the officer's decision to use deadly force must be "objectively reasonable" and take the severity of the alleged crime into account, the extent of the actual threat posed, and the availability of less severe alternatives. Also important to consider is that officers are trained that firing at a moving vehicle is generally prohibited because the vehicle itself does not presumptively constitute a threat that justifies deadly force. When threatened by a moving vehicle officers are to move out of the way instead of using lethal force, unless exposed to another threat, such as a gun.

The video tells the truth. At the time the officer shot Ms. Young, she had clearly turned her steering wheel to the right, opposite of where the officer was standing, and she was pulling away from her parking space at a slow rate of speed. No officer could reasonably believe the vehicle posed an immediate threat and that there was no apparent means to avoid being in its path.

But that didn't prevent the officer from shooting Ta'Kiya Young to death for an alleged misdemeanor crime when his deficient tactics precipitated the use of deadly force that was contrary to police training and applicable legal standards of appropriateness.

I'm well aware of the sentiment that had Ms. Young complied with the officer's commands, the shooting could have been avoided. Social media posts were reminiscent of this attitude, some even written by cops under a pseudonym with comments like, "It could have all been avoided if she listened instead of refusing to do what she was told," as if "contempt of cop" justifies the use of deadly force, and "I'm personally happy she got what they all deserve…nothing (but) a bullet," an overtly racist statement said. This mindset has broad influence, festering even at the highest ranks of law enforcement.

Officers aren't judged by how well they handle situations when people comply willingly. That's easy. The real test is how they respond when someone fails to follow commands. It's in those moments, under stress and in rapidly unfolding tactical scenarios, that an officer's training and judgment matter. Staying calm is key, because clear-headed decisions lead to better outcomes. Training should focus on critical thinking strategies that guide officers toward the best possible results while avoiding emotions that cloud their judgment. Blaming someone's noncompliance to justify poor decisions doesn't cut it.

Every leader must understand the importance of acting during and after a high-profile incident. The first step is to pinpoint the problems, clearly define the issues, and communicate the purpose and importance of a plan of action in a straightforward and concise manner. What matters most is the truth. But what we got from the Blendon Township police chief were disingenuous words that served only to create a further divide. Public trust is utterly reliant on clear decisions about the facts with no chance of misinterpretation. But in this case, the public statement was fraught with self-serving inaccuracies:

I want to brief the community on a tragedy that recently occurred, which resulted in the unfortunate loss of life of a local woman. Last night, Blendon Township police officers were assisting a driver locked outside of her car in the Kroger parking lot on Sunbury Road. As the officers were helping, a Kroger employee pointed out to one of the officers that someone who had stolen bottles of alcohol from the store was at that moment fleeing. Store employees later reported that several suspects had been stealing items, but that the other suspects had fled in other cars. However, this particular female suspect, who had been pointed out to the officers, was in a Lexus sedan with no license plates and parked in a handicap spot right in front of the store. The woman started the car. One officer approached from the driver's side and ordered the woman to stop and get out of the car. She ignored the order. Another officer came from in front of the car and also ordered the woman to get out of the car. Despite being ordered to get out of the car more than a dozen times, she refused to do so.

The woman put the car in gear and accelerated forward. The officer, who was directly in the path of the oncoming car, fired one shot through the front of the windshield. The body camera footage that I've reviewed also confirms that the officer was directly in the path of the car. The car kept moving, and officers ran after it for about fifty feet. It then came to a stop on the sidewalk outside the store. Because the driver's door had been locked, officers immediately broke the driver's window so that they could attend to the woman and begin medical assistance. They also immediately called for emergency medical services.

The officer who fired the shot sprinted to his car to get a trauma kit, which he quickly employed. A passing emergency room doctor assisted. The woman died at Saint Ann's Hospital, which was the closest emergency room. I wanted a thorough and independent review of this incident. That's why I immediately asked the Ohio Bureau of Criminal Investigation to handle the investigation. Our department is fully cooperating with them. Out of an abundance of caution, I placed both officers on administrative leave. While this woman had previously been charged with crimes involving theft and fleeing from the police, our officers did not know that at the time. Following the Bureau of Criminal Investigations work, I will do the normal review to determine if policies and procedures were followed. In every case, we hold employees accountable if they violate policies, procedures, or the law. We will release the body camera footage of this incident as soon as the necessary legal redactions can be made. Recent changes in Ohio law regarding the rights of victims to have personally identifying information protected, as well as statutory redactions of certain items that must be blurred, make the release of this kind of video complicated.

Nonetheless, we will act with as much transparency as we legally can. Every loss of life is a tragedy. The family of the woman who died is understandably upset. I've personally spoken with a member of the family, and I will continue to keep them informed about what is happening. The next steps in this matter will come from the Ohio Bureau of Criminal Investigation, which is actively reviewing all of the facts. The community deserves to know the truth. We are committed to transparency and accountability in everything we do.

It's critical to address incidents like this with open, honest dialogue, not with biased summaries that mislead and raise more questions than they answer. Unfortunately, the police chief seemed focused on protecting his officer rather than providing clear, straightforward answers to obvious questions. It's baffling why he made certain statements, knowing full well that the officer's body camera footage would eventually come out and directly contradict some of his claims. For instance, the chief stated that the officer "came from in front of the car," a categorically false claim. It seems this was an attempt to deflect criticism of the officer's actions, notably why he placed himself in front of her car in the first place. But the footage clearly shows the officer walking from behind the vehicle to stand in front of it, an act entirely of his own volition.

The word choice of "accelerated" to describe how Ms. Young pulled her vehicle out of her parking space invokes a false sense that she was moving at a high rate of speed, which conflicts with the video that depicts her car moving slowly. But most disturbing is the claim that the officer was "directly in the path of the oncoming car," and the body camera footage the police chief reviewed "confirmed" this conclusion. The officer clearly was not directly in the path of the car at the time he decided to shoot, likely due to the omitted fact that Ms. Young can be seen in the video turning her steering wheel fully to the right and out of the path of the officer before the vehicle begins to move.

Further damaging the department's reputation is the fact that the involved officer remained on the payroll for nearly two years, despite clearly violating policy without justification—actions that directly contributed to a needless loss of life. He was only placed on unpaid leave when budget constraints made it untenable to continue paying a charged officer while other department members faced layoffs.

The shooting officer's body camera footage confirms that he was not in the path of the car, as it shows his left hand on the hood and his arm fully extended across the front of the vehicle at a forty five degree angle, directly from the driver's side, front corner panel area. This is a position consistent with the expectation that officers are to move out of the way of oncoming vehicles. This is corroborated by the other officer's body camera footage that shows the shooting officer standing at the front portion of the driver's side, front quarter panel, at the time he discharged the single round that killed Ms. Young.

What this officer did to Ta'kiya Young and the department's callous response to the incident exposed this officer's inadequate training, questionable decisions, and calculated deception by the police chief. When police officers' conduct fails to meet societal expectations, it diminishes public trust in law enforcement and makes the job of all officers more unsafe.

At the heart of this case is the officer's decision to use deadly force, a decision that should be scrutinized without bias. Yet the department's reference to Ms. Young's prior arrest record was an obvious attempt to deflect criticism. It had no bearing on the appropriateness of the officer's actions but was clearly intended to cast Ms. Young in a negative light and manipulate public opinion. This pattern of misleading statements, cloaked in police jargon or euphemisms, undermines any claimed commitment to transparency and accountability.

The 2024 indictment of the officer by a Franklin County grand jury for the murder of Ms. Young and her unborn child lays bare the devastating consequences of unchecked power within law enforcement and reinforces an urgent demand for accountability. Like the Tyre Nichols tragedy and countless others, this case highlights the systemic failures that demand immediate and transformative change. Who can argue the public's frustration when the law enforcement agencies' response was so disconnected from reality? In this instance, the officer will have to answer in criminal court for his decision to use lethal force.

Ms. Young's death reflects the broader realities of policing in the United States. Each year more than 1,000 fatal police shootings occur. Yet the arrest rate for officers involved in questionable use-of-force cases remains alarmingly low, around 2 percent. While I don't advocate for the indiscriminate prosecution of officers, far too many incidents warrant prosecutorial accountability to rebuild the public trust we so critically need.

As Sir Robert Peel famously said, "The power of the police to fulfill their functions and duties is dependent on public approval of their existence, actions, and behavior, and on their ability to secure and maintain public respect." These aren't just statistics, they're human lives lost through a system that, far too often, fails to hold its own accountable.

In a further display of this disconnect, the police chief refused to release the identities of the involved officers, citing a law meant to protect the privacy of victims. Astonishingly, he claimed that the officers themselves were the victims in this case, despite the reality that the shooting officer was later indicted for murder. This decision reveals a troubling misalignment with the facts and highlights just how deeply police culture can distort accountability. By framing the involved officers as victims, the chief's actions further eroded public trust and reinforced the perception that law enforcement leadership prioritizes protecting its own over confronting the truth.

The shooting officer's indictment marks a step in the right direction. Still, it must be just one part of a larger effort to build accountability into the foundation of law enforcement. With over 18,000 law enforcement agencies in the United States, consistency in training, oversight, and accountability remains a significant challenge. National standards tied to federal funding could help bridge this gap, ensuring all agencies operate with the same commitment to professionalism and transparency. The Blendon Township shooting echoes the themes of this chapter and the broader lessons from the Tyre Nichols case: Without accountability, we can't move forward.

* * *

The shooting of Eddie Irizarry by the Philadelphia Police Department on August 14, 2023, stands as another clear example of the troubling patterns in American policing, raising pressing questions about tactics, transparency, and trust. Eddie Irizarry, a twenty-seven-year-old Puerto Rican-born man, was killed following what began as a traffic stop for reportedly "driving erratically." Struggling with schizophrenia and having limited English proficiency, Irizarry found himself at the center of an encounter that would tragically end his life.

When reviewing the footage of the incident, it was impossible to ignore the inadequate police tactics and the toxic culture it exposed, a culture of law enforcement protecting its own over maintaining public credibility. The sequence of events that led to Irizarry's death began with a minor driving infraction. After Irizarry parked on the side of the road, officers approached his vehicle. One officer drew his firearm and immediately rushed to the driver's side window, creating a situation fraught with unnecessary peril. This action, coupled with the officer's proximity to Irizarry, begs the question: did the officer reasonably believe a potential deadly threat existed, or were his actions shaped by assumptions tied to the neighborhood?

The shooting took place in Philadelphia's Kensington neighborhood, an area plagued by one of the city's highest rates of drug activity that's widely considered the epicenter of the region's fentanyl crisis. Once known for its open-air drug markets, Kensington has long struggled with rampant opioid use, homelessness, and crime, making it a focal point of Philadelphia's efforts to curb the overdose epidemic.

Given this backdrop, the officer likely suspected Irizarry was connected to the drug trade, which might explain why he drew his gun and rushed to the car, likely to prevent the destruction of narcotics evidence. But even if true, such reasoning fails to justify the deficient tactics employed that deviated sharply from training and protocol. Instead of de-escalating the situation, the officer's aggressive actions did the opposite, leaving little room for a measured assessment of any potential threat. The police tactics used during this encounter were a major factor in the tragic outcome.

Compounding the tragedy was the Philadelphia Police Department's initial public statement about the incident. The department claimed Irizarry had exited his car, brandished a knife, and lunged at the officer, prompting the use of deadly force. This account painted a picture of self-defense that justified the shooting. And you guessed it, the release of security surveillance video told an entirely different story. The video showed Irizarry sitting in his car with the doors closed and the windows rolled up when the officer fired six shots at him within seconds of approaching. At no point did Irizarry leave his car or pose an immediate threat.

This blatant contradiction between the department's statement and the video evidence caused a nationwide uproar. Whether the original story was intentional deception or the result of poor communication, it underscored a disturbing lack of accountability within the department.

Why would the department release such a false account, knowing that video footage could eventually come to light? It's hard to imagine it was anything but intentional. The inaccuracies, such as claiming Irizarry exited the car and lunged with a knife, were not minor errors, they were pivotal details that shaped public opinion of the shooting. As we've established, leadership in law enforcement requires transparency, especially in the aftermath of critical incidents. Yet in this case, the focus again appeared to be on protecting the officer involved rather than addressing the public's concerns and delivering an honest account of what happened. When police accounts of events are demonstrably false, it becomes nearly impossible for the public to trust law enforcement. If the information the police provide is unreliable, how can communities know investigations will be unbiased?

In this case, the shooting officer was charged with murder and related offenses, but the damage had been done. The department's initial story and the officer's refusal to cooperate with the investigation highlighted far-reaching issues that extend beyond this single incident. The Eddie Irizarry shooting is another sobering reminder of the critical need for law enforcement agencies to prioritize accuracy, transparency, and accountability in every interaction. For the Irizarry family, true accountability must seem inexplicably elusive. Although the officer involved in this case was found guilty of voluntary manslaughter and several lesser charges, the judge handed down a sentence well below the standard minimum and immediately granted parole. This decision drew strong condemnation from the city's district attorney and profound disappointment from Irizarry's family, who struggled to comprehend how his life could be deemed so insignificant.

* * *

In the American West, settlers would circle the wagons as a defensive maneuver, placing what was most valuable inside the circle while creating a barrier against external threats. Today, police organizations employ a similar tactic, not to safeguard the public but to shield themselves from scrutiny. They go to great lengths to protect their own yet, paradoxically, they are just as willing to cast officers to the wolves when it's politically expedient or advantageous in swaying public opinion. Unfortunately, placing optics over principles often comes at the expense of doing what's right. In moments like these I've been called upon to provide expert testimony in defense of officers facing suspension, termination, or even criminal charges.

One such case involved an off-duty LAPD officer who, in June 2019, shot a man to death at a well-known, nationwide wholesale store. The officer had been standing in line for a food sample, holding his toddler son, when he was blindsided by a punch to the back of his head.

The officer is a first-generation Mexican American raised in South Los Angeles. He was thirty at the time of the shooting and had about eight years on the job. By all accounts, the officer lost consciousness, causing him and his one-and-a-half-year-old son to fall to the concrete floor. Moments later the officer regained consciousness and observed the man who had punched him standing several feet away. Having perceived what he described as a loud sound and a flash of light at the moment he was punched, he believed he had been shot and thought he saw a gun in the man's hand. But the man had no gun. In defense of his life and the life of his son, the officer drew a gun he carried off duty and shot the man, killing him.

It was a terrible circumstance for all involved. But what was to come was even more dreadful. The shooting had gone through the LAPD administrative adjudication process, and the shooting was deemed out of policy with Chief Michel Moore recommending the officer be terminated.

According to a *Los Angeles Times* article, Chief Moore's leadership, which began in June 2018, faced significant criticism. Moore joined the LAPD in 1981 and rose through the ranks to become chief. Some viewed his leadership style as insular and overly centralized. The article cited concerns about favoritism, a lack of transparency in promotions and assignments, and a reluctance to entertain differing viewpoints from the command staff.

I was brought in as a police use of force and investigation expert to testify during the officer's Board of Rights hearing. The board, whose members are appointed by the Los Angeles Police Commission, serves as the independent arbitrator of discipline.

It's important to understand that the man who attacked the officer had an intellectual disability, something the officer had no way of knowing, and the investigation quickly lost objectivity amid sympathy for the deceased's family. The case was investigated by the Force Investigation Division, a unit I supervised for seven years as its longest-serving lieutenant at the time. Reviewing its report in preparation for my testimony, I found the contents deeply disturbing.

The report, which is supposed to present a clear and objective account of events based on the preponderance of the evidence, failed to meet that standard. Instead of organizing all the evidence, both incriminating and favorable, in a logical and chronological manner, it was poorly constructed, misrepresented the facts, and unfairly implied the officer's guilt.

It went so far as to assert that the officer had been untruthful. During his investigative interview, the officer reported making critical statements to one of the initial responding officers, statements that reflected his state of mind at the time of the shooting. While those comments were not captured on the officer's body camera video, this was not evidence of dishonesty. The officer had simply been mistaken. He had made his statements to witnesses immediately after the incident, not to the responding officers.

What matters most is that the statements were made, not to whom they were directed. Those comments, given voluntarily and so soon after the shooting, bolstered the officer's credibility and supported his version of events. Yet, the report was crafted in such a way that it misled the reader into concluding he was lying.

Even more troubling was the deliberate omission of evidence. A photograph of the officer's head injury, along with a detective's documented observations of "redness" and a "swollen area" where the officer was struck, was initially included in the report but later removed by someone within the chain of command.

And the manipulation didn't stop there.

Despite medical records confirming the officer's diagnosis of "acute head trauma, cervical sprain, loss of consciousness, and a concussion," and the fact that his prescribed medication and discharge instructions aligned with standard concussion protocols, the final report, astonishingly, claimed the officer sustained "no injury."

Graham v. Connor, the landmark Supreme Court case, established that an officer's use of force must be evaluated based on the "objective reasonableness" standard. In this case, acknowledging the officer's injury was critical to understanding how it may have impacted his perceptions and decision to use deadly force. Yet there were no medical expert reports, a glaring omission and a departure from prior practice. I suspect the omission was intentional, as an expert opinion likely would have provided exculpatory evidence supporting the reasonableness of the officer's actions and decision to use deadly force. The initial doctor's diagnosis of head trauma and concussion, along with prescribed medication to treat nausea related to the concussion, were similarly excluded from the report.

The purpose of a Board of Rights hearing is to ascertain the truth, so why did the department object to me testifying as an expert witness on the grounds that I was purportedly biased? At the time I had twelve years of combined experience in the investigation and adjudication of use-of-force cases, experience unmatched by anyone else in the department. I suspect the objection was because my insight would expose the nefarious measures taken by the department to influence the outcome.

The objection was overruled. But despite my testimony, the organizational efforts biased the adjudication process, as they were intended to do. The predetermined outcome set into motion several politically motivated decisions that influenced events for several years. I suspect the department wanted to get rid of the officer because it was politically expedient.

The California Attorney General's Office charged the officer in August 2021 after the Riverside County District

Attorney declined to file charges. The officer was charged with one count of voluntary manslaughter and two counts of assault with a firearm for wounding the decedent's parents. He faced up to thirty years in prison. The criminal trial was held in December 2023. In January 2024 the jury deliberated and declared a mistrial, voting nine to three in favor of acquittal. On February 9, 2024, the prosecutor announced the case would not be retried.

Despite no longer being a member of the LAPD, the officer overcame the unjust treatment he received and is living the next chapter of his life. I have always been a believer in the truth because it always prevails.

* * *

As my career progressed I became exposed to instances where political pressure complicated or influenced critical management decisions in the highest ranks of the department. This could not have been more evident than when I testified in a civil lawsuit case.

It was approaching midnight on March 19, 2010, and two partner officers were nearing the end of their workday when they heard a loud "bang." It was not a gunshot but a sound described as more like someone had "slammed something." To investigate, the officer who was driving made a U-turn. He and his partner then saw a man wearing a hoodie and walking away from them on the east sidewalk. Unbeknownst to them, he was a twenty-seven-year-old autistic man. As they got close to him, the passenger officer, while seated in the police car, asked the man an innocuous question like, "Hey, how are you doing?" or "Hey, are you okay?" The man gave the officers what was described as a "mad look" and began "ruffling his waistband," which caused the passenger officer to believe he was arming himself. The passenger officer yelled, "Waistband! Waistband!" to inform his partner of the perceived deadly threat, and then he drew his gun. A surveillance video from a nearby business shows the man suddenly turned toward the officers and made a throwing motion. That motion caused the passenger officer to believe the man was taking a shooting stance and, in response to the perceived deadly threat, he fired one round from the passenger seat of the police car.

Simultaneously, the driving officer hastily exited, which caused him to forget to put the car in park. As he exited he heard a gunshot, and with the belief that the passenger officer had been shot, he fired one round. Although the driving officer's shot missed, the passenger officer's round struck the man in the head, killing him.

The investigation revealed the man was unarmed. He had a cellphone case clipped to his waistband. Worthy of consideration is the fact that his cell phone was later recovered from the sidewalk. When assessed in combination with surveillance video, it became evident that the passenger officer likely perceived the cell phone to be a gun.

Significant to the public outcry was that the decedent had a mental capacity much younger than his biological age. Despite the fact that officers were unaware of the decedent's cognitive limitations and that the incident was captured on surveillance video that corroborated the officers' version of events, the tenor of the Honorable Board of Police Commissioners, the final adjudicator of officer-involved shootings, was that of retribution.

Chief Charlie Beck, who had succeeded Bill Bratton as LAPD Chief in 2009, recommended to the Police Commission that the shooting be deemed "in-policy," an opinion shared by the Inspector General's office, the civilian oversight entity of the department that submits comparison recommendations to the commissioners. But the commissioners' thoughts were made clear when, during a recess from their closed session I overheard one of them comment, "I don't care what the adjudication standards are. I want those officers fired." As if it were not already predetermined, the commissioners found the single round fired by each officer to be "out of policy." And despite a relatively low standard that was clearly met in this instance, they also found the passenger officer's drawing of his firearm to be "out of policy." The commissioners have the final say in such cases, but the chief of police has the authority to determine what discipline, if any, is meted out. And he did as he saw fit.

He issued the officers an official reprimand, which is a written admonishment that would indefinitely remain in their personnel packages. Then, likely to appease members of the police commission, he placed the officers on a list of those prohibited from having public contact. Although there were issues with the tactics used by the officers, he clearly did not believe they warranted termination but instead found a middle ground to ease the political pressure.

After being restricted from public contact for five years following the shooting and being denied overtime, promotions, and the ability to work off-duty, the officers filed a discrimination and retaliation lawsuit against the City of Los Angeles.

Despite Chief Beck's recommendation that the shooting be found appropriate, the department's position was that the officers' tactics were troubling, and there was no confidence in their ability to perform in the field. But no remedy was provided beyond the indefinite public contact restriction.

Generally, deficient tactics are meant to be addressed through remedial tactical training. As I testified in court for this case, I knew of no officer who was restricted from field duty for this duration of time solely because of his or her deficient tactics. In fact, I could cite numerous instances in which the opposite was true.

The appearance was that the department arbitrarily punished these officers more severely because of the public outcry resulting from the fact that they had shot an unarmed, autistic, Black man. My testimony and the testimony of others established that the penalty imposed on the two officers was excessive when compared to the discipline imposed in similar cases.

The jury ruled in favor of the officers and awarded cumulative damages of nearly $4 million. But the verdict and the damages won were overturned on appeal because the officers' argument relied on the decedent's race in support of the discrimination claim. This case demonstrated the unintended consequences that political influence can have on decisions made by law enforcement officials, even when decisions are made with good intentions.

* * *

Toxic culture within law enforcement often reveals itself most vividly in the aftermath of tragedy. The death of Frank

Tyson on April 18, 2024, while in the custody of the Canton, Ohio, Police, is a striking example, shedding light on the erosion of confidence in law enforcement. Tyson, fifty-three years old, was involved in a single-car crash in which he fled the scene before officers detained him. Police reports claim he resisted arrest and became unresponsive after being restrained in handcuffs.

What really happened was far more disturbing: Officers allowed Tyson to remain handcuffed in a prone position while he repeatedly pleaded for help. Despite his cries of "I can't breathe!" officers failed to act.

Over five minutes passed with Tyson lying motionless before officers finally checked on him. By then, it was too late. Despite efforts that included CPR and multiple doses of Narcan, Tyson was pronounced dead later that evening.

This police failure was another unforgivable example of a culture that often prioritizes control over care. Officers are trained not to leave a handcuffed individual in a prone position and to monitor detainees in distress. Yet Tyson's pleas were dismissed as an inconvenience rather than as a medical emergency. Such disregard highlights a dangerous mindset in law enforcement, one in which humanity takes a backseat to authority, even when life is at stake.

Body camera footage captured Tyson's desperate cries, painfully echoing other tragic cases in which systemic failures and indifference led to clear deviations from policy designed to protect against preventable deaths. This case illustrates the circumstances of Tyson's death as well as the deeper culture within law enforcement that enabled the tragedy.

In the wake of Tyson's death, the two involved officers were charged with reckless homicide. In a related hearing, the courtroom once again became the stage upon which the undercurrents of this toxic culture played out. Over fifty uniformed Canton Police officers filled the courtroom while additional officers watched via video in an overflow room. Such an overwhelming presence offered a symbolic bond of solidarity with their colleagues under scrutiny. The sight of so many officers, on or off duty, raised questions about their intentions and applied implicit pressure on the judicial process.

A Cleveland-area attorney representing the Tyson family addressed this issue directly during his remarks before Stark County Common Pleas Judge Kristin Farmer. Speaking with measured resolve, he urged the judge to remain impartial:

> *We would ask that the presence of over fifty law enforcement officers gathered here today not influence, in any way, that decision," He said. "In my years as a prosecutor and in my years in courts, I've never seen what I've seen today. It's concerning that the presence, the concept of presence, is being used in this way as taxpayers are paying for these officers to be here.*

The Tyson family attorney acknowledged that some officers might be off duty during their attendance, but his statement highlighted the broader issue: "It's a troubling use of presence."

To me, the sheer number of officers in attendance reflected a culture that prioritizes solidarity over accountability.

For the Tyson family, the courtroom scene likely deepened their grief, raising heartfelt questions about the challenges of achieving meaningful change. The officers' show of unity, while legal, symbolized the very culture that enables tragedies like Frank Tyson's death to occur while shielding those involved from scrutiny. This case demonstrates that toxic loyalty within police ranks can undermine public trust, even in democratically sacred spaces designed for impartial justice.

* * *

While some might dismiss this next example as insignificant, it speaks to a broader issue: When officers mishandle even routine enforcement, it calls everything into question. It shouldn't take a nationally publicized incident to make us pause and consider how our police operate.

In a small East Coast town, it has been reported that officers frequently issued citations to drivers making U-turns in the downtown business district. Despite being permitted by state law, there was a city ordinance prohibiting U-turns, but no signs were posted, a requirement under the state vehicle code. Drivers, trusting they had committed a violation, often paid their tickets without question. Even traffic courts were likely to uphold the citations under the mistaken assumption that proper signage was in place.

When the department finally recognized the mistake, it didn't acknowledge the error. Instead, it installed the required signs and backdated their posting to a year and a half earlier, an act that raises far more concerns than it resolves. What should have happened is simple: admit the error, refund the fines, and correct any driving records impacted by the invalid citations. But that's not what happened.

A similar pattern emerges with jaywalking tickets. Pedestrians are routinely cited for crossing streets outside crosswalks, but officers often overlook the specific requirements for enforcement. For a valid violation, the crossing must occur between two adjacent controlled intersections, either with traffic signals or stop signs, without an uncontrolled intersection in between. In the absence of this specific circumstance, state law allows pedestrians to cross streets as long as they don't impede traffic, but many are ticketed anyway.

It's not unreasonable to expect officers to know the laws they enforce. These examples, seemingly minor, lead to larger questions. If mistakes happen here, where else are they happening? People must know they can rely on their police to be fair, consistent, and knowledgeable. If trust is broken over something small, it's only natural to question everything else.

The stories in this chapter, whether making national headlines or slipping under the radar, illustrate recurring failures within law enforcement. They expose the consequences of weak leadership, inadequate training, and a culture that prioritizes self-preservation over accountability. When these elements collide, preventable tragedies occur, and the truth is often the first casualty.

These patterns reveal a simple fact: we cannot train or policy our way out of a broken system. Progress requires bold, sustained change, a reimagining of leadership, accountability, and transparency. Leaders must embrace their responsibility to create a police culture in which integrity and empathy drive decision making, not fear or unchecked power.

Change begins with moral courage. Without it, progress will remain out of reach, and the next tragedy will be just a matter of time.

To rebuild trust, law enforcement must answer critical questions like these: What values guide their actions? How do they respond when those values are betrayed? And most importantly, what steps will they take to prevent these failures from happening again?

Chapter 10:
The Uvalde Massacre

We don't rise to the level of our expectations,
we fall to the level of our training.

—Archilochus

On May 24, 2022, an eighteen-year-old gunman, armed with a semiautomatic rifle, entered Robb Elementary School in Uvalde, Texas, and killed nineteen children and two adults. Uvalde, a city of just over 15,200, most of whom are Latino, joined a growing list of American communities shattered by mass shootings. It was the deadliest school shooting in Texas history, and while we have seen incidents with more deaths— Virginia Tech in 2007, where thirty-three were killed, and Sandy Hook Elementary in 2012, where twenty first graders and six adults were massacred, Uvalde became a defining moment of failure in American policing history.

That defining moment of reckoning began with a simple yet staggering question: how did the gunman stay inside the school for over an hour while children were being shot and killed?

In the immediate aftermath of the shooting, law enforcement leaders hijacked the moment to grandstand an overinflated narrative of valor and heroism, celebrating the police response while sidestepping the mounting questions posed by the public and the press. Reports of officers running toward danger filled the headlines, but the facts didn't align with the staggering loss of life.

I suspected the truth was far less noble long before the full details emerged. I believed Uvalde was another instance of police leadership prioritizing public relations over transparency, further eroding community confidence in the process. Those suspicions were echoed across social media, where countless voices expressed confusion, heartbreak, and outrage as they asked how such a catastrophic failure could have unfolded.

What followed was a series of revelations that laid bare a systemic breakdown demanding attention and action. The U.S. Department of Justice launched an investigation into the police response, and in January 2024, the findings were released. The conclusion was unequivocal: The Uvalde massacre stemmed from "cascading failures of leadership, decision making, tactics, policy, and training."

Every aspect of the police response proved catastrophically inadequate, from the event's classification to the actions, or lack thereof, taken by individual officers.

The DOJ pinpointed the officers' most critical mistake, misclassifying the situation as a "barricaded standoff" instead of the active shooter event it was. That fundamental error reshaped the response and led to a deadly delay in direct action. Rather than immediately confronting the gunman to end the attack, the police hesitated, waiting for what they perceived as a more strategic moment. But in a scenario where an elementary school was under siege for over an hour, there was no "right moment." Every second of inaction cost irreplaceable lives.

Attorney General Merrick Garland emphasized the gravity of the failure, stating unequivocally that officers responding to active shooter situations must "immediately enter the room to stop the shooter with whatever weapons and tools they have with them." That directive isn't optional. It's the foundation of active shooter training, the same training I received and taught, specifically designed in the aftermath of Columbine to prevent such failures. And yet at Uvalde's Robb Elementary, officers hesitated. They failed to act. And children died.

Among the most staggering aspects of that failure was that some of the officers on the scene were also instructors of Immediate Action Rapid Deployment training, protocols specifically designed for those exact scenarios. Those were individuals who had taught others to respond aggressively, decisively, and immediately when lives were at risk. But in their critical moment, they failed to follow their own training.

Almost all the officials in charge that day have been fired or have retired. Police Chief Pete Arredondo was even indicted on multiple charges, including a misdemeanor dereliction of duty related to the failures in police response and delays that led to the severity of the tragedy. But accountability after the fact cannot undo the harm, not just to the children and families of Uvalde but also to the civic trust in law enforcement across the country.

How could trained officers allow such a tragedy to unfold under their watch? The victims were not heartless individuals but neighbors, friends, and community members. The answer lies in a familiar combination of deficient training, poor leadership, and a culture of complacency that prioritizes caution over courage.

The Uvalde massacre yet again exposed a culture of complacency and illuminated systemic failures that require immediate and comprehensive action. When lives are on the line, there's no room for excuses or complacency.

Some might view a critical stance as disloyal to law enforcement. I believe the opposite is true. Genuine loyalty lies in confronting hard truths. Without a willingness to recognize and address shortcomings, progress remains out of reach. For law enforcement to rebuild trust and strive for excellence, it must embrace accountability and commit to meaningful change.

Throughout my career—as an officer, investigator, trainer, and consultant—I've seen firsthand the consequences of poor preparation and complacency more times than I'd like to remember. I taught IARD tactics, deployed them in active shooter situations, and oversaw mass shooting investigations, including the 2013 attack at LAX.

On November 1, 2013, a gunman entered Terminal 3, targeting TSA officers, killing one and injuring two before being neutralized. Armed with an assault rifle and over one hundred rounds, he moved through the terminal, asking travelers, "Are you TSA?" before bypassing or shooting them. The chaos disrupted one of the world's busiest airports, delaying hundreds of flights.

That incident reinforced the need for proactive threat detection and decisive response. The shooter exhibited clear warning signs like anger and erratic messages to family members, yet no intervention occurred. But responding officers acted without hesitation, running toward gunfire to prevent further loss of life. Their swift action stands in stark contrast to Uvalde, where delays and inaction proved fatal.

The LAX attack underscores the critical importance of training, readiness, and the mindset required to confront threats head-on. As we analyze Uvalde, the same lessons apply: Officers must be prepared to act, not just in response to violence but in preventing it.

So how did we reach this point, a time when the number of school shootings has reached a scale impossible to comprehend? The Uvalde shooter's past was filled with glaring warning signs and red flags that were either ignored or missed by a society too indifferent or inattentive to intervene. This pattern, repeated in countless mass shootings, exposes fundamental failures in both prevention and intervention.

The young Uvalde shooter, for example, had a troubled history marked by behavioral issues, mental health struggles, and a fractured family life. He had recently dropped out of high school after enduring severe bullying with peers reportedly nicknaming him "school shooter." Isolated and socially withdrawn, he worked in fast food jobs, using his earnings to purchase two AR-15-style semiautomatic rifles, thousands of rounds of ammunition, and accessories designed to make his weapons even more lethal.

Federal investigators later uncovered additional troubling details. The shooter had made direct threats of violence, including alarming posts on social media. Just ten days before the Uvalde massacre, an eighteen-year-old gunman in Buffalo, New York, killed ten Black people in a racially motivated attack. The Uvalde shooter's response? He began speaking openly about his violent intentions. Coworkers reported hearing him express suicidal thoughts and disturbing remarks, yet no meaningful intervention occurred.

On the morning of May 24, 2022, the shooter sent chilling text messages to a fifteen-year-old girl in Germany he had met online. He confessed to shooting his grandmother in the face and declared his intent to "shoot up" an elementary school. Armed with a weapon of war and a calculated plan to cause unimaginable harm, he drove his grandmother's pickup to Robb Elementary School, crashed it near the campus, climbed over a fence, and entered the school through an unlocked door.

At every step along this young man's path to violence there were opportunities for intervention, moments where decisive action might have prevented tragedy. The warning signs demanded urgent attention from family, peers, and law enforcement, but they all went unheeded. This highlights the need for proactive threat assessments, mental health interventions, and open communication between schools, communities, and law enforcement agencies. Preventing tragedies like Uvalde requires acting before a shooter enters the building, not after the first shots are fired.

One particularly alarming revelation came as the gunman approached the school. An officer armed with a rifle and fully aware of the suspect's imminent danger requested supervisory approval over the radio to use lethal force. His hesitation, seeking off-site authorization, underscored a troubling gap in the officer's understanding of deadly force protocols. The appropriateness of lethal force requires that the threat be imminent. It's unimaginable that this officer felt he needed his supervisor's authorization to fire.

Studies show that in four out of five school shootings, someone knows the shooter's intentions beforehand, yet opportunities for proactive intervention remain underutilized.

Addressing these lapses requires robust community engagement and effective threat assessment strategies.

Once inside Robb Elementary, the gunman met little resistance. Moving through the halls, he entered two connected fourth-grade classrooms and began his rampage. Officers arrived quickly but retreated after encountering gunfire, waiting for reinforcements instead of advancing. What followed were seventy-seven gut-wrenching minutes of devastating inaction.

The decision to classify the situation as a "barricaded standoff" rather than an active shooter event defies logic. Yet Uvalde officers acted as if they had the luxury of time, waiting for SWAT teams to arrive from over sixty miles away while children called 911, pleading for help.

A *Texas Tribune* investigation revealed that officers, despite being armed with rifles similar to those of the shooter, felt outgunned, so they hesitated to act. Such a catastrophic failure highlights the role of fear, indecision, and poor leadership in compounding the tragedy.

Amid this mayhem, Angeli Gomez, a mother of two students at Robb Elementary, took action that will forever stand in contrast to the inaction of law enforcement. When Ms. Gomez heard about the active shooter she rushed to the school, only to encounter a horrific scene: gunfire echoing through the building, the screams of terrified children, and desperate parents begging officers to intervene. But the police did nothing.

Determined to save her children, Ms. Gomez attempted to get past the officers, but she was physically restrained and even handcuffed. She pleaded with the officers, convincing them to remove the handcuffs under the pretense that she would calm down. The moment she was free, Ms. Gomez took matters into her own hands. She jumped a fence, raced to the school, and banged on a classroom window to get the attention of her eldest son's teacher. Through sheer courage and quick thinking, she helped evacuate her son and his classmates, leading them to safety.

But she didn't stop there. Knowing her youngest son was still inside, she returned to the school and tried to open the door to his classroom. Overwhelmed with desperation, she jiggled the handle frantically. Instead of aiding her efforts, officers nearby admonished her, urging her to "calm down." But her persistence paid off when the officers finally began evacuating the children. Among the terrified students was her youngest son, who ran into her arms calling out, "Mom! Mom!"

Ms. Gomez not only saved her two children but also many others. Her inspiring bravery in the face of unimaginable terror highlighted a profound failure: a mother, armed only with determination and love, did what an entire police force, armed and trained, would not.

And yet the response from the Uvalde Police Department after the incident was as appalling as its inaction during it. Instead of honoring Ms. Gomez for her courage, the department harassed her. She was pulled over and accused of transporting illegal immigrants, a baseless claim meant to intimidate her. Police cars parked outside her home, their flashing lights aimed at her and her mother as they left the house for walks. Those acts of retaliation were a shocking display of insensitivity and deflection, a desperate attempt to silence a bold, brave woman who had exposed law enforcement's deadly failures.

Those catastrophic failures in Uvalde extended beyond individual officers to the systems meant to guide them. The breakdown in applying nationally recognized, unified command protocols when multiple agencies are involved revealed leadership deficiencies, poor coordination, and lack of preparedness.

Unified command is a foundational principle in emergency response, developed to prevent the exact kind of confusion and inaction that unfolded in Uvalde. It traces its roots back to the Incident Command System (ICS) created in the 1970s after devastating wildfires in California exposed the dangers of fragmented agency responses. Emergency managers saw that disjointed efforts led to delays, miscommunication, and unnecessary loss of life, so they built a standardized framework that prioritized interagency coordination, clear leadership structures, and a unified chain of command. Over time, the ICS became the standard for emergency response across the United States.

In practice, unified command brings multiple agencies together under a single operational framework, ensuring a coordinated response of necessary personnel and resources. Each agency contributes its expertise toward a shared goal. This is especially critical in mass casualty incidents, large-scale natural disasters, and active shooter situations, exactly the kind of crisis Uvalde faced. When unified command works, it prevents redundant efforts, eliminates communication breakdowns, and ensures rapid, coordinated action. But when it fails—whether due to leadership failures, poor training, or political friction—the results can be catastrophic.

After the initial inaction to neutralize the shooter, the Uvalde leadership failures were on full display. Officers cited locked doors as obstacles and made no effort to breach windows or engineer alternative entry points, tactics that should have been second nature under proper training and command. Instead of decisive leadership, they hesitated. Instead of coordinated action, they froze. The very structure designed to guide them either didn't exist or wasn't followed.

This failure wasn't just about poor decisions on the ground; it reflected a deeper breakdown in leadership and account-ability. Simply having a unified command structure on paper isn't enough, it must be actively maintained, understood, and led with competence. When it isn't, lives are lost.

* * *

The systemic failures during the seventy-seven minutes of inaction at Uvalde didn't end with the tragedy, they continued in the institutional response. The *Prado Report*, rather than providing accountability or addressing critical tactical shortcomings, only compounded the damage.

In the aftermath, the City of Uvalde commissioned a report investigating the police response. The investigator, retired Austin detective Jesse Prado, produced a 182-page document concluding that no punishment was warranted for the more than twenty city officers involved. Prado said the officers "acted in good faith and did not violate department policy."

Many regard the report as a farce. It fails to address the real issue: tactics. Policies govern what officers can do, but tactics determine what they should do in rapidly unfolding, highly stressful situations. Evaluating the police response in Uvalde without scrutinizing their tactics is meaningless. All officers had received IARD training just two months before the shooting. And yet, when it mattered most, they froze. One officer's body camera captured him saying, "I don't want to get clapped out today." That sentiment—an unwillingness to risk his life for the children in that school—tells us everything we need to know about how badly the system failed.

The *Prado Report's* glaring omissions and weak conclusions serve as yet another example of the cultural decay that has taken hold in law enforcement. The report absolved officers of responsibility by narrowly evaluating policy compliance and avoiding any meaningful critique of tactics. But the public wasn't fooled. Parents, survivors, and concerned citizens across the country understand that policy alone doesn't save lives. Instead, it's the tactics and actions taken in alignment with proper training and the courage to act when it matters most that make the difference. This is the true standard by which law enforcement responses must be evaluated.

When officers freeze, falter, or prioritize their own safety above those they are sworn to protect, trust evaporates. The damage to the relationship between law enforcement and the community cannot be overstated. And it isn't confined to Uvalde. When the world watched officers stand idle as children were slaughtered, it became a stain on the entire profession.

The Uvalde response exemplifies what happens when complacency and a lack of preparation permeate police culture. Officers on the scene were woefully unprepared, psychologically and tactically, for the scenario they faced. The excuse of being "outgunned" rings hollow when their hesitation allowed the gunman to operate unchecked for over an hour.

Active shooter tactics were designed for a reason: to neutralize threats quickly and decisively. Officers are trained to prioritize the lives of victims, not their own safety.

But training alone isn't enough. A critical failure of leadership in Uvalde exacerbated the confusion. Command structures broke down, communication faltered, and no one took control of the scene. Officers deferred to others, assuming someone else would step up and make the hard decisions. But leadership in law enforcement is not about waiting, it's about acting. When seconds matter, indecision kills.

This failure speaks to a larger issue within policing: the need for strong, decisive leadership at every level. Effective leadership in law enforcement is about setting the tone, taking responsibility, and inspiring others to act. In Uvalde there was no such leadership. Officers waited for someone else to take charge while children bled out on the other side of a door. While tactical training for active shooter situations has improved since Columbine, Uvalde exposes its critical limitations. Training must be comprehensive, realistic, and ongoing. Officers must be taught not just the mechanics of entry, breaching, and threat neutralization but also the mindset required to act decisively in life-and-death situations.

Too often, training is treated as a box to check rather than a mission-critical investment. Formal classroom instruction and perfunctory drills are only a beginning. Officers need scenario-based training that replicates the chaos, stress, and split-second decisions they will face in the field. They need to train in environments that reflect the real-world settings they may encounter, like schools, and practice with the tools and resources they will have at their disposal.

The Uvalde officers were trained just weeks before the shooting, yet their failure to apply that training demonstrates that training must become instinct. Officers must rise to the level of their preparation, which must be rigorous, immersive, and continuous. Anything less is unacceptable.

Perhaps the most haunting statement captured on body camera footage was from that Uvalde officer who said, "I don't want to get clapped out today." It's an admission of fear, a fear that froze officers in place while children died. And while fear is a natural human response, it's one police officers must overcome. That's the job. That's the expectation. Law enforcement, like military service or being a first responder, isn't for everyone. It requires people who are willing to confront danger without hesitation, even when it comes at significant personal risk. On May 24, 2022, the officers at Robb Elementary were called to do the hardest part of their job, and they failed. The conscious decision to prioritize self over the lives of helpless children is unforgivable.

This is not an indictment of every officer. Across the world, countless men and women in law enforcement demonstrate extraordinary courage and selflessness daily. I've known many and lost a few of these noble officers. Uvalde must serve as a wake-up call. The public expects, and deserves, officers who will act with bravery, skill, and resolve in the face of mortal danger. Anything less dishonors the oath officers take.

The tragedy of Uvalde cannot be undone. Nineteen children and two teachers lost their lives, and countless others were forever scarred. To honor their memory, we must commit to meaningful change.

In 2023 alone there were 349 school shootings in the United States, according to the K-12 School Shooting Database. Between 2009 and 2018, the U.S. experienced fifty-seven times as many school shootings as other high-income countries, according to Statista. These figures underscore a uniquely American epidemic that demands a multifaceted response with law enforcement playing a critical role in addressing these crises in real time.

* * *

Proactive intervention is also essential. Organizations like Sandy Hook Promise emphasize the importance of creating trusted networks within schools and communities where concerns can be reported without fear of stigma or retaliation.

Building these networks requires law enforcement to engage consistently with students, parents, community volunteers, and educators. School resource officers and crossing guards, for instance, should be more than just a security or safety presence, they should actively participate in the school community, fostering relationships that encourage open communication with the kids in their community.

Mental health resources also must be integrated into intervention strategies. According to the National Institute of Mental Health, 16.5 percent of U.S. youth aged six to seventeen experience a mental health disorder each year, and many lack access to adequate care. By working together with school counselors and social workers, officers can help identify at-risk individuals and intervene before a crisis develops.

Technology is beginning to play an increasingly pivotal role in law enforcement's ability to respond to school shootings.

Virtual reality simulations provide officers with immersive environments to practice high-stakes decision making. Unlike traditional drills, VR training can replicate the chaos of an active shooter scenario, enabling officers to hone their skills in dynamic, realistic conditions.

Real time surveillance systems also enhance situational awareness. Advanced school security cameras can transmit live footage to responding officers, offering critical insights into a shooter's location and movements. Metal detection systems equipped with Artificial Intelligence (AI) further streamline security processes, reducing the risk of human error while quickly identifying threats by determining the difference between a keychain and a handgun in someone's pocket.

While some argue that increasing the number of armed personnel on school campuses is the solution, evidence suggests otherwise. A 2021 study in *JAMA Network Open* found that schools with armed guards experienced a 2.83 times higher rate of deaths during shootings compared to those without armed personnel. This raises questions about the efficacy of adding more guns to already volatile situations.

Instead, I once again suggest resources be directed toward evidence-based practices, such as conflict resolution training and anonymous reporting systems that have been shown to reduce the likelihood of violence. Empowering educators and students with tools to recognize and report threats can be more effective than having a physical security presence.

The failures in Uvalde serve as a striking reminder that even well-trained, well-intentioned officers can falter without proper reinforcement of their skills and mindset. Attorney General Garland emphasized that active shooter responses must prioritize immediate engagement. Delays, like those observed in Uvalde, are unacceptable and deadly.

The Department of Justice's report on Uvalde revealed that training must become second nature, ingrained so deeply that hesitation is eliminated. Such training requires continuous reinforcement through drills, leadership, mentorship, and a strong emphasis on the mission to protect lives above all else.

As school shootings continue to devastate communities across the United States, it's imperative that law enforcement agencies adopt a comprehensive, coordinated approach to training and preparedness.

For additional insights and strategies, organizations like The Violence Project and Sandy Hook Promise offer invaluable resources on reducing gun violence and improving safety protocols. Let Uvalde serve as a call to action for all of us committed to creating safer schools, campuses, and communities.

As the dust settled in Uvalde, the systemic failures exposed an unsettling reality: When leadership falters, when training is inadequate, and when hesitation replaces decisive action, the cost is measured in lives lost. The tragedy exposed the consequences of complacency and poor preparation, highlighting the urgent need for law enforcement to reevaluate not just policies but the very culture that allowed this failure to unfold. True accountability isn't about assigning blame in hindsight, it's about ensuring that no other community endures the same heartbreak.

Yet Uvalde is not an isolated failure. In early January 2025, three of America's most iconic cities—New Orleans, Las Vegas, and Los Angeles—faced crises of their own, each testing the limits of their emergency response systems. The way those cities handled, or mishandled, their respective disasters offers a striking contrast to the failures in Uvalde. Some responses minimized chaos, demonstrating the power of leadership and preparation, while others compounded disaster through indecision and disorganization. These events provide a powerful lens through which to evaluate what works, what doesn't, and why effective leadership in public safety is more critical than ever.

Chapter 11:
The Tale of Three Cities

By failing to prepare, you are preparing to fail.

—Benjamin Franklin

The first two weeks of January 2025 felt like a series of shocking wake-up calls for three iconic American cities: New Orleans, Las Vegas, and Los Angeles. Known for their rich histories, vibrant cultures, and distinctive identities, those cities became focal points of three distinct crises, each unfolding with a mix of urgency and chaos. The streets of New Orleans, usually alive with jazz and revelry, were stained with blood and tragedy when a rented pickup truck plowed through a jubilant crowd in the French Quarter, leaving behind a horrible scene. Hours later, Las Vegas was rocked by an explosion outside the Trump International Hotel where a Tesla Cybertruck was intentionally detonated with makeshift explosive materials, killing its driver and rattling an already wary public.

Meanwhile, in Los Angeles, just over a week after the New Year's Day tragedies in New Orleans and Las Vegas, wildfires erupted across the city, devastating neighborhoods and exposing deep-rooted failures decades in the making. The annual threat of Santa Ana winds escalated the fires into a full-blown crisis, triggering chaotic evacuations, gridlock, and a glaring collapse of municipal coordination. As residents fled for their lives, many abandoned their vehicles, and with them, the remnants of their old lives, on the choked city streets.

Each city's response, or lack thereof, offers critical lessons in crisis management, from communication failures to operational lapses. This chapter examines these three unusual occurrences, their underlying causes, and the urgent need for a proactive, coordinated approach to public safety. The chapter highlights the contrasts in leadership, preparation, and response between the cities, offering critical insights into how systemic failures, complacency, and fragmented coordination exacerbate crises. In contrast, proactive strategies and strong leadership can mitigate their impact. By analyzing these events, the chapter underscores the importance of preparedness, accountability, and transparent communication in safeguarding communities.

* * *

New Orleans is defined by its resilience. That was never more evident than in the aftermath of Hurricane Katrina. But on New Year's Day 2025, the city became the epicenter of a preventable tragedy that exposed the same systemic failures in preparedness and response that had devastated the city two decades earlier. A man driving a rented pickup truck exploited glaring gaps in the city's security measures, turning Bourbon Street into a scene of devastation. Homemade explosives hidden in coolers planted along his route of destruction an hour earlier went unnoticed, and poorly maintained barriers offered little resistance as the truck plowed into the festive crowd, leaving fourteen dead and dozens injured. The attack culminated with the driver exiting the vehicle and opening fire on officers, who ultimately neutralized him.

In my estimation, the tragedy was compounded by long-standing issues that had been developing for years. Let me elaborate: On the day of the attack, surveillance footage revealed a gaggle of officers talking in a circle near the attack site, but they were oblivious to the threat that was already unfolding.

Yes, they ran toward the danger once the carnage began, but by then it was too late. They shouldn't have been standing in a group to begin with. They were responsible for actively monitoring the area for anything unusual. They were not there to have a good time. Worse, two officers were seated inside their parked patrol vehicle that was being used as an inadequate makeshift barricade. The officers were unaware of their surroundings as their vehicle failed to stop the oncoming truck, reinforcing a hard truth about policing often emphasized in even the earliest police training: "The car is a coffin."

Using a patrol car as a barricade isn't merely ineffective; it deviates from best practices. Exacerbating the problem was the officers sitting idle in the vehicle because it limited their situational awareness and reaction time. Sitting in a police car creates a false sense of security but, in reality, it renders the officers incapable of performing their most basic function— actively monitoring the area for potential threats. The entire response appeared unfocused, unprepared, and completely vulnerable.

Officers should never sit idle in a patrol car during an event. Instead, they need to stay on their feet and be engaged and vigilant with their heads on a swivel. Compare the scene in New Orleans to what we see in New York City, which has embraced creative solutions for securing busy public spaces like Times Square. New York officials repurpose garbage trucks to protect large crowds during high-profile events like the New Year's

Eve ball drop. That's smart policing and good civics, using the resources you already have to keep people safe.

The New Orleans attacker's placement of coolers one hour in advance, a clear security risk in a crowded space, went completely unnoticed. Basic proactive footbeat patrolling could have made all the difference. The length of the French Quarter is slightly less than one mile, comprised of just thirteen short blocks. Had his act been observed or had the suspicious coolers been identified, the tragedy could have been averted. Officers must actively scan their surroundings, stay engaged, and avoid the traps of complacency. Disengaging from duty to participate in a large group chat during a high-risk event was a critical failure that reflects a deeper cultural issue.

The leadership and communication failures in New Orleans were equally staggering. After the attack, New Orleans Police Department (NOPD) Police Superintendent Anne Kirkpatrick admitted the city's bollard system, critical for protecting high-density pedestrian areas, had been nonfunctional for years. Her response? An acknowledgment that the barriers were being repaired for the Super Bowl, so they were unavailable for the New Year's celebration. That kind of deferred accountability isn't just a failure of leadership, it's a dereliction of duty. Protecting lives should always be number one.

Another issue was the involvement of multiple agencies. When multiple jurisdictions are involved, the local police department, in this case the NOPD, should act as the incident commander, setting strategies, defining objectives, and delegating responsibilities.

Without insightful leadership, confusion and inefficiency prevail, as was painfully evident during the deadly events of early January 2025. A 2019 report by Interfor International found that unified command's theoretical benefits often falter amid entrenched political bickering and organizational silos.

The report, commissioned by the French Quarter Management District, described the security apparatus in New Orleans' French Quarter as a "patchwork" plagued by "internecine politics and bickering" among law enforcement agencies, private security firms, and other stakeholders. These dynamics hindered efforts to consolidate security measures and left critical vulnerabilities unaddressed, such as the malfunctioning bollard system on Bourbon Street. The report highlighted an alarming lack of coordination with one stakeholder likening the disparate agencies to "fiefdoms," each vying for control and resources. Even recommendations for improved vehicle barriers and centralized oversight went largely unheeded, underscoring the systemic resistance to change.

During the tragic events of New Year's Day 2025, these unresolved issues manifested in real-time failures. Surveillance footage showed the attacker's vehicle easily bypassing a barrier that was not deployed, illustrating the consequences of years of neglect. The infighting and lack of cooperation that the report warned about had left the city ill-equipped to respond cohesively to a high-risk, preventable incident.

Such political and organizational dysfunction undermines the very purpose of unified command: to ensure seamless collective action during emergencies. The lessons from New Orleans reveal that until stakeholders prioritize collective safety over territorial disputes, the theoretical advantages of unified command will remain unrealized, leaving communities vulnerable in their moments of greatest need.

* * *

Vehicle ramming attacks are not a new phenomenon, but their frequency and impact have grown significantly in recent years, particularly in developed countries like the United States. The tragic events in New Orleans on January 1, 2025, are part of a disturbing global trend. Such attacks leverage everyday vehicles, often rented, to inflict maximum casualties, transforming ordinary objects into weapons of mass destruction.

Historically, terrorist groups like al Qaeda and ISIS have championed vehicle ramming as a tactic because it's simple and lethal. Manuals and propaganda published by these organizations explicitly instruct followers to use vehicles as "mowing machines," targeting crowded pedestrian areas to demoralize and terrorize communities. In the United States, vehicle ramming attacks have accounted for a disproportionate share of fatalities in recent years, making them one of the most pressing threats for law enforcement to address.

The New Orleans attack bore many hallmarks of those tactics: a rented pickup truck used to ram a crowd, explosives planted inside the vehicle, and the driver armed with firearms to escalate the carnage. The attacker followed a playbook that has been used repeatedly, from the devastating attack in Nice, France, in 2016 to the ISIS-inspired ramming on a bike path in New York City in 2017.

Just weeks earlier, on December 20, a rented car plowed through a crowded market in Germany, killing 6 and injuring more than 200. The suspect, a Saudi doctor who had been a permanent resident of Germany since 2006, was arrested immediately after the attack. Interestingly, this individual did not fit the typical profile of extremist perpetrators. He identified as an ex-Muslim who was openly critical of Islam and who had expressed far-right views on social media. Such incidents underscore a critical lesson: Vehicle attacks are a predictable and increasingly versatile method of mass violence, adaptable to different motivations and ideologies. Such attacks highlight the urgent need for robust security measures and proactive strategies to prevent such tragedies.

For New Orleans, the prevalence of vehicle attacks should have been a wake-up call long before this tragedy unfolded. The failure to secure pedestrian areas with robust barriers and proactive surveillance reflects a lack of preparation for a well-documented threat.

The lessons from New Orleans are clear. Law enforcement agencies must move beyond reactive measures and adopt proactive strategies to mitigate the risks posed by vehicle ramming attacks. This includes regular training on identifying potential threats, the strategic placement of physical barriers, and interagency coordination to ensure a unified response. Vehicle attacks may be simple in execution, but their predictability and rising popularity offer an opportunity for prevention, an opportunity that New Orleans tragically missed.

The failures in New Orleans didn't stop at the local level. National leaders quickly entered the fray, and misinformation amplified the communication crisis. Initially, the FBI released a statement declaring that the attack was "not a terrorist event." Later, its assertion was reversed, and the agency confirmed that the tragedy was inspired by the Islamic State. This misstep left a significant void, allowing political figures and commentators to fill the gap with speculation based on their own agendas, further inflaming an already tense situation.

One of the most pervasive false claims was that the pickup truck used in the attack had recently crossed into the U.S. from Mexico, fueling the narrative that the perpetrator was an undocumented immigrant. That misinformation tapped into broader fears about border security and immigration.

"Biden's parting gift to America—migrant terrorists," Donald Trump Jr. wrote on X, formerly Twitter, amplifying an early erroneous Fox News claim. "Shut the border," he continued. GOP Rep. Marjorie Taylor Greene echoed those sentiments, blaming the tragedy on lax immigration policies. The quick spread of such rumors exemplifies how misinformation can take on a life of its own, gaining momentum before the facts have a chance to surface.

The FBI eventually clarified that the attacker was a U.S. citizen who had rented the vehicle domestically, but by then the damage was done. The story of an "illegal migrant terrorist" had taken root in the public consciousness, reinforced by some high-profile figures and media outlets.

As Mark Twain famously said, "A lie can travel halfway around the world while the truth is still putting on its shoes." This quote aptly captures the challenges law enforcement officials face in combating misinformation during crises. Once falsehoods are introduced into public discourse, they are notoriously difficult to retract. In this case, the initial confusion surrounding the attacker's identity and motive not only eroded trust in the FBI's communication but also became a flashpoint for political polarization.

This misinformation did more than distort the facts. It turned a national tragedy into a political battleground. Critics of the Biden administration and Democratic leadership seized on the attack to advance their own agendas, framing the incident as a failure of border security and national defense. Meanwhile, defenders of the administration accused the critics of exploiting a tragedy for political gain, further deepening partisan divides.

Adding to the complexity was the role of social media in amplifying and distorting narratives. Platforms like X became echo chambers where unverified claims spread rapidly, often bolstered by prominent figures with millions of followers. The speed and scale of this dissemination outpaced efforts to correct it, leaving many Americans with a distorted understanding of the events in New Orleans.

This situation highlights a broader issue we discussed earlier: the role of leadership in managing narratives during a crisis. Leaders at all levels must understand the importance of delivering timely, accurate information and the risks of leaving a vacuum for speculation. Inconsistent messaging, combined with politically charged commentary, only erodes public trust in the institutions responsible for public safety.

In the aftermath, New Orleans Mayor LaToya Cantrell admitted the city's bollard system could only withstand impacts of up to 10 mph, a glaring shortcoming for safeguarding Bourbon Street during large-scale celebrations. While individual officers were praised for their bravery, the NOPD leadership's public response fell short, appearing to deflect attention from deeper organizational problems.

Highlighting heroism is important, but major public displays of interagency grandstanding cannot substitute for accountability. Officers shouldn't break their arms patting themselves, or each other, on the back while foundational problems remain unaddressed. For me, the paycheck that came every other Wednesday was more than sufficient thanks. Without meaningful change and a rededication to excellence, trust in the NOPD and other law enforcement agencies nationwide will continue to erode, deepening the damage.

Ultimately, the tragedy in New Orleans became a microcosm of the challenges facing modern crisis management: the intersection of misinformation, political opportunism, and the erosion of credibility with the public. Addressing these challenges requires not only better communication practices but also a commitment to fostering transparency, accountability, and a willingness to get things done across all levels of government. The stakes are too high to allow the truth to be overshadowed by agendas and speculation.

* * *

Hours after the incident in New Orleans, across the country in Las Vegas, a Tesla Cybertruck exploded outside the Trump International Hotel, killing its driver, an active-duty Army master sergeant. The circumstances were tragic but starkly different than those in New Orleans.

The master sergeant, suffering from PTSD, had rented a Cybertruck days earlier and filled its bed with fuel canisters and fireworks. Before the explosion, he shot himself, leaving behind notes that framed the act not as terrorism but as a "wake-up call" to what he perceived as America's looming collapse.

The response in Las Vegas couldn't have been more different from the one in New Orleans. The Las Vegas Metropolitan Police Department moved swiftly, evacuating the hotel and securing the area to minimize harm. Sheriff Kevin McMahill provided clear, concise updates in press briefings, openly sharing what was known while acknowledging the unknown.

The sheriff's handling of the post-incident press conference was masterful. One person, deliberate and intentional in his delivery, spoke clearly about what they knew and what they didn't. That kind of professionalism and confidence sets the standard for what law enforcement should aspire to in a crisis. That was an example of everything to do. New Orleans was an example of everything not to do before, during, and after the incident.

* * *

In emergency management, rare events that carry the potential for significant disruption, damage, or loss of life are often referred to as "unusual occurrences." These can include natural disasters like wildfires and earthquakes, man-made incidents such as terrorist attacks or industrial accidents, and even large-scale public events that require heightened coordination and preparedness. While these occurrences may be infrequent, their impact is magnified by their dynamic nature, complexity, and need for swift, coordinated responses.

Like many major cities, Los Angeles is no stranger to unusual occurrences. The city routinely faces challenges ranging from earthquakes to civil unrest and the annual threat of wildfires fueled by the infamous Santa Ana winds. Yet, when an unusual occurrence materialized in the form of unprecedented wildfires in early January 2025, the city's response fell far short of what was required.

The wildfires consumed entire neighborhoods, forced chaotic evacuations, and exposed a glaring lack of municipal coordination. The tragedy claimed the lives of an untold number of people, displaced thousands, and underscored the critical need for proactive leadership and robust emergency management systems.

While the Santa Ana winds are a recurring phenomenon and well-documented risk, the response to this particular crisis revealed systemic failures. Hydrants in Pacific Palisades ran dry at critical moments, leaving firefighters scrambling to contain the inferno. The LA fire chief had earlier suspended hydrant inspections that could have identified problems in time to fix them. A large reservoir in Pacific Palisades was out of commission at the time of the wildfires, leaving a multi-million-gallon water source unavailable. Residents, desperate to evacuate, faced hours of gridlock with no police officers available to direct traffic or ease the flow of vehicles. These issues were compounded by years of inadequate preparation despite repeated warnings about the growing vulnerabilities posed by the winds and the region's evolving environmental risks.

In a desperate effort to break through the jam, officials used a massive bulldozer to push abandoned cars aside on Palisades Drive, carving a path for emergency vehicles to reach those in need.

Traci Park, the LA City council member representing Pacific Palisades, addressed the overwhelming frustrations of her constituents in an interview on CNN. She described the scene on the ground as "apocalyptic" and emphasized that these weren't just her constituents, they were also her friends and neighbors. Park acknowledged the systemic issues, saying, "We already know that when we have a fire event, our communication systems go down…there are particular bottlenecks when it comes to evacuating." She also highlighted the chronic underinvestment in critical infrastructure: "We have the same number of fire stations and firefighters that we had fifty, sixty years ago, but our calls for service have tripled."

Park pointed to the December release of the *Standard of Cover* report that revealed the city's lack of preparedness for major emergencies. "We know from that report that we are so understaffed that our response times are twice the national standards," she said, further noting that Los Angeles needs at least sixty-two new fire stations just to meet the city's average daily demand. Her comments painted a vivid picture of a city struggling to keep up with its growing vulnerabilities, emphasizing the urgent need for improvements in public safety and infrastructure.

As Park concluded, she committed to ensuring accountability and transparency and made a promise to her constituents: "We will convene as many top leaders in as many town halls as it takes to get residents the answers they deserve." Her remarks reflected the pressing need for a collaborative, forward-thinking approach to prevent such tragedies.

When I turned on the news, the scene was surreal and haunting, an unrecognizable version of the streets I used to drive to visit friends. A massive red bulldozer roared forward, shoving abandoned vehicles to the side like matchbox cars, their windows clouded with ash and their once-shiny exteriors dulled by layers of soot and smoke. Luxury cars and everyday sedans were pushed unceremoniously into haphazard piles along the roadside, a testament to the chaos and desperation unfolding.

The normally familiar and orderly road had become a cataclysmic wasteland, choked with the remnants of panicked flight. Thick, orange-tinged smoke hung low, muffling sounds and reducing visibility as the glow of the approaching flames cast eerie shadows through the haze. It was a scene that looked more like a disaster movie than the reality of the beautiful city I once called home.

Adding to the institutional breakdowns was a stark failure in first responder readiness. Despite well-documented fire risks and high wind warnings, Los Angeles Fire Department leadership failed to take proactive measures to ensure adequate staffing and resources. According to the *Los Angeles Times*, Fire Chief Kristin Crowley opted not to hold over nearly 1,000 firefighters from the prior shift, leaving critical personnel unavailable as the fire spread. Compounding this misstep, the *Daily Mail* said the department severely underutilized its resources, staffing only five of more than forty available engines that could have been deployed to high-risk areas. Not surprisingly, area residents reported not seeing any firefighters attempting to put out the initial fire, even as it grew rapidly.

Despite official claims of pre-staging resources, internal planning documents obtained by the *Los Angeles Times* revealed that fire officials had outright rejected requests to deploy additional engines to vulnerable areas. Instead, reinforcements were only called in after the fire had already begun tearing through the landscape. As *Daily Mail* sources within the LAFD noted, the failure to mobilize resources in advance was not just an oversight; it was a systemic failure. The decision to delay action turned a manageable crisis into a catastrophic one, amplifying destruction and underscoring the urgent need for accountability in emergency response leadership.

According to CNN, the fallout from those failures culminated in Mayor Karen Bass's decision to fire Crowley in late February 2025. The mayor cited Crowley's mishandling of the crisis as a key factor in the firing. The move sparked controversy, with some viewing Crowley as a scapegoat for broader systemic issues, including budget cuts and years of underinvestment in fire department resources. Critics, including prominent business leaders and firefighter unions, argued that leadership failures extended beyond Crowley. They pointed to Mayor Bass's own absence during the critical early hours of the fire as she was on an official trip to Ghana. Her delayed return and perceived lack of preparedness ignited a firestorm of backlash with figures like Elon Musk using social media to openly criticize her leadership, labeling the mayor as "utterly incompetent."

The shake-up at the highest levels of emergency management underscored the urgent need for a more proactive, centralized approach to crisis response, one that prioritizes readiness, coordination, and accountability before disaster strikes.

Piling on the outcry over the city's inadequate response, prominent business mogul Rick Caruso harshly criticized LA's handling of the wildfire crisis. Caruso labeled the city a "third world country," pointing to failures in maintaining water reservoirs that left firefighters struggling to combat the spreading flames. His remarks, while controversial, echoed a broader frustration among residents and stakeholders about the city's systemic unpreparedness. As evacuation orders displaced over 30,000 residents, Caruso's critique sparked a renewed conversation about municipal mismanagement and the city's inability to meet the escalating challenges of recurring natural disasters. His comments are a reminder that leadership failures not only erode public trust but also exacerbate the human and economic toll of such crises.

While some critiques were politically charged, they exposed legitimate concerns about leadership gaps during crises. The National Weather Service had issued fire weather warnings before Bass's departure, signaling the potential for catastrophic conditions. The absence of proactive measures, coupled with the challenges of coordinating a response from afar, highlighted the limitations of the city's governance structure. Critics argued that Bass's handling of the crisis, including her reliance on prepared remarks during critical press conferences, underscored the need for a more assertive executive approach in times of emergency.

But Bass's defenders pointed to the systemic nature of the crisis, emphasizing that the fires were not solely a result of city policies but rather a culmination of decades of environmental risk, urban planning decisions, and regional vulnerabilities. The mayor herself promised a comprehensive review of the response, acknowledging the need for improvement while cautioning against divisive rhetoric.

Christian Grose, a political scientist from the University of Southern California, observed that Mayor Bass's expertise has historically been in fostering legislative agreements behind the scenes, a skill set that contrasts sharply with the bold, decisive public leadership expected of big-city mayors during crises. Grose told the AP, "This moment demands a true executive who will stand up and say, 'This is what we're going to do.'"

Another layer to the crisis was State Farm's decision to withdraw fire insurance coverage in high-risk areas like Pacific Palisades just months before the wildfires. In fact, state authorities listed the Palisades as one of the five Southern California areas with the highest potential for wildfire risk. In July 2024, California Department of Insurance spokesman Michael Soller said about 1,600 policies were dropped in Pacific Palisades. Other insurance data found that State Farm also dropped more than 2,000 policies in the Los Angeles communities of Brentwood, Calabasas, and Hidden Hills. The reason cited was the increased frequency of natural disasters, inflation, and challenges in the reinsurance market. Letters sent to policyholders identified those areas as presenting "substantial wildfire hazards."

The timing of this withdrawal raises troubling questions: What did State Farm know that the City of Los Angeles apparently chose to ignore? The insurance company's decision, likely informed by extensive risk assessments and predictive models, highlights a glaring disconnect between private sector insights and public sector preparedness. The lack of action from city officials to address the risks identified by insurers like State Farm underscores a broader failure to acknowledge and mitigate the dangers posed by recurring natural disasters.

In the aftermath of the Los Angeles wildfires, misinformation flourished, with figures like president-elect

Donald Trump pointing to policies protecting the endangered Delta smelt as the culprit for water shortages faced by firefighters. Critics alleged that environmental regulations limited water access, while others blamed diversity, equity, and inclusion policies, Governor Gavin Newsom's immigration strategies, or even billionaire influence on climate policy. Local officials claimed the temporary loss of water from three tanks and fire hydrants was due to high demand, not environmental policy. Yet those narratives persisted, illustrating how complex crises are often oversimplified in public discourse.

At the heart of LA's problem was the absence of centralized leadership to oversee and unify efforts across the multiple agencies involved in disaster response. The lack of a dedicated emergency management director (EMD)—a role specifically designed to coordinate preparedness and responses to unusual occurrences—was glaringly evident in Los Angeles. Unlike Beverly Hills, where a full-time employee ensures seamless coordination and proactive planning, Los Angeles relied on a fragmented approach that left residents and first responders to navigate the crisis with little guidance.

The Los Angeles wildfires remind us of the stakes involved in preventing and managing unusual occurrences. Proactive planning, clear leadership, and seamless coordination are non-negotiable when facing crises of this magnitude. However, a critical question remains: despite the red flag fire conditions stretching along the Southern California coast, why has the LA area been so disproportionately affected?

Other municipalities have demonstrated the effectiveness of mitigation measures, from improved resource allocation to community education and infrastructure upgrades. What lessons can Los Angeles draw from these examples to ensure that it's better equipped to face the mounting challenges of climate-driven disasters? The answers lie not only in leadership but also in a willingness to honestly confront underlying weaknesses to prevent future catastrophes.

* * *

The crises in New Orleans, Las Vegas, and Los Angeles in the early days of January 2025 reveal an undeniable reality: leadership, preparation, and interagency coordination determine not only how a city responds to an "unusual occurrence" but also how its people recover. Each city's experience offers critical insights, some cautionary, others inspiring, about the systems and decisions that shape outcomes long before a crisis begins.

In New Orleans, complacency and years of deferred action culminated in a preventable tragedy. The failure to maintain functional barriers in high-risk areas, coupled with an unfocused and uncoordinated police presence, made Bourbon Street a soft target.

That failure was not borne of a single bad decision but rather a culture of neglect that allowed critical safeguards to erode over time. While individual officers showed commendable bravery in confronting the attacker, the broader lack of preparation for such an event exposed deep cracks in the city's infrastructure and leadership. The result was not only a devastating loss of life but also a painful reminder of the cost of complacency.

Las Vegas, by contrast, showcased the power of proactive leadership and swift, decisive action. In the wake of the

Cybertruck explosion, authorities responded with gravitas and professionalism. The area was secured, the public was reassured, and Sheriff McMahill's clear and concise communication set a standard for crisis management. His updates conveyed critical information and restored trust, demonstrating how strong leadership can stabilize turmoil and guide a community through its darkest moments. Las Vegas exemplified what is possible when preparation and leadership work hand in hand.

Los Angeles offered yet another lesson, this time in the dangers of fragmented coordination and systemic underinvestment. Decades of neglect had left the city's fire infrastructure ill-equipped to manage the unprecedented wildfires fueled by the Santa Ana winds. Hydrants ran dry, pumps became inactive, key reservoirs were out of service, and chaotic evacuations in the Pacific Palisades neighborhood highlighted a glaring lack of planning, staging, and resource allocation.

The absence of a centralized leadership figure, like an emergency management director, further exacerbated the crisis, leaving residents and first responders to navigate the disaster with little guidance. While some efforts demonstrated ingenuity in the moment, they also underscored the reactive nature of the response.

Those failures highlight missed opportunities to maximize mitigation measures. In places where winter weather is expected every year, like the Midwest, road conditions during a storm are so much better where snowplows are maintained and ready to treat the roads with salt ahead of time. It doesn't stop the storm, but it mitigates the consequences of it. On the other hand, Los Angeles dropped the ball by failing to remove brush, ensuring fire hydrants were working, or planning and communicating evacuation routes for citizens. Simple, proactive steps like those could have softened the blow of a disaster that ended up being far worse than it needed to be.

What unites these three stories is a common thread: The outcomes of crises are not determined solely by the events themselves but by the decisions, investments, and leadership that precede them.

As Benjamin Franklin famously said, "An ounce of prevention is worth a pound of cure." Proactive measures, such as maintaining barriers, conducting thorough risk assessments, and ensuring clear lines of communication, can mean the difference between tragedy and resilience. Las Vegas showed how preparation and leadership can be achieved, while New Orleans and Los Angeles underscored the devastating consequences of complacency and disorganization.

The lessons from these cities should hit us all like a gut punch. While we can't prevent every crisis, we absolutely can control how devastating the impact is. Law enforcement officers and city leaders must stop waiting for the worst to happen before they act. It's not complicated, proactive measures like investing in infrastructure, prioritizing interagency collaboration, and empowering leaders who can step up and communicate clearly in the chaos aren't optional, they're essential. We have a choice. Will we learn from these failures, or will we keep making the same mistakes, leaving a legacy of lives lost and trust broken in the process?

But here's the thing: Not all crises come from the outside. Some hit much closer to home. What happens when someone is so crushed by despair, is so unsupported that they see no way out but to force someone else's hand? The devastating reality of "suicide by cop" puts law enforcement in the kind of moments you don't forget—emotionally charged, ethically complex, and life-altering for everyone involved. In the next chapter we'll examine those deeply personal crises and explore what it will take to do better, because waiting to act isn't an option.

Chapter 12:
Suicide by Cop

The American people have this to learn: that where justice is denied, where poverty is enforced, where ignorance prevails, and where any one class is made to feel that society is an organized conspiracy to oppress, rob, and degrade them, neither person nor property is safe.

—Frederick Douglass

On the morning of Thursday, February 22, 2024, in Columbus, Ohio, Colin Jennings seemed subdued, his movements lethargic, his words sparse. His boyfriend, Chris Stone, noticed the mood shift immediately. Colin had been battling depression and anxiety for years, but he'd been preparing for a job interview at 11:30 the next morning, which could be a pivotal opportunity to rebuild his life. Instead, Colin picked up a knife.

Chris had seen such responses before, so he promised he would act decisively the next time Colin attempted to harm himself. He would call for help, no matter the consequences. Keeping his word, Stone dialed 911, putting the call on speakerphone so Colin could hear the dispatcher. He hoped such transparency would diffuse the situation.

The emergency call lasted nearly ten minutes. Stone repeated, three times, that Colin was experiencing a mental health crisis, and he pleaded for someone trained to handle such situations to intervene. Yet when the Columbus Police Department arrived, it was not mental health professionals who stepped out of their vehicles but uniformed officers with weapons drawn.

Body camera footage captures the moments that followed: Colin, knife still in hand, moves toward the officers. His voice, filled with desperation, echoes through the footage: "Shoot me. I want to die." Colin charged once but stopped. When he charged a second time, the officers fired multiple rounds, killing him.

Chris Stone's call for help ended in the death of the man he loved. Three weeks later, overwhelmed by guilt and grief, Stone ended his own life.

What began as a plea for assistance, a hope that someone could de-escalate Colin's mental health crisis, spiraled into a double tragedy. Colin Jennings became yet another name among the countless individuals whose lives have been lost in incidents known as "suicide by cop," a phenomenon that accounts for over a third of police shootings in the United States.

Colin's story is not isolated, it's a devastating example of how systems fail both individuals in crisis and the officers responding to them. According to the *American Journal of Psychiatry*, incidents like this stem not only from individual despair but also from systemic gaps in law enforcement training and resources.

In this chapter we confront the heartbreaking realities of suicide by cop. We'll explore the neuroscience of mental health crises, delve into the underlying issues contributing to such tragedies, and discuss actionable changes that could turn law enforcement into an instrument of compassion rather than a tool of tragedy.

Colin Jennings was more than a statistic. He was a young man with aspirations who had a partner who loved him and a future worth fighting for. The question is this: how do we ensure that cries for help lead to healing rather than death?

* * *

More than one-third of the 1,163 police shootings in 2023 involved suicide by cop, incidents in which individuals intentionally provoke officers to respond with lethal force, reports the *American Journal of Psychiatry*.

This sobering reality is something Dr. Lisa Feldman Barrett, a globally recognized authority in psychology and neuroscience, highlighted during a recent conversation we had while I was researching this book.

As a University Distinguished Professor at Northeastern University and the Chief Science Officer for the Center for Law, Brain & Behavior at Massachusetts General Hospital, Dr. Barrett is one of the top 0.1 percent of the world's most cited scientists. Her expertise includes advising law enforcement and legal professionals on the critical intersections of neuroscience and public safety. Her groundbreaking research on emotion and decision making under stress sheds light on the physiological challenges involved:

> *In neuroscience, one of the things that we often see is up to 36 percent of officer-involved shootings are suicide by cop. The question to me is, how can you have law enforcement officers who don't know how to regulate themselves? They're absolutely oblivious to the impact of their presence and their deployment of weapons, whether it's a firearm, a beanbag, or 40-*

millimeter sponge rounds. How can you be unaware of the impact that these weapons have on the person you're actually trying to help?

All too often these incidents end tragically.

From a neuroscience perspective, we see that, while police often use force believing it's necessary for self-defense, we must also consider how violence against officers influences their response to perceived threats.

When I retired as a lieutenant after thirty years with the LAPD, I acquired expertise in the investigation and adjudication of more than 700 lethal force incidents.

Consider just one. LAPD officers responded to a radio call in which the person reporting advised that her estranged husband was experiencing a mental crisis, and despite violating a restraining order, he returned to her apartment and refused to leave. She just wanted him out, not for him to die.

After the officers drew their guns, her husband was cooperative at times, but at other times he exhibited signs of a mental break with reality. But the officers were focused primarily on what they wanted to accomplish, and that was get this guy outside the apartment so they could take him into custody. Fifteen minutes into the police encounter and after several taunts in which the husband called for the officers to shoot him, the husband retreated into the kitchen and reached for a knife, which prompted the officers to tase him.

Importantly, throughout the encounter the officers maintained a sufficient distance and had multiple obstacles between themselves and the individual in crisis, raising questions about the necessity of lethal force in that moment. The neuromuscular incapacitation from the taser caused the husband to drop the knife and fall to the floor. But when he rose to his knees and again reached for the knife, the officers fired six rounds, killing him.

Such instances are unique in that stressful life events or conflicts, such as despondence over a relationship breakup, domestic violence, terminal illness, or loss of a job, are present at the time the incident occurs in over 70 percent of cases. A temporary existential crisis causes suicidal behavior—a sense that life is futile or meaningless—brought on by negative emotions or a sense of isolation, not from psychosis or mental illness.

I've seen so many of these shootings in which officers were either oblivious to or ignored the unmistakable signs that a person was suicidal and made no effort to consider the needs of the person in crisis, as was evident in this case. Even more concerning, I've seen officers and the organizations they serve avoid accountability through an accepted mindset that "bad things happen to those who make bad choices."

But law enforcement must move beyond the avoidance and the delusion of such reasoning and reevaluate their responsibility to those whose behavior suggests a desire to die at the hands of the police. Essential to notice are random acts of violence, behaving aggressively toward officers with no apparent reason, and expressions of the desire to die, like "kill me" or "shoot me."

Officers should prioritize gaining voluntary compliance by using effective communication to build trust and establish a personal connection. Relying on traditional training that emphasizes force often escalates situations instead of defusing them. It's crucial to recognize the overwhelming impact of multiple uniformed officers arriving with weapons drawn, especially on someone in a mental health crisis. Such a scenario would be anxiety-inducing for anyone, so imagine the heightened distress it causes for someone with suicidal tendencies.

For years, law enforcement agencies have introduced programs aimed at improving interactions with individuals in crisis. The Cleveland Division of Police recently expanded its Co-Responder Team program, rolling out Toyota RAV4 vehicles that look different from standard patrol cars. The goal was to make officers and clinicians more approachable when responding to mental health crises. While changing how police present themselves in these situations is a step in the right direction, it falls short of addressing the deeper issue, the entrenched police culture that dictates how officers approach these calls in the first place.

A different uniform, a softer-colored vehicle—such changes are superficial solutions to a deeply rooted problem. Crisis response is not about optics, it's about how law enforcement fundamentally understands and engages with individuals in distress. The challenge is not about the tools available but about how and when they're deployed.

While some efforts to modify law enforcement's handling of these incidents have occurred, they have predominantly underperformed in changing how most of these encounters unfold. Take the LAPD for example. The department has operated a mental health response unit for over a decade, pairing officers with clinicians to handle crisis calls. Yet despite these efforts, the percentage of officer-involved shootings involving individuals in crisis has remained largely unchanged.

Why? Because these teams, while valuable, don't replace the initial officers who arrive on the scene. If those officers don't approach the situation focused on empathy and de-escalation, tragic outcomes will persist.

So how do law enforcement agencies determined to achieve police accountability continue to overlook their failures in handling incidents of suicide by cop?

I discussed that issue and related topics with Dr. Judith Andersen, a health psychologist at the University of Toronto whose research focuses on how stress impacts the health and occupational performance of cops. She has conducted field research on the responses of police officers who experience trauma and severe anxiety and how they react in those situations. Here are some of the observations she shared with me:

> *What we've seen is that officers with the current training and practices tend to rush into a mental health call and escalate the situation with a person with mental illness. One would think that the goal would be to create time and distance and stand back. This stepping back would create a barrier between the person with the mental trauma and any other pedestrians or bystanders who were in the vicinity and let the scenario de-escalate. So you're not rushing, and you can have more time to assess. Is this person autistic? Can they not hear us? Are they having a vision or hallucination?*

Dr. Andersen and her colleagues have conducted numerous studies to examine how officers respond to high-stress scenarios, particularly those involving split-second decisions. In a controlled environment study designed to assess how officers would handle a volatile situation, she recounted an incredibly revealing example:

We did a controlled study where the officers went on a call for a guy who was on probation and who wasn't supposed to be drinking. When they arrived, they saw that he was drinking and had a friend there, and it was a very noisy environment. Then he threatened to commit suicide, and he had a knife and put it to his own neck and counted down. And if the officers had just said, you know, please put the knife down—the other guy wasn't in the picture anymore, so no one else was at risk—then perhaps he would have put the knife down. But so many officers, and even highly trained officers, were more likely to shoot the guy as he was committing suicide.

Dr. Andersen's findings reveal a critical gap in U.S. police training: the failure to prioritize de-escalation and situational assessment over immediate displays of force. In other countries, such as the UK and Finland, police responses to suicidal behaviors often prioritize creating time and distance to avoid escalation. Here's more from Dr. Anderson:

The kind of thinking we found there is that if there's a person who is exhibiting those suicidal behaviors, just give them time and distance. And if they're going to commit suicide, they're going to commit suicide, but you don't kill them. But the police in North America are, from what I've seen in the training that we've reviewed, escalating the situation. They are coming up to a mentally distressed person, and suddenly, the taser light is shining on them, or the police are in the face of the distressed, shouting commands. It's too much sensory overload for a person already in crisis.

She also observes that the police escalation can provoke a reaction from the mentally distressed person, which then justifies the police killing, a killing that wouldn't have happened if the police had moved back and de-escalated.

This is not to suggest that police should avoid using force when faced with a serious threat. There are moments when the use of lethal force is both justified and unavoidable.

But all too often these incidents end tragically through the use of unnecessary force, a result of inadequate training or, perhaps, a police culture not aligned with that training. When correctly managed, many such incidents can be resolved by means other than deadly force and without undue danger to officers or the public.

Despite the frequency of these tragic incidents, the reality is stark: Only 15 percent of the 18,000 police departments nationwide provide their officers with intervention training designed to improve how these situations are handled. Furthermore, there is no national training mandate for suicide-by-cop incidents, which leaves agencies to develop their own standards—thus, many don't. Too often, the standards that exist are only applied after an officer unnecessarily takes a life in a high-profile case, when a continued emphasis could have made an incident like this avoidable altogether.

The countless number of poorly handled incidents captured on video reveals a troubling pattern: Officers often approach such situations with a rigid mindset, perceiving individuals in crisis as threats rather than as fellow human beings in need of help.

Addressing this issue demands a fundamental shift in how law enforcement and the communities they serve perceive their role in responding to individuals in crisis. Only by recognizing this shared responsibility can we improve the outcomes of these often tragic encounters.

Officers must seek essential information that delves deeper into the individual's background like their mental health history, whether they're on medication, when it was last taken, whether they have exhibited similar behavior, what de-escalation methods have been effective, and what specific factors tend to aggravate or calm them. This critical information is often best provided by family members or those reporting the crisis, and it offers valuable context that can guide officers in responding appropriately.

Equally important is understanding how uniforms, more than one officer on the scene, and visible weapons like firearms, tasers, or beanbag shotguns can exacerbate a person's anxiety. Officers must approach such situations with awareness of the psychological impact of their presence and strive to defuse tensions rather than inadvertently escalate them.

Current efforts to improve crisis response have often fallen short due to a lack of meaningful connection between mental health professionals and law enforcement. This disconnection leads officers to misinterpret behaviors as immediate threats, driving an overreliance on force. Training programs frequently emphasize rapid responses to perceived dangers, reinforcing a hypervigilant mindset that undermines opportunities for de-escalation.

Effective crisis management requires a shift in focus that prioritizes trust, communication, and the guardian mindset.

Officers must learn to dissociate themselves from the default reliance on force and emphasize strategies that protect life and foster collaboration.

Without proactive changes in training and culture, avoidable tragedies will continue. There is an urgent need to integrate mental health expertise with law enforcement practices to provide officers with the tools, knowledge, and support necessary to navigate these complex situations with patience and understanding. Failure to meet that need will not only be measured in lives lost but also in the erosion of trust between police and communities.

* * *

Dr. Andersen and her team also have studied how dealing with persons with mental illness works in Canada, and it could be there that we find a way forward. Dr. Anderson's Mental Health and Policing Working Group set out to assess how the police in Canada encounter people with mental illness. Her goal was to develop a working paper that documents the nature of these interactions.

In another paper her team explored some of the existing policing programs and initiatives in Canada. In that second paper Dr. Andersen and her team examined what we know about mental health screening tools, non-escalation and de-escalation training, and crisis intervention. The team reviewed the nature of the intervention, examined the evidence base for each aspect of the police engagement, and then developed a scientific analysis of what we know and what we need to know.

To improve police responses and outcomes for individuals with mental illness, Dr. Andersen and her team found that more

Canadian police services are adopting mental health screening tools. Such tools aim to better identify mental health issues and provide more effective, tailored responses. Whether it involves taking steps to deescalate a situation, implementing suicide precautions on-site, or ensuring proper care on the way to a mental health facility, the goal is to handle such encounters with greater competence and compassion.

It seems like an obvious step for U.S. police forces to learn from how other countries handle individuals with mental health issues. Fortunately, some departments are starting to do just that.

Dr. Andersen's team discovered two primary types of mental health tools police services employ: screening tools used by frontline officers to assist in decision making when dealing with people in mental distress and, after the fact, additional screening tools to assess both the general health and mental health status of individuals taken into police custody.

Dr. Anderson's team relied on studies from the United Kingdom for their data because Canadian data was unavailable. But the team did find several Canadian news items announcing the adoption of a mobile mental health screening tool by, among other agencies, the Royal Canadian Mounted Police, Ontario Provincial Police, York, Ontario Regional Police, and Sarnia, Ontario, Police. The tool is called the InterRAI Brief Mental Health Screener (BMHS), and it's intended for those who aren't mental health professionals, such as law enforcement personnel, who are likely to deal with individuals with mental health needs.

The tool's InterRAI (International Resident Assessment Instrument) element refers to a nonprofit organization comprised of an international team of researchers who develop means to help people with mental illness.

While the initial reason for the system was to provide police officers with an evidence-based tool to standardize their observations and assist in expressing reasonable grounds to believe a person has a mental disorder, it soon became apparent there were other benefits.

One of the most significant benefits of the BMHS is its ability to bridge the communication gap between emergency department staff and police officers. The assessment form employs terms such as "hallucinations" and "delusions," language that has become familiar in everyday discourse but that remains critical for precise communication in mental health crises. With the average Canadian police recruit being twenty-seven years old and holding a college degree, officers are more equipped than ever to use psychological terms effectively.

The BMHS was derived from the comprehensive, ten-page RAI Mental Health form, a tool employed in Ontario hospitals and other jurisdictions worldwide. Recognizing the impracticality of using a lengthy form in the field, researchers developed the BMHS in 2007 as a streamlined alternative tailored for police use. Consisting of forty-six targeted questions, the BMHS allows officers to quickly and accurately assess individuals in crisis.

The impact of the BMHS extends far beyond immediate encounters. Once completed, the form is forwarded to local mental health agencies, even if the individual is not transported to a hospital. Such a procedure ensures that people in crisis are connected with the care they need before their situation escalates into a potentially fatal confrontation. Police officers who have used the BMHS have reported that it makes describing complex behaviors easier. During a training session one officer noted, "This helps me put into words that really weird stuff I'm looking at."

This ability to translate the weird stuff into actionable data creates a more effective relationship between law enforcement and medical professionals. A specialist from the Niagara Ontario Health System noted that before adoption of the BMHS, interactions between police officers and nursing staff were often confrontational. Now, those relationships have shifted toward collegiality as both sides work from a shared understanding.

The success of programs like the BMHS and New Jersey's ARRIVE Together highlights the transformative potential of integrating mental health expertise into policing. These initiatives show how creative approaches can save lives, reduce harm, and build community trust.

The ARRIVE Together program, launched in 2021, pairs law enforcement officers with mental health professionals to respond to crisis calls together. The goal is to prevent violent escalations and divert individuals in crisis toward treatment rather than jail. As New Jersey Governor Phil Murphy explained, "The vast majority of law enforcement officers are not trained to be experts in dealing with mental health crises, and responding to an individual in crisis alongside a trained mental health professional is proving that we can achieve more successful outcomes than when we ask police to step into these fraught situations alone." The results speak for themselves. The program has eliminated the use of force in nearly 250 mental health calls in Cumberland County alone.

It's a powerful illustration of how improving the approach, rather than doubling down on force, leads to better outcomes. Police are no longer solely responsible for managing these high-stakes situations; instead, they work alongside professionals trained in de-escalation and intervention. But this success begs the question: What can we learn from countries where police rarely rely on firearms to maintain public safety?

* * *

During a visit to London to research this book I observed British officers in action and learned about their training, particularly their adherence to Sir Robert Peel's Nine Principles of Policing. Those principles, as I've noted earlier, center on public trust, minimal force, and community cooperation, and they remain at the heart of British law enforcement today.

One particularly striking example was a pro-Palestinian demonstration near Trafalgar Square. British officers, drawn from various precincts across London, approached the volatile situation with a calm, composed, and measured demeanor. They prioritized dialogue and de-escalation, engaging the crowd with respect and restraint rather than resorting to force or aggression. They were there to help people's voices be heard safely and without too much disruption. The results speak volumes: Tensions were defused without violence, and public confidence was preserved.

Such an approach is deeply ingrained in the British policing philosophy Peel championed. To illustrate, police in England and Wales discharged firearms only five times between April 2019 and March 2020. While some might attribute that number to the unique circumstances of the first year of the COVID-19 pandemic, it's important to note that there were only thirteen such incidents in the preceding year, an incredible contrast to the thousands of instances in the U.S. during the same periods. Of course, this disparity is partly influenced by the significantly lower prevalence of firearms in English society compared to American society. Even so, the massive difference underscores the British emphasis on de-escalation and nonlethal responses that reflect a deliberate operational philosophy centered on minimizing harm and boosting community confidence.

Moreover, according to the College of Policing, force was used in only 0.07 percent of all recorded police interactions in England and Wales in 2020, further underscoring their law enforcement's commitment to minimizing harm and fostering public trust. Studies indicate that British officers face fewer injuries during encounters with armed individuals compared to their counterparts in countries where lethal force is routinely employed. While the absence of widespread firearms in British society significantly contributes to those lower numbers, it's crucial to acknowledge that British police regularly face incidents involving weapons other than firearms—knives, hammers, hatchets, and other potentially lethal objects. These are the types of incidents that, in the US, often lead to the use of lethal force. The ability of British officers to de-escalate such situations reflects the impact of comprehensive training and a commitment to restraint. By prioritizing dialogue and alternatives to lethal force methods, British policing sets an example for handling high-risk encounters while safeguarding both the public and the officers, fostering a safer and more trust-driven approach to law enforcement.

I also traveled to Paris, France, where I observed law enforcement in one of Europe's most dynamic urban environments. At Gare du Nord, one of the busiest train stations in the world, I accompanied a task force on the homeless. The officers approached their work with a refreshing level of compassion and humanity. Rather than resorting to force or intimidation, they engaged in respectful communication, balancing the immediate needs of public safety with a focus on the dignity of those experiencing homelessness. They guided individuals to critical resources such as shelters, hot meal services, and medical care, showcasing a holistic approach to addressing societal challenges.

In Paris, I also spent time with officers from the 9th District Police Station during random investigative searches. Their professionalism was marked by a calm, nonchalant demeanor and a deliberate avoidance of unnecessary displays of authority. The French officers demonstrated how trust and cooperation can be cultivated through restraint and respect, a marked contrast to the usual demeaning commands and displays of authority in U.S. law enforcement. Like my mother emphasized, "It's not always what you say, it's how you say it."

The differences in the approach of British and French policing versus what I've observed in the U.S. highlight more than just procedural variances, and they reflect fundamentally disparate philosophies. Officers acted as mediators and protectors in London and Paris, emphasizing dialogue. By contrast, U.S. law enforcement often relies on control and force, which can escalate tensions rather than defuse them. As a result, U.S. officers require a paradigm shift from the warrior mentality to the more appropriate and effective guardian mindset that underscores the central theme of this book: the importance of prioritizing trust, empathy, and synergy in law enforcement. Programs like ARRIVE Together, alongside the restraint and professionalism demonstrated by officers in

London and Paris, offer a compelling blueprint for what policing can and should look like in America.

* * *

The ARRIVE Together program exemplifies a shift toward a guardian mindset that prioritizes trust, empathy, and restraint. In Cumberland County, this approach has delivered remarkable results. Here's what New Jersey State Police Superintendent Patrick Callahan observed when discussing mental health crisis calls:

> *We knew from data across the country that 50 percent of these calls end in use of force—half of them. You think about that. You know how many uses of force we've had in Cumberland County? Zero—not one.*

Rather than cutting resources, programs like ARRIVE Together highlight the need for smarter, more targeted investments. Calls to "defund the police" oversimplify a deeply complex issue and divert attention from the real problem: the lack of adequate resources, training, and mental health integration within police departments. The goal shouldn't be to dismantle law enforcement but to equip it with the tools to handle modern challenges effectively and humanely.

Strategic investments in de-escalation training, integrated mental health teams, and tools like body-worn cameras have already proven their worth. Research shows that body-worn cameras alone reduce use-of-force incidents by nearly 50 percent and complaints against officers by almost 90 percent. New Jersey Governor Phil Murphy emphasized the effectiveness of these measures when he made the following remarks:

Responding to an individual in crisis alongside a trained mental health professional proves that we can achieve more successful outcomes than when we ask the police to step into these fraught situations alone.

The path forward is not about defunding, it's about reallocating resources so they can make the most impact. Programs like ARRIVE Together and tools like the BMHS offer a roadmap for change, demonstrating that better outcomes are possible when law enforcement adopts a proactive, collaborative, and compassionate approach.

The examples from New Jersey, Canada, and Europe show that law enforcement can evolve with the proper focus and mindset. This transformation from a reactive, enforcement-driven model to one rooted in guardianship represents the future of effective policing. At its core, this evolution demands transparency, accountability, and a relentless focus on preserving life.

Each mishandled crisis response is not only a personal tragedy but a blow to the integrity of our systems. The cost of inaction is far too great because it's measured in lives lost and communities fractured. Change isn't optional, it's an urgent necessity.

Section III.
Reimagine Policing:
The Path Forward

Chapter 13:
Reimagine the Path to Better Policing

The strength of the team is each individual member. The strength of each member is the team.

—Phil Jackson

To fully understand the challenges and opportunities within modern policing, it's essential to hear from more people who have lived it than just me, officers with various upbringings, experiences, insights, and commitments to improvement. In this chapter I bring the perspectives of two of my esteemed colleagues and friends from the Los Angeles Police Department, Juli Munson and Brian Gilman.

Juli and Brian represent two distinct yet complementary paths in policing. Juli, a former attorney who joined the LAPD at age thirty-five, brings a sharp legal mind and a passion for training younger officers. Brian, a Dartmouth graduate and retired lieutenant with military experience, offers a blend of intellectual rigor and practical wisdom forged over decades of service.

Through their stories you'll gain an insider's behind-the-scenes view of the complexities of police work: the triumphs, the struggles, and the systemic issues that hinder progress. Their reflections reveal not only the challenges of policing in America but also a roadmap for building a better future by fostering education, leadership, and innovation.

* * *

I first met Juli in 2011 when she was forty-nine. Right away, she struck me as someone who had it together—fit and polished, always looking professional in her uniform. Juli wasn't the kind of person who shared everything with everyone, but there was a noticeable warmth that made people want to know her better.

We both lived east of Los Angeles in a bedroom community popular among law enforcement officers at the time due to its affordable housing. Each morning, Juli and I took the same train into the city. During our walk from Union Station to police headquarters, I often saw her carrying her young son, gently yet purposefully navigating the morning rush to drop him off at daycare. There was something deeply nurturing about how she cared for him, not overbearing, just quietly steadfast. She reminded me of my own mother.

Eventually, we started talking during those commutes, and it didn't take long to realize we had a lot in common. Like me, Juli had lost her mother to cancer at a young age. Her father was a civil engineer and a Korean War veteran, just like mine. And then there was her son, adopted and biracial, who added another layer to the many conversations we shared. It felt natural, like we were meant to become friends.

At that time I was responsible for overseeing the adjudication of deadly force incidents for the chief of police. Juli stood out immediately as exceptionally bright and naturally insightful. She had a way of thinking critically and creatively, qualities I often struggled to find in others I worked with. Her legal background was the icing on the cake, adding depth to her already sharp analytical skills. It didn't take long before she joined my team, where she excelled at tackling some of the most complex cases with a mastery that impressed almost everyone. Over the years, our working relationship grew into a lasting friendship.

But not everyone in the LAPD was as quick to see Juli's value. From the start she faced resistance from many of her colleagues, opposition rooted not in her capabilities but in the closed-off nature of police culture. Some of the reasons for that pushback would have been laughable if not for what they revealed about the insular mindset still slithering in the dark shadows of law enforcement. Here's how Juli describes her experience:

> It was kind of a funny evolution, leaving the practice of law to be a cop, and while I thoroughly enjoyed my time as a patrol officer, my favorite time in my career was as a training officer. I loved teaching younger officers how to do the job. And, you know, there were always things about being a female and entering the force, but that wasn't what my colleagues seized upon. I didn't graduate from the Police Academy until I was 35 years old. And so straight away on my first day there in my training, the officers were very suspicious of me. 'You're a lawyer; what are you doing here? You took a huge pay cut. You must be a spy. You're going to be recording me and reporting on me' and all this kind of stuff.

Juli laughed as she recalled the paranoia. Then she continued:

So I got people who wouldn't work with me. I had trained grown-ass men that wouldn't work with me, which was crazy to me. I'm like, 'Dude, I'm just out here like everybody,' but no one believed that anyone would give up the practice of law to be a cop. And so there were a lot of suspicions surrounding that.

As time passed, Juli's fellow officers abandoned their suspicions when they saw how committed she was to police work and to getting the best out of them, not spying on them:

They finally realized that I wasn't a spy, which was a much more sexy thing to be than an ex-lawyer, but they finally understood the bottom line: I just wanted to be a cop.

* * *

Brian is an intelligent, articulate individual who exudes intellectual gravitas. Despite his impressive credentials, he remains unassuming, carrying himself with a quiet yet confident demeanor. His upbringing in an academic environment, with his father serving as the president of Occidental College in Los Angeles, shaped his thoughtful and well-rounded perspective.

We worked together at the Use of Force Review Division and Force Investigation Division. He's several years my senior and worked many of the same patrol divisions I did. He proved to be a mentor of sorts. I often sought his organizational insight as I tried to avoid the internal politics of the department that he was so skilled in navigating. His combined academic, military, and law enforcement credentials are unmatched and serve as the lens through which he views today's policing challenges.

Brian enrolled at Dartmouth in September 1973 but dropped out after a couple of years to figure out what he wanted to do before returning to graduate in 1979. He came to policing directly out of college. Brian recalled some of those first years after Dartmouth in a recent conversation:

> *It was during my junior year that I initially got a job working for the campus police as a student worker. One of the guys had a brother who was working for the police department, and he told me that they were looking for 'paid reserve' officers who worked a lot of road jobs, such as traffic control. I took the job, and before long, the chief offered me a full-time spot. My idea was to get some money in the bank and then maybe go to law school. One thing led to another, and until I decided that I probably didn't have a future as a cop in small town Vermont, I went into the military, and then from the military, I went to the LAPD.*

Brian served in the United States Army, Infantry Branch, and was honorably discharged as a captain.

Like Juli, Brian was in his thirties and had some life experience when he joined the LAPD. He retired as a lieutenant. But unlike Juli, nobody thought he was a spy. Brian's age, compared to his immediate peers, and his life experience made him a standout of sorts. Let him tell it:

> *I went right out of the [police] academy and into the [LAPD] 77th Division. And we would go to an armed robbery at a convenience store or liquor store, and I'd*

be ready to put up the crime scene tape and start dusting for prints, and my training officer would look at me with a huge eye roll. 'Responding' just meant scratching out enough information for a crime report and then moving on to the next call. LAPD in the late 1980s was completely different than today. We were overrun by the crack epidemic and gang violence, so I learned very quickly to do what was needed. It was just part of the culture. If it didn't come from the LAPD, then it kind of was dismissed. So I didn't spend a whole lot of time telling cop stories from Vermont.

Both Brian and Juli experienced meaningful change in their long police careers, but they also saw some things that never seem to change in law enforcement, but that need to.

When Brian started his LAPD career he was based in South Los Angeles. Until the 1920s, South Los Angeles was one of the city's most desirable areas. It has changed, as neighborhoods do, and become a predominantly Black community, one that faced racism that residents often met with rage, including the infamous 1965 Watts Riots. In the years following those riots, South LA was afflicted by an expanding gang crime problem that reinforced institutional ideas about who exactly the police were serving and protecting.

"There was still very much a 'them versus us,'" Brian said. "It was disconcerting to me because I just had that feeling that this is not the way we should be treating people."

Brian shared a vivid memory from his time as a probationary officer working the midnight to 8 a.m. shift. While patrolling his assigned division with his partner, they spotted two ordinary Black residents walking down the sidewalk at 2 a.m. Brian explained what happened next:

Now, is that unusual behavior? I don't know. I mean, I don't go walking around my neighborhood at two in the morning, but there was no evidence whatsoever that they were gangsters or up to no good. But my partner said, 'Hit him with the light.' Meaning at the time, our police cars had these handheld lights. So I pointed the handheld spotlight out the window and lit them up from the waist down. Enough to illuminate them. My partner, and not in a malicious way, said, 'Hit him in the face.' In other words, shine a very bright spotlight right in their face.

Brian complied, although reluctantly, his gut churning at the injustice.

I mean, to me, that was just a shitty thing to do, right, because you could do it. And that was just sort of my first inkling of how we were really disrespecting these people in this neighborhood and beyond.

Juli, on the other hand, faced challenges rooted in how her colleagues perceived her, issues that stemmed from her excellence on the job. Here's how she explained it:

The LAPD is not that interested in growing and fostering the success of exceptional people. They handpick people who reflect their agenda. And if that's not you, even if you're more outstanding than other people, they don't really care. They're not really trying to foster greatness. Maybe, because of my background as a lawyer, I just have a little bit better ability to communicate and analyze the situation. I'm going to apply the law better than a non-lawyer colleague. That's nothing against them. But instead of the bosses saying, 'You know, she's an awesome resource, and I'm really glad she doesn't give a shit about ever becoming a supervisor,' they gave me a rough time.

Juli didn't want to become a sergeant or be placed in any kind of supervisory role because she believed the LAPD command structure wanted followers, not leaders, but she also saw a more sinister aspect of the 'circle the wagons' policy so common to police leadership:

That's why women don't come forward with sexual harassment. I never said anything because I didn't know what they would do if a female colleague said she was being sexually harassed. Well, I did have a pretty good idea. They would say, 'Okay, we need to protect you and take you and transfer you to another division while we investigate,' but the guy who was accused of sexual harassment gets to stay put. So you basically lose your position at that division. Then you go to another division where everybody knows that you're there because you alleged sexual harassment against an officer at your previous division, so no other guys at your new division will talk to you. So, tell me, what woman is going to say anything?

Juli points out that she did enjoy her police work, but even that enjoyment came with a cost because of precisely what I saw when I started: nobody wanted you to do more or do it better than what they were doing. Hear it from Juli:

You put me in an intellectual environment where I'm studying, where I'm reading volumes of transcripts, and

*you're applying law to the narrative, and it was fun.
Everybody hated my guts because I actually made them
have to be better than what they were willing to be. Or
perhaps they couldn't be, which is fine. Not everybody
can be great at something. I can't be a SWAT officer.
Hallelujah. I don't want to be a SWAT officer. But I
know that I'm suited for this. And so just let me flourish
and excel in this. 'Nope, can't do that. Because you're
making everybody else look bad around you. We have
to put you back down in a hole, so just serve your time
and be quiet.'*

There's a lot of that attitude that holds police back from
achieving a culture where excellence is expected, and its
achievement is embraced. The system is designed so you're
both controlled and controllable.

Brian was invited to visit Manchester, England, in 2007 as
part of that city's Peace Week shortly after two gang-related
shootings rocked the city. Brian saw another culture and
another police force firsthand, one in which most officers didn't
carry a gun. Brian brought what he learned back to Los Angeles:

*I was a gang lieutenant down in the Newton division
at the time. I was hosted by the Greater Manchester
Police. And they also hosted another guy
euphemistically called a street preacher. He was like a
gang intervention person but more faith based. And so
the two of us went over. A good amount of our time was
spent going to little meetings. Where we heard again
and again that they had a gang problem in Manchester
that sort of identified with the LA Bloods and Crips. The
level of violence in Manchester was minuscule*

compared to anything that we would see in Los Angeles. But it was absolutely frightening to the people of Manchester and their police because they're just so unused to gun violence. It was a tremendous time, and I learned a lot. And when I came back home, nobody was interested in hearing about it at all, because it didn't come from LAPD. Any sort of specialized experience was intimidating to people.

Both Juli and Brian think policing in the U.S. can be improved, and both agree that the way to do that is through education. Only 30 percent of U.S. police officers have a four-year college degree. People with an education are harder to control, fool, and indoctrinate and are more likely to think independently. In Germany, people must study and train for three years and earn a university degree to become police officers. Juli offered another observation:

I don't think you need law enforcement officers in uniform to show up to somebody's house to write reports. I think that's just an incredible waste of a resource to go and write a report on something that happened a long time, or even an hour ago.

Report writing could be a completely different profession than being a street cop. Then leave the gun-toting officers to the actual contact with criminals in action.

Juli's point is one that I echo: The police must reassess how they allocate and deploy their resources. She provides a compelling example that underscores both the necessity and the means to achieve it:

You don't have to pull a black and white out of the field to investigate a rape. The rape happened the day before; there's no suspect in the vicinity, so why are you taking out a two-person patrol car to handle that? It should be another specialized team. Then you free up officers to actually deal with situations that are happening right now, not stuff that's over with.

Juli is absolutely correct about the misuse of uniformed officers. There's a better way than to take a two-officer patrol unit out of the field so they can conduct a rape investigation.

Human resources should be better managed to maximize the trained skills of department personnel. Specially trained investigators, rather than beat cops, should be used to conduct investigations. Leave the cops on the streets. Juli speaks for many when she makes the following points:

I mean, one of the best examples you can get is a death investigation. Somebody smells a stinker (a person who has been dead for a few days), and you've got a whole car tied up the entire day with a dead guy. And even if the guy has a knife in his back, you don't need a first responder to be there. You need that first responder responding first. You don't need them tied up with the dead guy with a knife in his back just to hold the scene for detectives to show up. So I think that the resources of the first responder aspect of it should be reallocated and maybe a separate position established that can deal with everything that's not immediate. It would be less dangerous, and it would need more intellect. So it would attract those people who want to participate in law enforcement without feeling that intense danger aspect. A lot of people don't want to be in law enforcement because they don't want to get shot at, beaten up, or charged by a raging mob. They don't want to engage in high-crime situations. This scenario would answer that call for a division of labor and allow more people to participate in law enforcement at a more intellectual level.

Brian shares Juli's perspective, and he spent his LAPD career honing his intellect to better serve both the community and his fellow officers. He strongly believes that by looking beyond our borders and learning from the policing practices of other countries, we can create a more effective and forward-thinking approach to law enforcement here at home:

I'm a big proponent of the European model where they treat law enforcement as a profession and not as a vocation like we do here in this country. If you look at the basic tenets of professions like medicine or law, you have to have higher education. How can you say, when the LAPD is the third largest municipal law enforcement agency in the country, that the basic educational requirement to become an officer is a basic GED?

Brian wrote his master's thesis in the early 1990s, arguing that college should be a prerequisite for entering a career in law enforcement:

If I were king for a day, I would look at raising the education standards because I think we all realize that would only benefit candidates. We could have a Police College where you study for four years, and you not only learn the stuff that they teach in the police academy, such as tactics and firearms proficiency, but you also would spend more time dealing with courses in sociology and psychology, in crisis resolution, in communication skills. We need to treat policing as a profession and not just a vocation where you only need a high school certificate to serve and protect our complex world.

Juli makes the same point Brian and I make: The police must be prepared to face the worst of humanity. Juli put it like this:

As the LAPD evolved as a department, I was seeing more educated candidates coming in, and it's a delicate balance because you want a candidate who is thoughtful, but you don't want them so thoughtful that they don't know how to act, or how to react. Sometimes you have to have courage. Fear is fine, you can have fear. If you don't have it, that's a concern. You need to have fear to be able to assess danger. But you have to be able to do your job despite it. And you have to push through in spite of the danger. And you may acknowledge it, but you cannot react because of fear. You have to know the rules and the parameters on which you're functioning as a law enforcement officer and apply those correctly. The 'Oh, shit!' after-the-fact revision doesn't work. It's too important of a decision whether to put your hands on somebody, or use a taser, or use your weapon. It's too important of a decision to get it wrong. You really need to get that question right. And if you're not 100 percent sure, then you need to kind of reassess, take the time to reassess. And I know that's easy to say. As you know, I'm not in the middle of danger right now. And a lot of those decisions are split-second decisions. And you have to react, and that's when it goes back to training. How do you react in those situations? You have to know if it's appropriate to use lethal force or not. It's a mix of brains and understanding your fears and, of course, courage.

* * *

Juli and Brian's insights underscore the need for change, not through superficial tactics but by reevaluating the very foundation of policing. Their call for education, specialization, and a commitment to fostering excellence in officers resonates deeply at a time when the public demands accountability and trust from those sworn to protect and serve.

Through their stories we see the cracks in the system and the light that can shine when officers like Juli and Brian challenge the status quo. Their willingness to share their struggles and triumphs reveals a shared truth: The path to better policing begins with investing in better officers. It's not just about improving tactics or training, it's about creating a culture that values critical thinking, emotional intelligence, and empathy.

Chapter 14:
The Toughest Issues in Policing Today

Perfection is not attainable, but if we chase perfection, we can catch excellence.

—Vince Lombardi

It's a story every officer knows, one of the countless routine moments that can turn critical in an instant—a suspect flees, an officer in pursuit, a violent confrontation, a barricaded suspect refusing to surrender, a decision made in seconds that may be scrutinized for years. By morning, the headlines have already framed the narrative: another department under fire, another city divided.

We've told these stories before. We've walked through the tragic missteps, the tactical failures, and the moments when things went right. We've examined mass shootings, botched responses, officers making impossible choices with imperfect information. But as much as these events differ in their specifics, a pattern emerges, one that has less to do with any single incident and more to do with the way law enforcement, as a profession, responds to its own failures.

The fumbling press conferences will follow. Carefully crafted statements will be issued, state and federal partners will be congratulated, backs will be patted, and internal reviews will be launched. But behind the official responses and the public scrutiny, the deeper issue remains: the entrenched culture within law enforcement that resists change, shields mistakes, and punishes those who challenge the status quo.

Too often, departments treat criticism as an attack rather than an opportunity to improve. Instead of fostering accountability, many departments reinforce a system where outdated practices persist, mistakes are buried, and loyalty is prioritized over integrity.

Policing today isn't just struggling with public perception; it's struggling with itself. An internal culture of defensiveness has made it difficult for many organizations to evolve, even when overwhelming evidence shows that some of their approaches aren't working. Officers often see constructive criticism as a threat rather than a tool for progress, and leadership structures reinforce stagnation rather than innovation.

I attribute this, in part, to toxic police culture.

Such a culture is built on behaviors, attitudes, and unspoken rules that prioritize power and loyalty over accountability and trust. It fosters secrecy, shields misconduct, and discourages officers from speaking out against unethical practices. Toxicity thrives where aggressive tactics are glorified, mistakes are hidden, and leadership fails to model fairness and transparency. Insular attitudes hinder progress while suspicion of perceived outsiders is viewed as a threat to the protected status quo. Police insiders, whose experiences were shared in the previous chapter, have lived through those challenges.

Then there's the issue of misplaced loyalty, officers protecting each other at the expense of accountability. The old them versus us mentality isolates law enforcement from the communities they are sworn to serve. It fosters a mindset where admitting mistakes is seen as weakness rather than an opportunity to build trust.

Coupled with outdated training, inadequate support for officer mental health, and the struggle to recruit and retain the right people, these roadblocks keep policing stuck in the past. And unless law enforcement acknowledges these systemic failures and commits to meaningful change, the profession will continue to erode from within.

If policing is to remain effective and trusted, it must move beyond defensiveness and toward real progress. That means addressing these issues, not just to survive public scrutiny but to build a profession that lives up to its mission to serve the communities sworn to protect.

* * *

To reimagine policing, we need to search for solutions in a way that invites participation rather than encourages resistance from within. Law enforcement must encourage dissent from inside the organization while welcoming collaboration from external influences. Officers need to see themselves as part of the change, not as its target. Too often, the language used to criticize law enforcement alienates those within the profession, turning a necessary conversation into an unwinnable battle. That's why the way we talk about change matters as much as the change itself.

Words carry weight, especially in law enforcement, where clarity and perception are critical. The term "police reform" often lands with a thud, sparking resistance instead of reflection. Police reform suggests a broken system that implies blame that can alienate officers who feel under siege and create barriers to meaningful change.

I've avoided using "police reform" throughout this book for exactly this reason. It oversimplifies the challenges we face and frames the conversation in adversarial rather than constructive terms. I advocate for a focus on collaboration, a process in which law enforcement, community members, and policymakers work together to find solutions. This isn't about imposing change; it's about building trust and ensuring we listen to the diverse voices that lead to innovation.

The push for civilian leadership in police departments, the integration of AI, and evolving staffing models all represent necessary adaptations in modern law enforcement. Such changes don't signal a failing institution, they reflect a profession that, like any other, must evolve to meet the needs of the people it serves. The Department of Justice has long supported collaborative approaches to improving law enforcement, and with good reason. Research shows that when police departments and communities actively engage with one another, the results are safer neighborhoods and stronger relationships that lead to more effective policing.

This distinction is vital because the solutions we seek aren't one-size-fits-all. Communities differ, and so do their needs. By embracing collaboration over reform, we acknowledge the complexity of modern policing and the necessity of tailored approaches to building a better future.

True progress in law enforcement requires more than just policy adjustments or structural changes; it demands a shift in mindset. The future of policing isn't just about implementing new technology or adjusting staffing models; it's about ensuring that every decision, every innovation, and every adaptation is guided by the core principles that define effective policing: strategic coordination, proactive acknowledgment of challenges, effective response, and rigorous evaluation.

But true accountability must extend beyond individual officers to include departmental leadership. Too often there's an overt effort to limit the public's access to information in the hope that the news cycle will shift and allow negative incidents to fade from public memory. This tactic, combined with the disingenuous and cavalier handling of critical incidents by police executives, sits at the heart of the distrust many in society have toward law enforcement.

There's an important distinction between personal attacks and critiques of someone's actions. While criticism can be difficult to accept, when it's grounded in truth, it serves as a catalyst for personal and organizational growth and helps rebuild public trust.

I recently spoke to a lifelong friend from my time at Western Michigan, someone who knew me well during my hockey years. I confided in her about the harassment I endured as a member of the hockey team. She witnessed my struggles firsthand and knew how I stood by my principles, ultimately choosing to leave the team. When reflecting on that time she said, "You're committed to telling the truth, even when folks don't want to hear it. Being truthful, as hard as it may be to hear, is genuine, and that's what you are, genuine. You're not afraid to call people out and, in accordance with your virtues, to influence things for the better."

I appreciated her words, partly because they reminded me of a hard truth that's rarely spoken: Honesty is seldom rewarded in the moment. Being honest is often painful. And in some situations, it's punished. My father always told me, "A man is only as good as his word." That virtue should apply to those policing our communities, yet time and again I saw that being honest, speaking the truth, wasn't always welcome or honored.

* * *

Truth in law enforcement isn't just about calling out misconduct, it's about the willingness to hold ourselves to the highest standards, especially when no one is watching. It's about showing up prepared, physically and mentally, for whatever the job demands.

Yet too often policing treats preparation as a one-time event rather than an ongoing responsibility. Just as accountability shouldn't stop at an internal review, an officer's readiness shouldn't end with the academy. Training, both ethical and physical, shouldn't be just a requirement at the start of a career; it should be a lifelong requirement to uphold.

And yet when it comes to physical preparedness, departments routinely fall short. The expectation is that officers will be ready for anything, but the reality is that many are left to maintain, or lose, their fitness on their own. The consequences of that gap aren't just personal; they impact officer safety, public safety, and the effectiveness of policing itself.

Nowhere is this failure to prioritize long-term readiness more obvious than in physical fitness. Too many departments operate as if an officer's fitness is determined by a single academy test, as if passing one standard at the beginning of a career is enough to ensure preparedness for decades. Policing shouldn't be a profession in which you pass a one-time physical standard and then coast for the rest of your career. Effective policing demands sustained physical and mental preparedness, yet most departments impose no ongoing fitness requirements.

Academy physical tests are often treated as proof that an officer is ready for the job. In reality, those tests are nothing more than a baseline. Take the six-foot fence climb, a common academy requirement meant to simulate real-world obstacles. Assuming an officer who passes a fitness test once in the academy can meet those standards years later is unrealistic— that's not how fitness works.

Many officers in the field today couldn't clear that same fence, despite having met the requirement when they were first hired. Yet they remain on the job, responding to calls that demand physical exertion. A foot chase isn't just about climbing a fence, it's about sustaining a sprint, controlling breathing, and making critical decisions under stress. Fitness isn't a box to check once; it's a continuous requirement for officer safety and ability to effectively serve the public.

Too often, fitness declines as the years go by—long shifts, sleep deprivation, stress, and a culture that normalizes unhealthy habits take a toll. Officers work mandatory overtime, grab meals on the go, and cope with stress through alcohol or poor lifestyle choices. Without continued fitness training, even the most physically capable officers at the academy lose their edge.

Expecting officers to perform at a high level for decades without mandatory fitness maintenance is unrealistic. Unlike other public service professions like firefighters, military special operations, police departments rarely require ongoing physical testing or conditioning. In many cases, officers who passed a fitness test in the academy are held to no ongoing fitness standard, and often haven't trained seriously in years.

But beyond department mandates, officers must take personal responsibility for maintaining their physical health. Their body is an instrument of their job, one that needs to be cared for to ensure longevity and to prevent injuries. Every pursuit, every physical altercation, every split-second decision is affected by an officer's physical condition. Neglecting fitness doesn't just put the officer at risk; it puts colleagues and the public at risk too.

Chronic pain, mobility issues, and preventable injuries can shorten careers and diminish quality of life in retirement. The physical demands of policing don't disappear with time, and neither should an officer's commitment to staying in peak condition.

It's time for departments to rethink their approach. Passing an academy standard should be the beginning, not the end, of an officer's physical conditioning. Just as continuing education is required for tactical skills, ongoing fitness should be a nonnegotiable part of the job. Officers should be tested regularly, not just on whether they can climb a fence but on whether they can meet the real demands of policing: sprinting, grappling, sustaining effort in an aerobic situation, and making split-second decisions under physical strain.

Without accountability, expecting officers to be physically prepared for any scenario is wishful thinking at best, dangerous at worst. If policing values readiness, then fitness can't be an afterthought. It must be an essential part of the job throughout one's entire career.

In my own career, athletic performance wasn't just encouraged; it directly influenced the opportunities available to me. The Baker to Vegas Challenge Cup Relay, the world's most prestigious law enforcement running race, was my first such opportunity. Officers from across the globe compete in this 120-mile relay through the Mojave Desert with each team comprising twenty runners. The sheriff's elite running team, filled with deputies assigned to the Men's Central Jail, identified me as a formidable runner, so I earned my place on the team. For two years we secured bragging rights by winning the race and setting course records.

Before long, my hockey background came to light, and I was recruited to join the combined LAPD/LA Sheriff's hockey team. The pinnacle of this experience was competing in the International Police Winter Games, which took us as far as Davos, Switzerland, to face police organizations from around the world. Our team included standout players such as Victor Nechayev, the first player from the Soviet Union to play in the NHL. After retiring from professional hockey, Nechayev joined the LAPD as a tech reserve and Russian translator. In 1993 we faced off against the Ottawa Police Department in the gold medal game and emerged victorious. I scored the game-winning goal and was named tournament MVP, intertwining my hockey and law enforcement careers in an unforgettable way.

Later I turned to CrossFit, drawn by its high-intensity interval training, Olympic weightlifting, and calisthenics. Those challenges pushed me physically and mentally. My competitive drive then led me to the 2012 Nevada Police and Fire Games where I earned the gold medal in the CrossFit competition.

Competitive sports in this context taught me something law enforcement frequently overlooks: fitness is primarily about the ability to perform the physical demands of the job, and the body's response to stress can mean the difference between clear-headed decision making and critical mistakes.

* * *

Imagine an officer in a high-stakes foot pursuit with heart pounding and adrenaline surging. Every breath feels heavier, vision narrows, and the ability to think clearly diminishes. Officers face these physiological realities when under stress and exposed to physical exertion in the apprehension of a violent or non-compliant suspect. However, for those with poor physical fitness, the challenges become exponentially greater.

Dr. Lisa Feldman Barrett's insights on stress and decision making have been a recurring theme throughout this book, reinforcing how the brain processes unpredictable situations. As one of the world's most cited neuroscientists and an advisor on the intersection of neuroscience and public safety, her research has helped shape our understanding of how stress, fitness, and emotional regulation impact officer performance. During a recent conversation she highlighted a sobering reality:

When an officer's physiological state is compromised, the ability to perceive threats accurately, and respond appropriately, deteriorates.

Dr. Barrett explained how an officer's elevated heart rate, often due to poor physical fitness—can drastically impair their ability to perceive and process their surroundings. When the heart rate surges, the brain prioritizes managing the body's physiological stress over processing the environment. As a result, an officer can experience tunnel vision, hypervigilance, and impaired decision making, all of which compromise a desirable performance in critical moments.

I've seen how physically fit officers have a distinct advantage over their less fit counterparts. With lower resting heart rates and greater resilience under pressure, officers who are fit can stay calm, maintain focus, and make sound decisions, even in chaotic situations. Fitness isn't just about looking good, it's about the physiological readiness to effectively meet the demands of policing. Fitness isn't a luxury in law enforcement, it's a professional imperative.

Research on heart rate variability (HRV), a critical measure of how the body adapts to stress, further underscores the importance of fitness. Individuals with higher HRV demonstrate better cognitive processing and emotion regulation, which helps them remain composed so they can make effective decisions during high-pressure incidents.

Law enforcement can be one of the most physically demanding of professions, yet the toll it takes on an officer's health is often ignored. The INTERHEART study, which analyzed over 15,000 heart attack cases across fifty-two countries, identified nine key risk factors: smoking, poor diet, lack of exercise, hypertension, diabetes, obesity, abnormal cholesterol, alcohol consumption, and chronic stress that account for over 90 percent of heart disease worldwide. These same risk factors plague law enforcement, yet they're rarely treated with the urgency they deserve.

The numbers make it clear: Officers are twenty-five times more likely to die from heart disease than from a violent encounter. Nearly 80 percent of officers are overweight, with 30 percent classified as obese. Research published in 2013 in the *International Journal of Emergency Mental Health and Human Resilience* indicates that male law enforcement officers have a life expectancy 21.9 years shorter than the general U.S. male population. According to the CDC, the average life expectancy for a U.S. male in 2022 was 79.4 years. This means the average male law enforcement officer lives to be approximately 57.5 years old. Shift work, sleep deprivation, high cortisol levels, and a diet built around convenience all compound the problem. Despite those facts, too many departments continue to treat fitness as optional rather than essential.

Physical readiness isn't just about running after suspects, it's about survival. Officers train relentlessly for the slim chance of a gunfight but often neglect the much greater risk of a cardiac event. The INTERHEART study reinforces a simple truth: cardiovascular disease is preventable. The same principles that reduce heart attack risk worldwide apply to policing, yet too many officers overlook those principles. Addressing these risks isn't just about extending careers, it's about ensuring officers live long enough to enjoy retirement.

Departments spend millions on equipment, technology, and tactical training, yet many fail to invest in the most important resource, their personnel. Fitness programs, nutrition education, and routine health screenings should be the norm, not viewed as a disposable priority. Officers should demand better resources, but more importantly, they need to take personal responsibility for their health. The job takes a toll, and ignoring statistical warning signs won't make them go away. If law enforcement is serious about readiness, it must provide officers with ongoing training for both body and mind. A badge doesn't make anyone bulletproof, especially against the number one killer of police officers, heart disease.

When fitness is a priority, performance improves, communities benefit, and officers are better equipped, physically, mentally, and emotionally, to handle the demands of the job. Readiness in law enforcement isn't just about strength or endurance, it's about having the awareness, control, and resilience to make the right decisions when it matters most.

* * *

Earlier in this book I shared how working in the jails shaped my understanding of human behavior. That experience reinforced an innate truth I carried throughout my career: beneath the surface, all of us, even "hardened criminals," are driven by the same core emotions.

The most valuable truth I took from the jail environment was the power of emotional intelligence. To connect with someone, whether an inmate, a suspect, or a civilian in crisis, I had to understand and appeal to the emotions, hardwired into all of us, that drove their actions.

Psychologists like Paul Ekman and Robert Plutchik have identified those emotions as the foundational building blocks of the human experience. Our basic emotions—anger, fear, happiness, sadness, disgust, and surprise—are innate, automatic responses that have evolved over millennia to help us survive. Ekman's framework highlights six essential human emotions while Plutchik lists eight, pairing opposites like joy and sadness or trust and disgust. These emotions are nature's survival tools, triggering fight-or-flight responses, fostering cooperation, or safeguarding us from harm.

Take fear, for example. It operates like an internal alarm system, bypassing conscious thought to react instantly to danger. Imagine opening a drawer and a mouse leaps out. Before you even recognize what's happening, you've jumped back, slammed the drawer shut, and feel your heart pounding.

That immediate reaction stems from fear's neurological roots—automatic, unconscious, and designed for survival. This primal response isn't just a human trait; animals share it as well, underscoring its evolutionary nature.

Other emotions, like anger and disgust, are equally rooted in protection. Anger propels us to defend boundaries or confront injustice while disgust shields us from contamination or danger. Those emotions, though primitive, often trigger behaviors essential for survival. At the same time, they form the foundation for more complex feelings. For instance, frustration combines anger with helplessness, while contempt blends anger and disgust. Such nuanced emotions arise from the interaction of basic feelings with cultural and cognitive factors.

Even the objects of basic emotions vary by culture. Fear is universal, but what we fear is often shaped by our environment.

A student's panic over missing an exam reflects fear and the societal value placed on academic success. The interplay between biology and culture creates a rich, complex emotional landscape.

In law enforcement, understanding these basic emotions is invaluable. Recognizing fear, anger, or sadness in a suspect helps officers better manage conflicts, foster dialogue, and solve problems while avoiding unnecessary use of force. This emotional intelligence, rooted in the science of basic emotions, became one of my most effective tools for managing tense situations and preserving my humanity in even the most challenging circumstances.

By learning to appeal to core human emotions, I developed a policing approach grounded in empathy. Whether I was working with inmates in the jails, interacting with suspects on the streets, or supporting law-abiding citizens in need, I realized that understanding and compassion often could achieve what force and dominance could not. Those lessons shaped my broader perspective on the culture of force within law enforcement, a perspective I would carry with me for decades.

Further evidence of the impact of this insight was notable during a tense encounter where a domestic violence suspect's aggression softened after I acknowledged his fear of incarceration. Addressing his emotions directly rather than meeting his hostility with authority or force shifted the dynamic and allowed for a peaceful resolution. Time and time again, I found that empathy and emotional intelligence could de-escalate even the most volatile situations and resolve conflicts without the need for physical intervention. That realization formed the foundation of my commitment to challenging the culture of force in policing and fostering a more empathetic and effective approach to law enforcement.

But even the best policing strategies mean little if officers themselves are worn down by the weight of the job. Emotional intelligence is a critical component of effective policing. But without real support, the stress, trauma, and exhaustion of the profession take a toll on officers and the communities they serve.

* * *

Ignoring the importance of officer well-being weakens the entire profession. Officers are trained to handle crises, but few are given the tools to process the trauma they experience almost every day. The expectation is to compartmentalize, push forward, and suppress the emotional weight of the job. This outdated "stiff upper lip" mindset has come at a cost. And in Dallas, Texas, that cost became undeniable.

According to recent data, 20 to 30 percent of police officers struggle with substance abuse compared to about 10 percent of the general population. Suicide rates among officers remain significantly higher than the national average. In Dallas, after a rise in internal affairs complaints and alcohol-related incidents within the department, then-Chief Eddie Garcia recognized a deeper problem: Officer wellness was either insufficient or nonexistent. In 2021, he decided that he had to change this trend. He tasked one of his executive chiefs with researching the department's wellness initiatives, or lack thereof, and committed to implementing a proactive, department-wide solution. That vision led to the creation of the Officer Wellness Longevity Unit (OWL).

Assistant Chief Reuben Ramirez was OWL's architect. Unlike traditional wellness programs that rely on self-reporting or voluntary participation, OWL introduced a structured, proactive model that embedded mental and emotional well-being into the department's culture.

The centerpiece of OWL was the checkpoint model, a preventative system that leveraged informal leaders within the department to check on officers and civilian staff after any loss-of-life call. Those routine follow-ups weren't just procedural, they were an acknowledgment that cumulative trauma takes a toll. Rather than waiting for officers to reach a breaking point, OWL has helped normalize conversations about mental health, offering support before issues escalated into disciplinary problems or personal crises.

The OWL Unit has connected with over 4,200 Dallas Police staff members, and the results speak for themselves. Between 9 and 12 percent of those contacted have requested mental health resources, numbers that reflect a culture shift within the department. The message is clear: Seeking help is not a sign of weakness but a step toward longevity and resilience.

Beyond counseling and outreach, Dallas took an unprecedented step in addressing alcohol-related struggles within its ranks. The department implemented a first-of-its-kind alcohol leave policy, allowing officers to voluntarily enter a forty-five-day inpatient rehabilitation program before an alcohol-related incident could occur. The policy was designed to remove the stigma associated with seeking help by offering support without punitive consequences. To date, fourteen officers have used the program, and two have been promoted to supervisory roles, an indication that recovery and career advancement are not mutually exclusive.

Wellness training is another integral part of the Dallas department's leadership development program. New recruits at the academy, field training officers, and newly promoted supervisors all undergo wellness education to reinforce the importance of mental and emotional well-being at every stage of an officer's career. The Assist the Officer Foundation, a Dallas-based nonprofit, plays a key role in this effort by providing confidential counseling services to officers and their families. Since OWL's implementation, the foundation's counseling expenditures have increased exponentially, from $107,822 in 2021 to over $300,000 in 2024. Far from being an alarming statistic, this increase reflects a positive cultural shift, one in which officers are utilizing the resources available rather than suffering in silence.

The peer counseling model in Dallas builds on what some departments, including the LAPD, have found to be a critical support system for officers dealing with trauma, depression, or personal struggles. Working with volunteer peer counselors for the LAPD's officer wellness program, I saw firsthand how essential such programs are. Officers struggling with issues like divorce, alcohol abuse, PTSD, or depression had a place to go where they could speak openly without fear of it being reported to their commanding officers. The goal was simple: to provide a confidential, judgment-free space for officers to process their challenges with someone who understood the job.

This resonates at a personal level as I've lost officers to suicide, because of personal hardships and the cumulative trauma that has led to PTSD and mental health issues. I, too, have experienced sleep deprivation, digestive issues, and stress associated with exposure to critical incidents and the overall demands of the job.

Unlike formal departmental mental health resources, which some officers still associate with career consequences, peer counseling offered a level of trust and informality that encouraged participation. Many officers who would never have reached out to an official wellness unit felt comfortable talking with fellow officers who had walked in their shoes. Sometimes, simply talking through problems with someone who understands the job makes the difference between isolation and enlightenment. The LAPD program, like OWL in Dallas, reinforced a crucial lesson: Officers can't be expected to serve their communities effectively if they aren't supported themselves.

The impact of the OWL program extends beyond individual officers. By prioritizing wellness, the Dallas Police Department is investing in the long-term effectiveness of its force. Officers who are mentally and emotionally supported are better equipped to serve their communities, make sound decisions under pressure, and sustain fulfilling careers. The Dallas approach doesn't just benefit law enforcement; it strengthens public trust. When a department actively cares for its own, it fosters a culture of accountability, professionalism, and resilience.

What Dallas has done isn't a quick fix. It's a model for the future of policing, one in which officer well-being is a fundamental pillar of effective law enforcement.

If you're struggling, please know that you're not alone. Reaching out to a trusted friend, a peer, or one of the many resources available can make all the difference in the world. A single conversation, one moment of connection, can be the first step toward a whole new outlook.

Resources like Copline (1-800-COPLINE) provide confidential support for officers in crisis, and the Substance Abuse and Mental Health Services Administration (SAMHSA) helpline (1-800-662-HELP) offers assistance for addiction and mental health challenges. Organizations such as the International Association of Chiefs of Police (IACP) and the National Alliance on Mental Illness (NAMI) also have developed wellness programs and training resources tailored specifically to first responders.

Such initiatives are essential to the future of policing itself, so I'll say it again: Officers who receive wellness support are better equipped to engage with their communities, make sound decisions under pressure, and build trust and empathy with the public. Proactively investing in officer wellness isn't just the right thing to do, it's a critical step toward strengthening the profession for generations to come. Don't delay until the weight feels unbearable. Someone is always ready to listen and help.

* * *

True progress comes from a relentless commitment to self-improvement. Departments that refuse to examine their own shortcomings, whether in training, leadership, policies, or officer wellness, aren't just stagnant, they are a liability. But agencies that commit to accountability, invest in their people, and adapt to the evolving demands of the job will be the ones that define the future of law enforcement.

The U.S. Navy's Blue Angels don't just train to perform, they train to improve. They don't settle for good enough. Instead, after each flight, they conduct a meticulous debrief and analyze every maneuver with brutal honesty. Even the most experienced pilots aren't above critique. No mistake is dismissed. No weakness is ignored when the margin for error is non-negotiable; honest self-assessment to achieve maximum performance and optimal outcomes is imperative.

Policing should demand the same standard. The strongest police departments won't be the ones that insist they have nothing to fix, they'll be the ones willing to self-assess, to confront weaknesses, and to evolve.

But that evolution doesn't begin at the department level. It starts with the individual officer. The best officers, the ones who thrive in this profession, don't wait for change to be forced upon them. They train for it. They prepare for it. They hold themselves to a higher standard, not because they must, but because they refuse to be unprepared when it matters most.

Policing as a profession can either cling to outdated habits, excusing mediocrity under the guise of tradition, or it can evolve into something stronger and something smarter. It can become more accountable and, ultimately, more effective. That transformation won't be dictated by policy alone. It will be shaped by the officers who step up, who push themselves beyond the bare minimum, who refuse to let complacency define their careers.

If we want better outcomes, we don't just need better policies, we need better cops. We need officers who understand that strength isn't about force alone but about control, who recognize that their technical skills mean nothing if they can't keep their composure under pressure, who train for the moment when they don't have time to think or when instinct and discipline are all that stand between success and failure, life and death.

Policing is already changing. The real question is this: Who is willing to rise to meet that change? That's what the next chapter is about: "Building a Better Cop."

Chapter 15:
Building a Better Cop

A lie doesn't become truth, wrong doesn't become right, and evil doesn't become good just because it's accepted by a majority.

—Booker T. Washington

Knowledge is power. Understanding where policing has been is essential to shaping where it needs to go. The previous chapter focused on the roadblocks holding law enforcement back. Now, the focus shifts to solutions, what it takes to develop officers who are not only competent in their skills but also prepared for the evolving challenges of the job.

For decades, pop culture has imagined what the perfect cop might look like. Actor Peter Weller's portrayal in *RoboCop* (1987) gave us a vision of law enforcement stripped of human error, an indestructible officer with unmatched strength, speed, and tactical prowess. But what makes RoboCop compelling isn't just his machine-like efficiency, it's his internal struggle to reclaim his humanity, to think critically, and to make ethical decisions in the face of moral ambiguity. Real policing isn't about creating a troop of robotic enforcers, it's about developing officers who are physically capable, mentally resilient, and ethically grounded, humans who can think, adapt, and lead under pressure.

Gaps in training, leadership, and culture have long impacted an officer's ability to succeed. But lasting change doesn't come solely from department policies or public relations initiatives. The most effective officers take responsibility for their own development. They understand that learning doesn't stop after the academy and that preparation is ongoing. How they train, manage stress, and engage with their communities all contribute to their success, just as we discussed with officer wellness.

Policing is already changing. The real question is whether officers will take an active role in shaping that change for the better. Law enforcement has a tendency to cling to outdated habits, assuming past methods still apply in today's world. Stagnation is far more dangerous than adaptation. Officers who excel in this career are the ones who evolve, refine their approach, and push themselves beyond the bare minimum. This chapter is about what it takes to be one of them.

Dr. Danielle Sabo, a sociologist and research associate at Cleveland State University, echoed this urgency in a conversation with me:

> *As an educator, I stand back and say, okay, I want police officers who are educated. But that doesn't mean I want a force where we're saying you have to have a master's degree in order to become a police officer. I do feel strongly that there are certain courses police officers should be required to take. And I do not believe they're getting them in their current training because it is so wildly quick.*

Dr. Sabo's perspective highlights a critical issue: Too many officers enter the field without the depth of education needed to excel. That's not to say every officer should hold an advanced degree, but training should go beyond the basics. Situational awareness, de-escalation, mental toughness, and ethical decision making must be ingrained into every aspect of an officer's career.

This chapter explores what it takes to become a better officer—physically, mentally, and ethically. We'll examine where training falls short, where recruitment needs to improve, and how individual officers can take control of their own development. After all, no one is going to do it for you.

* * *

Let's start with training. Police training in the United States falls short compared to most other developed nations, creating critical gaps in officer preparedness. On average, U.S. recruits undergo only about eight hundred hours of basic training, about twenty-one weeks, around five months. By contrast, Japan requires fifteen to twenty-one months, Germany mandates two and a half years, Finland and Iceland set a minimum of two years, and Norway demands three years during which recruits earn degrees in criminal justice. And the disparity in training isn't just in its length: Many countries hold officers to higher educational standards. While most U.S. departments require only a high school diploma, many nations mandate a university degree or the equivalent.

Compounding the issue, the U.S. lacks federally mandated training minimums, leading to dramatic inconsistencies between states. Connecticut requires roughly nine months of training while Hawaii has no basic training requirements at all. Clearly, such inconsistencies result in widely varying levels of officer preparation.

Beyond duration and standards, the content of police training remains a concern. In 2018 about 82 percent of recruits were trained on identifying and responding to excessive force, yet little data exists on how effectively their training translates into real-world policing. Meanwhile, Nordic countries provide a compelling model for how comprehensive, well-structured training can enhance officer competence, reduce misconduct, and build public trust. If U.S. law enforcement is to meet the demands of modern policing, it must adopt a more unified, evidence-based approach to training, one that prioritizes both quality and consistency.

In Norway, for example, aspiring officers undergo a three-year program that integrates classroom education with a full year of immersive, hands-on field experience. Similarly, Finland blends two years of academic instruction with practical fieldwork, while Iceland requires at least two years of training that culminates in a police science diploma. Those programs focus on building a well-rounded foundation in law, community engagement, and tactical skills before officers take on their roles. But adopting similar training programs in the United States would necessitate overcoming significant challenges, including the decentralized structure of law enforcement and the lack of standardized national training requirements. Despite those obstacles, Dr. Sabo envisions a future where U.S. police training evolves to prioritize deeper education and hands-on preparation:

> *If you can do a four-year degree to become a police officer, that would make you that much better. There can be a report writing course where you spend an entire semester on different elements of report writing, a course where you become trained in forensic, experiential, and trauma and learn to understand all of these intersectional perspectives, such as why a victim*

would respond in a certain way or why crime happens in certain communities. It would be a place where you take a geospatial class and understand how communities and location and structures impact crime.

I had an entire set of 100 variables that I would code in these reports describing where the crime occurred. Was it an abandoned building? Was it on train tracks? Did the victim get transported before, during, or after the assault? All of that impacts the entire story, which impacts the prosecution of the crime. If police officers could learn about that before they get into the actual serving police force, I think that could be incredible. And, of course, you would still have to pass the courses at the police academy as well.

In our previous chapter on suicide by cop, Dr. Judith Andersen, a psychology professor at the University of Toronto, provided critical insights into how stress affects health and decision making in law enforcement. Her research focuses on the physiological and psychological toll of high-stress encounters, shaping a deeper understanding of officer performance under pressure.

Dr. Andersen's collaboration with a police college in Finland offered a firsthand look at a proactive approach to training, one that prioritizes stress regulation, decision making under duress, and practical strategies to foster better policing outcomes. By integrating science-backed methods, Finnish law enforcement has taken significant strides in improving officer well-being and reducing unnecessary uses of force. These lessons provide a compelling contrast to current U.S. training models and offer a glimpse into what's possible when policing evolves with evidence-based practices.

Studies have consistently shown that education plays a key role in improving officer decision making. For example, a 2010 study published in *Police Quarterly* found that college-educated officers are 40 percent less likely to use force on the job. While education alone doesn't make someone a good officer, it fosters the patience, adaptability, and decision-making skills essential for modern policing. Dr. Andersen shared more about Finland's education-focused approach:

> *They have three years of an immersive kind of undergraduate training for their police officers. They have all kinds of classes, from learning all the legal stuff to community public relations. They also have them, of course, on weapons and tactics. They also have integrated our research about stress physiology.*

Dr. Andersen said that the police are so effectively trained that when Finland conducts a "survey every couple of years, their police are rated the second favorite public service, right under firefighters." She points out that Finland is not immune to police shootings, but the Finns think about them differently than Americans typically do:

> *They train their officers to shoot the suspect in the arm or leg, which is unheard of. No one in Canada or the U.S. would ever say that's okay. They would say, 'No, you cannot train people to do that. Let's shoot first in their (body) mass,' and that's what they do. In Finland, they are so reticent to shoot they'll send a dog in before resorting to a firearm. So just the scope in training, the seriousness with which they [the Finns]*

value research and development and integration throughout their police training—it's a lifelong commitment to these officers—is radically different from North America. Police officers are valued, they're treated well by their employers and not thrown under the bus constantly like we see in Canada and the US.

The difference in approach between Finland's police and those in the United States stems from a foundational disparity: Finnish officers operate in a context where the likelihood of encountering an armed subject is significantly lower than in the United States. Meanwhile, American officers are trained to expect that any encounter could escalate into potentially fatal violence within seconds. That inherent fear shapes every U.S. policing interaction, influencing both mindset and behavior from the outset.

So how do we address this deeply ingrained way of thinking? Is the answer in fundamentally changing who we hire, or does the solution lie in reshaping how officers are trained to think?

Dr. Barrett, as I've pointed out, is one of the world's leading authorities in psychology and neuroscience, and she has revolutionized our understanding of the human brain. She emphasizes that retraining officers' brains is not just about skill development but about transforming their automatic responses under stress, enabling them to assess threats more accurately and make better decisions in high-pressure situations. Here are more of her thoughts:

What's the optimal type of training or length of training or things like that when the issue about the brain is that it's predictive?

Everybody in this country is exposed to events in their own lives, or in the newspapers or on television and movies. They're exposed to certain types of regularities that link skin color or other sorts of physical features with stereotypic actions toward those people. But race is completely socially constructed, because what people have done is they've imposed a function on skin color that it didn't evolve to have. And then a bunch of people have agreed that that's the function, and so it serves its social reality. Large portions of the population implicitly make those associations.

Dr. Barrett believes that if we're to change policing, we need to change how police officers think:

You'd want to hire people who are willing to accept the fact that the brain can do things that they're not aware of. People have to have that belief before they're actually motivated to reduce their bias. There's research to show that. More generally, I just think it's hard to answer this kind of question: How do you pick the people? How do you hire the people who will be right for the job? This is not just a problem in policing, it's a problem everywhere in HR.

If it were up to me, what I would do in a perfect world is what they do in Finland. You have to get what is functionally an undergraduate degree, and it takes three years of training. And really, at the end of that, you decide who can be a police officer and who can't because what you've done is you've watched these people for three years, and you've trained them.

Dr. Barrett points out that this long-term study of the officers in training gives the assessors the best chance to select the best cops:

> *You know, that's not how training works in the United States. You get more training as an electrician than you do as a police officer. And we're talking about people who are carrying firearms. And so I'm not sure it's a question of who to hire. It might be a question of how you hire.*
>
> *I think about the kind of training that people receive, and also how open they are to training, and how well they absorb that training. I don't think these are things that you can assess with a test. I think you actually have to observe people in the process and then make a determination. Because tests don't tell you very much, to be honest. The HR world is full of these tests where people make ratings about themselves, and all they're telling you is what they believe about themselves. It's like a multibillion-dollar business, these personality tests, and they have no validity at all in predicting how someone will behave on the job, whether you're a police officer or a judge or a lawyer or, you know, a professor or whatever. It's just not how humans function. Humans don't have that kind of insight into themselves.*

Currently, law enforcement uses a "de-selection" process that focuses on undesirable attributes. If you don't have a criminal record, your finances are in order, and you have no substantial history of drug use, you're likely to be considered for hire. There's no consideration of the identifiable characteristics that are indicative of someone being successful as a police officer. No one would argue that we want our officers to have emotional intelligence, empathy, moral reasoning, critical thinking, self-awareness, and interpersonal skills, but our current process doesn't help us identify these people.

For Dr. Barrett, improving hiring practices means focusing on how candidates are evaluated and the questions that guide the process:

What is the hiring process? When is the determination made? How much training will candidates receive, and how closely will they be observed? What criteria will be used to evaluate them including: How well do they learn? How quickly do they adapt? What does their learning process show about their potential? These are the kinds of questions we need to be asking.

Dr. Barrett also thinks we should pay police officers well, which would offer incentives to a wider talent pool:

It's perfectly reasonable to incent people to train. Incenting people by providing carrots always works better than providing sticks. So I don't think, in principle, that's a problem. I just don't think it's enough. People have to be willing to undergo certain types of training, and they have to be willing to admit that, or at least entertain the possibility that they might have habits of mind or habits of action that they are unaware of and that they have to curb. It helps to hire people who have an open mind. And people with an open mind will be more influenced by their training. And all things considered equal, people who are motivated to reduce prejudice tend to reduce prejudice in response to training, and people who are resistant don't respond to training very well.

* * *

Dr. Sabo sees technology as a way to revolutionize policing, particularly with the integration of AI. As a topic at the forefront of modern innovation and societal debate, AI holds immense potential to enhance the effectiveness and efficiency of law enforcement. Here's how Dr. Sabo sees it:

One of the most incredible ways that I think AI can be used, especially in a geospatial qualitative type of way, is this: Why can't we harness the technology to make AI transcriptions of what the police body cameras see, and the police could then write up a police report directly from the transcript of their body cam? Everyone is wearing body cams at this point. So why are we not taking that recording of video footage to AI, which can write it up in a way that is more like a police report format, and it's not missing things. It has everything for the human officer to work from.

When you're sitting down for an interview, you could actually be listening to the interview. And you could have a computer screen in front of you, and it's actually prompting and telling the officer what to ask next. The AI is actually interacting with the officer and guiding them based on what the subject being interviewed is saying.

Dr. Sabo sees the future of AI as a powerful policing component that wouldn't replace human police officers but would empower them:

AI is something that is going to make us more efficient and can be harnessed in a really positive way, especially in instances that can truly help out, such as writing in police reports.

While the integration of AI into policing offers exciting possibilities, it also raises legitimate concerns about accuracy and ethics. For example, if AI algorithms are trained on biased datasets, they could perpetuate existing inequities in law enforcement practices. Additionally, over-reliance on AI could lead to situations in which technology fails to account for the nuance and context of human interactions. These challenges underscore the need for rigorous oversight, transparency, and continual evaluation of AI systems. Establishing independent review boards and requiring ongoing testing and updates could help ensure that AI tools serve as a supplement rather than a substitute for human judgment. Furthermore, ethical guidelines must be developed to govern the use of AI in policing, ensuring that its implementation aligns with principles of fairness, accountability, and respect for civil liberties.

Dr. Sabo trains police officers, and part of that training is a group exercise in which they review an officer's report from a few years back:

Like maybe two years ago? Would you write the same report like this today? Would you want to be a victim reading this report? Why was it written this way? And how can we be better? Maybe with AI, we could have established a template for all reports that makes it easier and better for the officers, and more accurate.

* * *

Faced with rising costs and recruitment challenges, some police departments are exploring innovative staffing strategies that prioritize cost savings and operational efficiency. In January 2023 the Milwaukee Police Department commissioned a consultant's report highlighting a significant opportunity: by increasing civilian roles rather than sworn officer positions, the department could save millions. The report recommended adding 11 sworn officers and 116 civilians, demonstrating how reallocating traditional police responsibilities to civilian staff can achieve significant cost savings without compromising efficiency.

Without the transition, Milwaukee would have needed 133 new sworn officers and only 27 civilian hires, a far costlier approach given that sworn salaries average at least 50 percent higher than civilian equivalents. This strategy exemplifies how rethinking staffing models can achieve financial and operational benefits while allowing officers to serve in roles that align with their training rather than be assigned duties that are better suited for individuals without police expertise.

Police departments are increasingly considering adding civilian commanders to oversee divisions with significant civilian staff such as dispatch, records, property and evidence, finance, policy and accreditation, human resources, and forensics. In 2023 in Syracuse, New York, Mayor Ben Walsh proposed creating a civilian commander role to oversee department improvement. The civilian commander would hold equal authority and rank to sworn commanders, such as deputy chiefs, signaling a shift toward integrating civilian leadership into key operational areas.

Syracuse, a central New York city with a population of nearly 150,000, has long been the region's economic and educational hub. Mayor Walsh, an independent leader from a prominent local political family, has been at the helm since 2018, spearheading innovative approaches to governance, including this proposed improvement for the police department.

In addition to structural changes, technology is poised to revolutionize policing in unimaginable ways. Artificial intelligence offers the potential to enhance efficiency and accuracy across law enforcement functions. For example, AI is already employed in medicine to identify and diagnose cancerous tumors, in courts to condense 400-page legal briefs into concise, accurate summaries, and in accessibility tools that "see" for the visually impaired by describing their surroundings. With such capabilities, integrating technology and AI into policing could improve outcomes, streamline operations, and create a more effective system for officers and their communities. If these tools can benefit other sectors so profoundly, why not harness their potential to improve law enforcement?

* * *

Few leaders understood what it truly meant to modernize policing more than former LAPD Chief Charlie Beck. I know that firsthand because I worked with him when he was Captain at Rampart. I served as his officer-in-charge of the gang unit. Rampart, as you will remember, was still fighting to recover from one of the department's darkest scandals. Even then, Beck never shied away from confronting tough challenges. He understood that rebuilding trust wasn't just about arrests. It meant employing intelligence-led policing, establishing community partnerships, and harnessing cutting-edge technology to create lasting, meaningful change.

Beck spearheaded early versions of technology-driven policing, integrating comprehensive gang databases, advanced mapping tools, and strategic intelligence long before most departments even considered them necessary. I personally experienced this approach as we tackled the persistent crime and gang activity that plagued neighborhoods around MacArthur Park.

MacArthur Park's history mirrors the complexities of urban development, reflecting periods of cultural vibrancy, decline, and ongoing efforts towards revitalization. MacArthur Park has faced significant challenges; the area became associated with crime, including drug dealing and violent incidents.

By leveraging data, community collaboration, and innovative technologies, we crafted a successful model that later became recognized as a national best practice. Technology acted as a force multiplier. Surveillance cameras allowed a single operator to monitor the entire park and direct officers to crimes in progress in real time—an effectiveness that once required a full taskforce to achieve. In fact, our efforts in MacArthur Park received acknowledgment in a *Los Angeles Times* article for dramatically reducing violence and reclaiming the park as a safer, community-oriented space.

When Beck later succeeded Bill Bratton as LAPD Chief, he built significantly upon that foundation. Although CompStat provided departments with valuable data, Beck recognized spreadsheets and crime maps alone weren't enough. True progress demanded embedding transparency directly into daily operations. Beck advocated fiercely for tools like body-worn cameras, GPS vehicle tracking, and real-time monitoring systems years before such technology became standard nationwide. For Beck, it wasn't about public relations optics; it was about operational efficiency and integrity.

After retiring from LAPD, Beck was tapped to serve as Interim Superintendent of the Chicago Police Department (CPD), a decision that reflected his national reputation for modernizing police work. However, his influence in Chicago actually began years earlier when he sent his LAPD chief of staff to help establish the city's Strategic Decision Support Centers (SDSCs). These intelligence hubs were designed to use data and real-time analytics to prevent shootings, particularly in high-crime areas like Englewood. According to a *GOVERNING* report and CPD data, the SDSCs contributed to a 52 percent reduction in violent crime in that district. As interim superintendent, Beck continued strengthening the model, reinforcing what he had long believed: real leadership means anticipating problems, not reacting to them, and using technology to drive emerging police methods.

Real leadership isn't about hoarding effective strategies or waiting until public pressure forces your hand. It's about proactively embracing solutions, developing systems that yield consistent results, and demonstrating that well-applied technology makes policing safer, smarter, and more effective.

That same philosophy informs where policing stands today. Technology can no longer be optional; it is essential. Departments unwilling to adapt will not merely fall behind. They will entirely forfeit public trust. That's why innovative companies like Compliant Technologies and Illuno embody precisely the kind of partners law enforcement needs today. These organizations are led by professionals who truly understand the complexities of policing and are genuinely committed to solving real-world problems.

One profound failure in policing has been our repeated emphasis on de-escalation while continually equipping officers with tools inherently designed to escalate. Batons. Tasers. Beanbag shotguns. Firearms. Almost every option on an officer's belt carries risks of severe injury, psychological trauma, or, at minimum, devastating optics that undermine public confidence. What's missing, and has long been, is a reliable, humane middle ground; a tool that provides officers control without forcing them into impossible choices.

Compliant Technologies' signature device, the G.L.O.V.E. (Generated Low Output Voltage Emitter), directly addresses this decades-old gap. It's a genuinely non-lethal compliance tool tailored explicitly for the rapid, unpredictable nature of street encounters, where decisions must occur within fractions of seconds, and the people officers confront aren't always criminals. Frequently, people in these situations are merely non-compliant, frightened, confused, or experiencing mental health crises.

The G.L.O.V.E. emits a safe, low-voltage current designed to secure compliance without neuromuscular incapacitation or lasting physical harm. There's no blunt force trauma, no puncture wound, and most importantly, no tragic outcome like unintended death from cardiac arrest; scenarios I've witnessed far too many times throughout my career. Knowing what we now understand, not equipping officers with tools capable of safely de-escalating dangerous encounters is negligent.

Consider the tragic case of Officer Kim Potter, who fatally shot Daunte Wright during a traffic stop after mistaking her firearm for a Taser. Potter was convicted of manslaughter and served prison time. She testified tearfully that she intended to use her Taser but mistakenly drew her handgun instead. Now imagine if Potter had the G.L.O.V.E. already equipped on her hand, no reach, no draw, no fatal mistake possible. The tragic incident could have been resolved safely in seconds, sparing Daunte Wright's life and preventing irreversible trauma for all involved. That's what responsible, technology-enhanced policing looks like.

Further enhancing accountability, Compliant Technologies incorporates its innovative CD3 platform, automatically logging every G.L.O.V.E. deployment in real-time, ensuring transparent documentation that protects officers and agencies from false claims. This built-in transparency is precisely what the policing profession urgently requires today.

However, policing's shortcomings extend far beyond just the tools officers carry on their belts. One particularly glaring vulnerability remains with off-duty policing assignments—long an unregulated, opaque corner of law enforcement where handshake deals, cash transactions, and informal agreements create a hotbed for liability, corruption, and public scandals. The risks of this informal system become painfully obvious when looking at high-profile incidents involving meticulously orchestrated crimes targeting athletes and celebrities.

In recent years, organized crime groups have unleashed a wave of burglaries targeting some of the most famous names in sports, from NFL stars Travis Kelce, Patrick Mahomes, and Joe Burrow, to NBA icons Luka Doncic and Bobby Portis. These incidents aren't isolated or random; they represent a broader, disturbing trend of criminal sophistication. According to *The U.S. Sun*, these burglaries are executed by highly trained, transnational gangs, notably from Chile, Colombia, Peru, and Venezuela, who reportedly exploit lenient U.S. entry policies, including short-term visas that allow repeated, largely undetected entry. These organized syndicates are meticulous, well-funded, and operate with brazen efficiency rarely seen in traditional home burglaries.

These criminals don't simply break into homes; they strategically select targets based on publicly accessible information—professional athletes' game schedules, public travel itineraries, and social media posts flaunting luxury possessions. They employ advanced technological methods, such as GPS signal jammers that disable alarm and security systems, effectively rendering modern surveillance ineffective. These gangs meticulously test their equipment prior to operations to confirm that security alerts fail well before they make their move. Disguising themselves as construction workers, joggers, or gardeners during preliminary surveillance, they seamlessly blend into affluent neighborhoods to map out vulnerabilities without raising suspicion. Once the coast is clear, they strike swiftly, typically executing burglaries within a tight ten to fifteen-minute window, which minimizes risk of capture.

The scale and efficiency of these operations are staggering. The *U.S. Sun* revealed that burglars stole over $30,000 worth of jewelry from Luka Doncic alone, while several invaluable and emotionally irreplaceable items such as autographed jerseys and personal keepsakes were taken from Travis Kelce's residence. Joe Burrow's home was targeted precisely during an away game, which caused profound distress and highlighted the alarming effectiveness of these organized criminal tactics. NHL and NBA security officials have even issued unprecedented alerts warning athletes to heighten security and awareness in response to these highly coordinated attacks.

Despite clear evidence of these threats, the system of off-duty policing that should provide robust protection remains trapped in antiquated, informal arrangements. Without transparency or standardized oversight, athletes and other high-profile figures continue to rely on vague assurances rather than measurable security.

This is precisely where companies like Illuno step in to revolutionize off-duty policing. Illuno eliminates the opacity and informality inherent in traditional off-duty work, not through departments, but through vetted coordinators, officers, and the businesses themselves. By bypassing city procurement red tape and RFPs, Illuno delivers a modern, community-facing platform that brings structure to the vastly fragmented off-duty market, where most assignments happen informally.

Illuno doesn't rely on direct department approval. It empowers trusted coordinators and verified officers to provide law enforcement-grade protection to clients while ensuring transparency, accountability, and risk mitigation. Each security assignment is meticulously scheduled, logged, and insured through Illuno's centralized platform. This ensures full oversight, protecting everyone involved—the officers, the clients, and the community.

The app connects law enforcement with community needs, linking businesses and individuals seeking officers with vetted professionals ready to serve. It's an innovative solution for the off-duty industry, tackling issues that often leave officers and clients disconnected while navigating risks and liabilities on their own. For corporations, athletes, and public officials who are particularly attractive targets, Illuno guarantees legitimate, law-enforcement-grade protection without the politics. Every officer is rigorously vetted. Every shift is documented and insured.

Illuno's platform fosters balance and fairness by simplifying access to off-duty jobs for all officers. By leveraging a digital system, Illuno allows officers to view and select available jobs based on their availability and preferences, reducing favoritism and manual scheduling conflicts. This approach not only saves time but also supports a more organized and accessible process, enabling officers to secure work without unnecessary barriers. Additionally, the platform's design helps prevent overwork by spreading job opportunities across a wider pool of officers, promoting healthier work-life balance and consistent compensation.

As you can see, we're reaching a whole new level of sophistication and technological capability in international criminal networks. These organizations now employ advanced cyber tools, encrypted communication, and detailed digital surveillance to identify and exploit vulnerabilities in private security and law enforcement systems. This reveals an undeniable truth: law enforcement must modernize operational strategies and administrative processes to maintain any hope of staying ahead. Criminals adapt quickly. Law enforcement agencies and their support systems must adapt even faster.

Illuno and Compliant Technologies aren't just offering tools—they represent a reimagining of how modern policing can meet twenty-first century challenges. At its core, this conversation isn't just theoretical or administrative. This conversation is deeply personal and profoundly human. Each security failure represents shattered lives, broken trust, and the painful realization that preventable tragedies keep occurring. As Chief Beck demonstrated through proactive, tech-driven leadership at LAPD, true change comes from anticipating threats before they materialize, not after tragedies unfold.

We must choose accountability, transparency, and strategic innovation as our guiding principles. Implementing platforms like Illuno and adopting compliance technology from innovators like Compliant Technologies aren't merely operational upgrades. They are ethical imperatives. We must ensure officers have the tools and systems necessary to perform their duties safely and effectively. This is about restoring and preserving public trust. Most importantly, it's about protecting lives, both civilian and officer, from harm that proactive, transparent, intelligent solutions can effectively mitigate.

We have the technology, the knowledge, and the capability to meet these threats. Law enforcement leaders and organizational stakeholders must now exhibit the courage and foresight to integrate these solutions and prioritize public safety and officer welfare above tradition, inertia, and bureaucracy. The time for incremental adjustments has passed; what policing demands today is bold, comprehensive action.

* * *

Policing will never be easy, but it can be smarter. It can be more prepared. It can be better. As previously noted, that starts with officers who choose to rise to the challenge, not just meet the minimum standard. The best officers aren't waiting for policies to catch up. They're taking ownership of their training, sharpening their decision-making skills, and holding themselves to a higher level of accountability.

But individual effort alone isn't enough. Without meaningful structural changes, even the most dedicated officers will struggle against outdated systems that work against them. Training must evolve to reflect the realities of modern policing. Recruitment needs to prioritize critical thinking, resilience, and adaptability, as well as physical endurance. Leadership must recognize that building better officers means investing in their education, well-being, and long-term development.

There is no single fix, no shortcut to improvement. The path forward requires a combination of smarter hiring, deeper training, technological advancements, and stronger community relationships. Officers who embrace this mindset—the ones willing to learn, adapt, and lead—will define the future of policing.

Building better officers is only one piece of the puzzle. If the departments they serve are failing—if leadership is broken, policies are outdated, and trust is eroded—then even the best officers will be set up to fail. The next chapter tackles that reality head-on. Because no matter how skilled or prepared officers are, they are only as effective as the institution backing them. And when that institution is failing, it's time for a reckoning.

Chapter 16:
Fixing a Failing Police Force

It is not the strongest of the species that survives,
nor the most intelligent that survives. It is the one
that is most adaptable to change.

—Charles Darwin

A well-trained officer can only do so much in a broken system. Leadership, culture, and accountability shape policing just as much as tactics and training. Without strong leadership and clear priorities, departments stagnate and public trust erodes.

Nowhere is this more evident than in Ohio where a recent audit found that, of 300 police departments, only 5 were in compliance with the state's mandated training requirements. The sheer scale of this failure reveals a deeper, systemic issue. Departments are neglecting one of the most basic responsibilities of law enforcement, ensuring that officers are properly trained to do their jobs.

Much of this information was uncovered not by government officials but by citizen activist Mariah Crenshaw of the organization Chasing Justice. Through tireless research and public records requests, Crenshaw exposed Ohio's widespread noncompliance.

In 2017, Officer Larry McDonald of the East Cleveland Police Department was hired by the Cleveland Division of Police, despite being out of compliance with Ohio's required annual training. Years later he returned to the East Cleveland Police Department and, in early 2021, shot and killed nineteen-year-old Vincent Belmonte. A later investigation revealed that McDonald had been out of compliance during his entire prior employment with the Cleveland Police, meaning he was never eligible to serve. This failure raises serious questions about how departments screen and monitor officer training compliance, why gaps like this persist, and how an officer who didn't meet state requirements was still given the authority to police the public.

Millions of taxpayer dollars are allocated for officer education, yet there is no system in place to verify whether training is actually completed, let alone effective. Worse, many of these lapses go unchallenged because oversight is minimal. Police departments self-report compliance, and many officers complete mandatory training in absurdly short windows. Records show, for example, that courses on de-escalation and use of force have been completed in as little as three minutes. *Three minutes.* This is a result of law enforcement becoming reliant on e-learning. Officers receive training electronically with no active oversight ensuring that they are effectively completing the training as required. The shortcomings of this type of training have been highlighted by numerous officer depositions I've reviewed for civil lawsuits, in which officers admitted they had not completed the required electronic training despite signing off that they had.

The result? Officers continue to patrol the streets without the necessary knowledge to do their jobs responsibly. Departments fail to enforce training requirements, and communities pay the price. When a department lacks oversight, when leadership fails to demand compliance, and when training is reduced to a paperwork exercise rather than a meaningful process, public safety suffers.

This is where state oversight in hiring and training could provide a solution. Rather than relying on hundreds of individual departments to self-regulate, states could take a more significant role in screening, training, and certifying officers before they enter the hiring pool. A centralized system would ensure every recruit meets standardized requirements, eliminating the inconsistency that allows officers with inadequate training or troubling disciplinary records to move unchecked between departments. Such an approach would not only address compliance failures but also curb the common practice of officers who face misconduct allegations simply transferring to another agency to evade accountability.

This chapter focuses on the next step—fixing what's not working. That means rethinking recruitment, strengthening leadership, and making sure departments evolve with the job. The problems with law enforcement aren't just about individual officers, they're about a system that allows mediocrity, deficient training, and inconsistency to thrive.

Currently, police departments across the U.S. operate like islands, each setting its own hiring standards and training compliance. Yet each state is responsible for the certification of all officers. It defies logic that individual states do not maintain stronger oversight to make sure officers adhere to hiring and training standards.

By shifting hiring oversight to the state, officers would be drawn from a regulated pool, ensuring a uniform baseline of competency. Training centers operated at the state level could further this effort, offering continuing education and regional collaboration. Officers from various communities would train together, breaking down the insular cultures that sometimes reinforce problematic department norms. This model wouldn't federalize law enforcement, something widely opposed within the profession, but it would create a higher degree of accountability at the state level, ensuring public safety isn't compromised by lax or inconsistent hiring practices.

Policing is changing, whether agencies are ready or not. The choice is to adapt or be left behind.

* * *

Leadership is critical to the success of policing. A department's culture, priorities, and trajectory are all defined by its leaders. Without strong, visionary leadership, even the best-intentioned officers will struggle to succeed. True leadership requires humility and a willingness to learn. Leaders must recognize that they don't have all the answers, and that effective policing requires collaboration, both within the department and with the public. Strong leaders foster environments where officers feel empowered to voice concerns, propose solutions, and adapt to new challenges. Remember, it's not about being right, it's about getting it right, which requires diversity of thought and a willingness to hear conflicting opinions.

As previously discussed, Chief Bratton's strategy of integrating civilian experts into leadership roles diversified perspectives and improved decision making at the highest levels of the LAPD. This leadership model is a powerful example of the accountability needed to drive meaningful cultural change. By combining civilian insights with officer expertise, departments can better align leadership priorities with community needs.

Leadership also means accountability. Too often, poor decision making at the top trickles down to the rank and file, eroding morale and public confidence. Leaders must model the behavior they expect from their officers: integrity, professionalism, and a commitment to excellence. This includes holding themselves and others, regardless of rank, accountable for mistakes, not as a means of punishment but as an opportunity for growth. Otherwise, internal actions and behaviors will fail to align with the organization's stated values and fall short of community expectations.

This disconnect—what some refer to as a policy-practice divide—is central to understanding these failures. It's not about rooting out bad apples within law enforcement. I don't subscribe to the idea that problematic behavior in policing can be dismissed as the actions of a few rogue individuals. Instead, these incidents reflect a larger organizational culture: how officers are recruited, how they're trained, and how leadership governs their behavior. While the vast majority of officers may not engage in outright misconduct, the environment that allows such incidents to occur and recur is embedded within the system.

The policy-practice divide represents the gap between what officers know they should do and what they actually do when confronted with real-world situations. Departments may have strong policies emphasizing de-escalation, ethical decision making, and accountability, but if those policies are not reinforced through training, leadership, and department culture, they become nothing more than words on paper. Officers may be taught best practices in controlled training environments, yet once they hit the streets, the department's culture often dictates their actions. This culture, shaped by poor recruitment practices, inadequate training, and weak leadership, overrides their formal education and reinforces behaviors that should be unacceptable.

It has been said that if it's a mistake of the mind, it's forgivable. If it's a mistake of the heart, that's the policy-practice divide. This isn't about officers making split-second errors under pressure. It's about making conscious decisions to ignore what they know is right, choosing tactics and behaviors that contradict their training. That failure isn't just on the individual. It's also on leadership.

We saw this play out in the death of Frank Tyson. The policies were there, training on de-escalation, guidelines on use of force, and, most importantly, expectations for handling individuals in distress, but when it mattered, those policies didn't translate into practice. Instead of adhering to their training and assessing the situation, officers ignored policy, and the outcome was tragic. This is what happens when culture overrides policy. Law enforcement must cultivate a culture in which following procedures is the standard, not the exception, a culture that encourages officers to integrate empathy and compassion into every decision.

Leadership either closes the policy-practice divide or widens it. When command staff fail to hold people accountable or look the other way, they tell officers that culture, not policy, determines how they operate. This is where things break down. The best policies in the world won't change anything if leaders don't enforce them. Most importantly, this requires the organization's influence to resonate with officers on an emotional level.

Recruitment plays a major role in this issue. Too many departments still subconsciously prioritize traditional alpha male qualities over emotional intelligence and problem solving. This practice can attract candidates who are more likely to lean on force rather than pause to think situations through when time permits. Training reinforces reliance on tactics and weapons while giving communication and de-escalation little more than lip service. Even when officers do receive proper training, they quickly learn that department culture rewards aggressive action, not restraint.

* * *

To address the mounting recruiting challenges facing modern policing, agencies also must prepare to recalibrate their hiring practices, prioritizing the inclusion of civilian professionals for roles that do not explicitly require sworn officers. Currently, police agencies in the U.S. employ over a million individuals with about 70 percent being sworn officers and 30 percent civilian staff. But recruitment has become increasingly difficult in the wake of the pandemic and the negative attention drawn by high-profile departmental failures, some of which we discussed earlier. This staffing crisis, while concerning, presents a significant opportunity for improvement by integrating more civilian expertise into police work.

A 2019 survey by the International Association of Chiefs of Police (IACP) highlighted the significance of this issue: 78 percent of agencies reported struggling to find qualified candidates, and 65 percent noted a decline in the overall number of applicants. Additionally, 75 percent acknowledged that recruitment had become more challenging over the past five years. Although some progress has been made in recent years, with major city police departments stemming the loss of personnel, they have yet to demonstrate meaningful growth toward pre-COVID staffing levels. Of the 13 departments serving cities with populations over one million, 11 remain smaller than they were in 2019.

This moment calls for a reimagining of staffing models. Dr. Sabo has worked extensively with teams of both sworn officers and civilians and has seen firsthand the transformative potential of such collaboration. By broadening the scope of civilian involvement, departments can alleviate staffing pressures and foster more efficient and more community-focused policing practices.

Expanding civilian roles goes beyond support staff. It means reconsidering who is best suited for specialized tasks. For example, why rely on sworn officers to teach defensive tactics when civilian subject matter experts can provide the same training without perpetuating the toxic cultural norms sometimes found in police instruction? Civilian instructors bring a neutral, skill-focused approach that avoids the negative attitudes and beliefs officers may unintentionally carry into the classroom.

Similarly, civilian professionals can fill roles like piloting helicopters or operating other specialized equipment, often at lower salaries than sworn officers receive, which can free up significant financial resources that could be repurposed for recruiting, training, and retaining a more skilled and community-focused police force. Furthermore, retaining officers incapable of performing full-duty police work strains budgets and undermines operational efficiency.

Dr. Sabo, who has worked extensively with interdisciplinary teams, provides a vivid example of this collaborative potential:

We have a human trafficking task force here in Cleveland. It's made up of law enforcement, it's made up of prosecutors, and it's made up of victim advocates. And we're on the team too, but we're doing the data analysis part of it. One of the things that I love about this team is that when they do get a hint of victims that they are potentially going to go get, they immediately call the human trafficking victim advocate at the Cleveland Rape Crisis Center, who is on call 24/7. For every call they answer, they have been trained to understand all of the different intersections that a victim of human trafficking would need and which might be at play, such as drugs, alcohol, wanting to stay with your trafficker, wanting to still be in that lifestyle. Maybe they have been turned into sex workers.

The team understands all those things, and they also bring a victim advocate with them who is beautifully trained on trauma-informed care, who's going to be able to do the long-term follow-up and connect to this trafficked individual with all of their therapeutic care with every resource that they will need. And the advocate will address their more immediate concerns, such as finding them potential shelter for the night. Typically, these victims have children, and they need to find somewhere safe for all of them. The victim advocate is going to do all that work to ensure they get transportation, food, housing, all of that which takes that job away from the police and frees them up to do other things.

So I see the future of different teams like this, especially ones that are doing more mental health-related calls, which have an advocate with them, and a social worker, but also at the same time having more training for the police officers who partner with them. We are not investing in prevention; we're not investing in education and training. We're saying, 'Oh, let's put more money in ShotSpotter technology.'

ShotSpotter is a gunshot detection system that uses acoustic sensors to identify, locate, and alert law enforcement to gunfire in real time. In theory, it enables faster police response, improves accuracy in detecting gunfire incidents, and provides data to support investigations. But while this technology has potential, its impact on overall crime reduction is still a matter of debate, particularly when compared to investments in preventative measures or community-focused initiatives.

* * *

Compressed work schedules, such as twelve-hour shifts, have become common in many police departments. While they may appear efficient on paper, these schedules have significant drawbacks that undermine officer performance and community engagement.

Studies show officers are no more productive in twelve hours than when working eight-hour shifts. Instead, the longer shifts lead to fatigue, which impairs decision making, situational awareness, and overall vigilance. This fatigue is exacerbated by the fact that many officers commute long distances, further reducing their alertness and effectiveness on the job.

Fatigue isn't the only issue. Compressed schedules also limit the consistent presence of officers in the communities they serve. Fewer workdays mean fewer opportunities to build relationships with residents and address local issues. This disconnect runs counter to the principles of community policing that emphasize trust and collaboration between law enforcement and the public. It's not enough to just put a police officer in a black and white. It's a philosophical question of how best to police our communities.

Additionally, longer shifts can unintentionally encourage officers to treat policing as a part-time job. With more consecutive days off, some officers pursue side businesses, potentially diverting their focus and energy from their primary duties. While side pursuits are not inherently negative, they shouldn't come at the expense of an officer's commitment to serve the communities they are sworn to protect. Officers also have to testify in court beyond their normal work hours, further stretching their mental and physical limits.

The solution lies in returning to more traditional eight-hour, five-day workweeks. This approach reduces fatigue and increases opportunities for consistent community engagement. It also fosters a healthier work-life balance for officers, ensuring they are physically and mentally prepared to handle the demands of the job.

Moreover, standardizing work schedules could be legislated, much like rules preventing police strikes, to ensure that public safety remains the top priority. Departments must prioritize community needs over officer preferences when designing work schedules, because effective policing requires officers to be present and engaged.

* * *

While education is a powerful tool, it's not the only way to cultivate better officers. Life experiences—whether gained through government service, professional careers, or significant personal achievements—play an equally vital role. Officers like my friend Brian, who brought leadership and adaptability from his educational and military background, and Juli, whose legal expertise deepened her understanding of community expectations and the law, illustrate how diverse experiences enrich policing. Officers who take an unconventional route to the field often bring resilience, adaptability, and poise.

But it's essential to recognize that the value of these experiences increases when paired with education. In Brian's case, his military background was strengthened by scholarly achievements that equipped him with critical thinking skills and the broader perspectives necessary for modern law enforcement. Such a combination of experience and education is a crucial factor in building a well-rounded police force capable of addressing the complexities of today's society.

Departments also must move beyond a one-size-fits-all approach to managing their personnel. Law enforcement, like an NFL team, thrives on the unique contributions of individuals with specialized skills. As legendary Green Bay Packers coach Vince Lombardi said, "The achievements of an organization are the results of combined efforts of each individual." Just as a quarterback and a defensive lineman bring different but equally valuable skills to a football team, law enforcement officers should be utilized based on their strengths and expertise. Not every officer needs to be 6 feet tall and 200 pounds to excel in their role. This outdated mindset in which all officers are treated as interchangeable parts hinders the profession's ability to evolve and address challenges effectively.

Departments should develop recruitment strategies that value intellectual and experiential diversity. This effort could include hiring pathways that reward prior government service, civic contributions, specialized professional backgrounds, and other significant achievements. Such strategies send a clear message: law enforcement values a wide range of skills and perspectives, not just traditional notions of what a macho cop should be.

Financial incentives, such as tuition reimbursement or loan forgiveness, can be powerful tools to attract candidates who prioritize self-improvement and lifelong learning. These programs shouldn't just apply to degrees earned after entering the profession but also to academic debt accrued before joining law enforcement.

For many highly educated individuals, the financial burden of student loans steers them away from careers in public service where salaries may not be competitive with private-sector opportunities. Law enforcement agencies already offer signing bonuses and other financial incentives to boost recruitment, so why not redirect some of those funds toward loan forgiveness programs that encourage college graduates to apply? By doing so, departments could appeal to individuals who've already demonstrated the discipline and commitment required to complete higher education, bringing a broader range of critical thinking, problem solving, and communication skills into policing.

Additionally, supporting officers in pursuing advanced degrees while on the job would foster continuous learning and professional growth. Such investments not only benefit individual officers, they strengthen the entire department, equipping law enforcement with better decision makers, leaders, and community liaisons. In a field that increasingly requires critical thinking, crisis management, and cultural competency, attracting and retaining educated officers is an investment in the future of policing itself.

My experience pursuing advanced academic opportunities through the department involved programs comprised only of other law enforcement professionals, which limited the ability to be exposed to broader and more diversified opinions. The maximum benefit would be gained by officers attending traditional university programs. This could serve to prevent the "groupthink" that emerges when those from similar backgrounds create an echo chamber that stifles conflicting thought.

* * *

Diversity in law enforcement is not just desirable, it is essential. Officers who reflect the communities they serve foster trust, break down barriers, and strengthen public relationships. Yet significant disparities remain. As of 2020, data from the Bureau of Justice Statistics revealed that 61.2 percent of local police officers were White, 12.2 percent were Black, and 11.6 percent were Hispanic or Latino. Gender representation is also starkly uneven, with women making up only 14 percent of full-time sworn officers.

For law enforcement leaders to correct these disparities requires active outreach and partnerships with community organizations, colleges, and minority advocacy groups. But diversity should not be limited to race and gender. As previously noted, intellectual diversity, such as hiring candidates with psychology, social work, or technology backgrounds, also can bring fresh perspectives and drive innovation within law enforcement.

By becoming more diverse, departments can challenge groupthink and identify solutions to entrenched problems that might otherwise go overlooked. For example, officers with backgrounds in mental health can offer new approaches to crisis intervention while those with tech expertise can help departments adopt modern tools for crime prevention, community engagement, and the use of AI to enhance effectiveness and efficiency.

While embracing diversity is critical, it must be paired with targeted skill development to maximize its impact. Departments should offer robust training programs that help all officers develop the skills they need to succeed, regardless of their background. Doing so ensures that candidates from diverse experiences are not just recruited but also are supported.

In the end, a diverse and well-trained police force is more than a reflection of the community it serves; it enhances public safety. By combining education, life experience, and a commitment to diversity, law enforcement agencies can build teams that are not only competent but also deeply connected to the communities they protect. This approach, in turn, strengthens the profession's credibility and effectiveness in the eyes of the public.

Shifting away from toxic culture requires rethinking leadership, fostering open communication, and creating an environment in which professionalism, empathy, and accountability are celebrated as an integral part of law enforcement.

* * *

The case for creating an emergency management director role in any community is undeniable. Such a role is necessary to ensure public safety systems operate cohesively, efficiently, and proactively during crises. An EMD serves as the catalyst for coordinating efforts across multiple agencies, aligning resources, streamlining communication, and implementing strategies that prevent fragmented and reactive responses. In the context of the recent Los Angeles wildfires, an EMD would have made a measurable difference in both mitigating the scope of the disaster and protecting lives and property.

An emergency management director is responsible for unifying disparate agencies—fire departments, police, utility companies, public works, and health services—under a coordinated strategy. This individual's job is to identify and address vulnerabilities before they escalate, ensuring readiness and collaboration across all sectors involved in public safety. Fragmented responses, like those seen during the wildfires, often stem from a lack of centralized leadership and an absence of a cohesive strategy. Without someone ensuring interagency coordination, resources are wasted, critical warnings are missed, and delays compound the severity of the crisis. Most importantly, the EMD serves as an additional layer of accountability to prevent critical functions from falling dormant in the blind spot created by the minutiae of everyday organizational operations.

The EMD's duties extend far beyond simply organizing response efforts during emergencies. This role is essential for proactive planning, risk assessment, and readiness exercises. For example, the Los Angeles wildfires exposed glaring weaknesses in infrastructure and resource allocation. The Santa Ynez Reservoir, a key resource for firefighting, sat empty for nearly a year due to a torn cover, a repair that would have cost only $130,000.

An EMD would have prioritized such maintenance, ensuring the reservoir was operational well before fire season began. Similarly, the outdated tree-trimming schedules in Los Angeles, which operate on a fifteen-year cycle compared to two to five years in neighboring cities, could have been identified and addressed. These are not small oversights, they are systemic failures that magnify risks and provide an example of overlooked mitigation measures that can prevent disasters or reduce their severity.

When we consider ways to build better systems in law enforcement, it's essential to draw lessons from our experiences, particularly when it comes to unusual occurrences: earthquakes, mudslides, fires, and civil unrest. Despite the Incident Command System, it wasn't until after the 9/11 attacks that we saw the inclusion of law enforcement in incident management. Policing an effective disaster response relies on a structured concept to address systemic weaknesses and prevent cascading failures. In response to such challenges, I developed CARE—coordination, acknowledgement, response, and evaluation. Originally inspired by failures I observed during the Los Angeles riots, this model has far-reaching implications for law enforcement leadership and continual improvement.

The EMD role becomes even more vital in large municipalities like Los Angeles where the scale of operations and diversity of risks demand centralized oversight. This position would bring a structured, methodical approach to emergency preparedness and response.

The EMD would ensure that coordination is not an afterthought but a foundational principle of public safety. Agencies would no longer operate in silos but as parts of a cohesive system working toward shared goals.

While traditionally associated with disaster response, the principles of emergency management—coordination, preparation, and adaptability—are just as crucial in law enforcement operations. EMDs wouldn't just oversee responses to wildfires, earthquakes, or civil unrest. They would play a pivotal role in ensuring police agencies are equipped to handle crises efficiently. This efficiency would include integrating law enforcement into broader emergency plans, ensuring real-time coordination with other agencies, and leading proactive training initiatives that reinforce critical planning, tactical readiness, and public safety strategies.

A key function of an EMD's role would be standardizing multiagency drills, ensuring police departments are not only trained for active threats but also prepared to operate within a cohesive framework alongside fire, emergency medical services, and municipal leadership. By embedding policing into an emergency management structure, departments can shift away from reactive decision making and move toward preemptive crisis mitigation, reducing risk and enhancing public trust.

Coordination is particularly important during emergencies that require multiagency collaboration. For instance, during the LA wildfires, better coordination between fire departments and utility companies could have mitigated the delays in resource deployment that compounded the disaster. An EMD would have established preplanned communication channels and protocols to ensure seamless collaboration and would have ensured the pre-staging of resources, such as firefighting equipment and personnel, into high-risk areas identified through risk assessments. Police resources would have been incorporated into the evacuation plans, and effective community outreach would have been achieved to inform residents about egress routes to prevent the bottlenecks that occurred. While seemingly basic, these missed steps were the difference between efficiency and catastrophe.

Beyond logistical coordination, the ability of law enforcement officers to navigate high-pressure situations with sound judgment is equally vital. A 2011 study published in the *Journal of Criminal Justice Education* found that officers with a four-year degree were better arbiters of their authority than were those with lower levels of education, reinforcing the broader impact of higher education on ethical decision making. These findings highlight the importance of an EMD who not only coordinates resources but also ensures that training emphasizes critical thinking, crisis management, and problem-solving. Officers with a strong educational foundation are better equipped to assess risks, adapt under pressure, and apply discretion effectively. By prioritizing higher education and structured training programs, law enforcement agencies can cultivate a force that is more thoughtful, accountable, and capable of making decisions that enhance both public trust and operational effectiveness in the handling of unusual occurrences.

Acknowledgment is another critical responsibility of the EMD role. The emergency management director must have the foresight to recognize potential risks and take proactive measures to address them. This responsibility also extends to identifying warning signs in the private sector, such as when insurance companies begin pulling coverage from high-risk areas. These actions are not just business decisions; they are red flags that demand immediate attention and strategic planning. During the wildfires, red flag warnings from the National Weather Service were clear and urgent, yet the city's response was slow and disorganized. An EMD would have acted on those warnings with the urgency they demanded, ensuring that resources were mobilized and communities notified in advance.

Response, or the ability to execute plans effectively and with confidence, is a direct reflection of the preparation led by this role. Although this phase is significantly impacted by the efforts of coordination, it is more reflective of the actual implementation in real time. The emergency management director ensures that response plans are well-rehearsed and that all stakeholders are familiar with their roles during a crisis. It's one thing to have the operational plans, but it's another to effectively carry them out. The ability to do so prevents the kind of chaotic, reactive responses we all saw during the wildfires, when personnel were not strategically positioned as the planning would suggest, and critical resources were delayed.

Evaluation, the final consideration of the CARE concept, is where the EMD plays a pivotal role in learning from past incidents. Honest and transparent post-incident assessments should be standard practice, and the director would lead those evaluations to identify what worked, what didn't, and how responses could be improved. Such practice eliminates the urge for department heads to protect the organization from legitimate criticism and the groupthink often present in the rationalizations used to avoid accountability. The overarching commitment must foster a culture of continuous improvement. For instance, in the aftermath of the wildfires, a comprehensive evaluation led by the EMD could have highlighted, without a tinge of bias, the infrastructure failures, communication breakdowns, and resource gaps that need to be addressed.

The qualifications for the EMD role are equally important. The emergency management director must possess a strong understanding of municipal operations including budgets, inter-agency processes, and city infrastructure. Proven experience in crisis management is essential, as is a track record of coordinating multiagency responses to emergencies. Advanced education in emergency management, public safety, or related fields provides the theoretical knowledge necessary for success. Additionally, leadership and communication skills are critical for fostering collaboration across departments and engaging effectively with the public. Most importantly, the director must maintain a neutral perspective, unbound by allegiance to a single agency, so they can prioritize the greater good without being influenced by departmental politics.

This position should report directly to the mayor or city manager, giving the EMD the authority to bypass bureaucratic bottlenecks and act swiftly during emergencies. By positioning this role at the highest level of municipal leadership, cities can ensure that public safety remains a top priority and that decisions are made without unnecessary delays. The person in this position would have authority over all other department heads.

While cost is often cited as an objection to creating such a role, the EMD should be viewed as an investment in public safety rather than as an expense. Potential funding sources include municipal budgets, state and federal grants, public-private partnerships, and the reallocation of resources from less effective programs.

The success of similar roles in other cities demonstrates the value of such a position. Beverly Hills, for example, has an emergency management director who exemplifies what this role can achieve. EMD Pamela Mottice Muller has implemented a comprehensive emergency management model that ensures coordination between police, fire, public works, and utility departments. Her work has allowed Beverly Hills to act quickly and cohesively during crises, avoiding the kind of disjointed responses seen in Los Angeles. The success of this role in Beverly Hills highlights the need for larger municipalities like Los Angeles to adopt similar models.

An EMD wouldn't just improve how cities respond to disasters, they'd prevent many crises from spiraling out of control in the first place. By focusing on risk mitigation, resource allocation, and strategic planning, this role creates systems that are resilient, adaptive, and trustworthy. For large cities like Los Angeles, the time for change is now. Without an EMD, the systemic failures that magnify crises will continue to undermine public safety and erode trust in leadership. The creation of an emergency management director position is not just a recommendation; it's an imperative.

* * *

Training, often seen as the solution to many of law enforcement's challenges, is only as strong as the culture it operates within. As demonstrated throughout this book, training alone doesn't fix systemic issues. Training must be reinforced through complementary policies, active supervision, and genuine community involvement.

Dr. Robin Engel, a leading scholar at The Ohio State University, highlights the potential of well-implemented training programs. Her 2019 study on de-escalation training with the Louisville Police Department demonstrated significant improvements: Use-of-force incidents dropped by 28.1 percent, citizen injuries decreased by 26.3 percent, and officer injuries fell by 36.0 percent. These results underscore the importance of equipping officers with tools to manage high-pressure situations effectively.

Similarly, mentorship programs in Camden, New Jersey, have shown that pairing senior officers with younger recruits to focus on relationship-building and de-escalation fosters accountability and creates a culture of collaboration. These efforts demonstrate that successful training depends as much on internal support and organizational buy-in as on external tools.

Yet even the best training programs can succeed only if officers are open to learning and growth. Dr. Lisa Feldman Barrett emphasizes that effective training requires participants to acknowledge the possibility of unhelpful habits or mindsets and a willingness to change them. "It helps to hire people who have an open mind," she explains. "People who have an open mind are going to be more influenced by their training."

This fact highlights a critical challenge in that not all officers are equally receptive to training. Many studies showing positive outcomes involve volunteers, individuals already inclined toward growth. Reaching those resistant to change requires leadership to set the tone, making it clear that ongoing learning and self-awareness are non-negotiable aspects of the profession.

Addressing the deeply ingrained warrior mentality in policing also is essential. This mindset, which prioritizes control and dominance over alliance and discretion, often undermines the goals of community policing and de-escalation. Shifting this culture requires a commitment from leadership to reimagine the role of law enforcement in society.

Officers need to be trained not only in tactical skills but also in emotional intelligence, communication, and cultural competence. They must learn to navigate complex social dynamics and recognize when a collaborative approach can achieve better outcomes than a show of force. Leadership plays a pivotal role here, modeling behaviors that value discretion and empathy while holding officers accountable for actions that deviate from those principles.

Finally, training programs must incorporate continuous evaluation and adaptation. It's not enough to check a box once. Departments need to regularly assess the effectiveness of their training initiatives and make necessary adjustments based on feedback, data, and evolving community needs. This iterative approach ensures that training remains relevant and impactful.

The days of imposed authority and groupthink initiatives are over.

By addressing these cultural and structural barriers to effective training, law enforcement can begin to move beyond outdated paradigms and embrace a model of policing that prioritizes collaboration, accountability, and shared responsibility.

Without the intellectual resources of universities, law enforcement runs the risk of becoming or maintaining a state of intellectual sterility. Universities are in many ways the social research and development centers of our society. While police can perform this function, there are few institutions outside of universities that are so well equipped to provide the research and the empirical evidence necessary to guide decisions. Remember how the findings of my contagious fire research were ignored to achieve a predetermined result? Another glaring example of how culturally inflexible law enforcement can be.

I also see a need for law enforcement leaders to be dedicated to creative encounters with the community. And that means proceeding with an open mind about how they can reach the same goal. The development of officers to their fullest potential as people, as intellectuals, and as professionals, can only be accomplished through planned and unplanned creative encounters.

What does that mean? It means there will be the usual police business within an organizational structure with officers participating in the department's planned routines, briefings, reports, and improvement program. Within that structure, there will be planned and unplanned creative encounters between the community and law enforcement. Those encounters would be openings for change that would generate the most opportunity for growth. Police departments need to have that room for the unplanned encounter, such as an opportunity to suggest a better way to do things, whether from experience or from community input. It could simply be an opportunity to be heard. The encounter would grow from there, engaging members of the department to consider a new idea. Then they could accept the idea and deploy it or reject it constructively and come up with something better.

An organization must experience internal and external disagreement and dissension if it is to develop as an acute social participant, and it must encounter diversity of thought if it is to grow in spirit and practice. You will recall when I was learning how to shoot with the LAPD that I dared to ask why its method was different from what I had learned with the LA County Sheriff's Department. The question directly related to officer safety, as the tactical concepts were at odds. Both couldn't be correct. Wouldn't one of the methods taught, at least statistically, put an officer in harm's way?

Despite the use of inclusive bodies to identify policing best practices, law enforcement often misdiagnoses the issues and fails to implement meaningful change. City officials need to be educated as to what prompts law enforcement decisions. On the other hand, police executives need to have greater awareness of community-identified problems viewed as of great importance. One of the problems is that police leaders are not politicians by training, and quite often inclination. Could politicians and police executives benefit from an examination of each other's practices, perspectives, and philosophies? Certainly worthy of consideration.

Effective law enforcement is rooted in trust, and trust is built through consistent, meaningful interactions, not through one-time gestures or high-profile initiatives. Community engagement is not a luxury or an afterthought but an essential factor in fostering collaboration and building the relationships necessary for effective policing. Departments must prioritize opportunities for officers to connect with residents beyond enforcement roles, creating partnerships that emphasize prevention, understanding, and shared responsibility.

Programs like Sandy Hook Promise demonstrate the potential of early intervention and collaboration. Such initiatives create trusted networks within schools and neighborhoods, enabling law enforcement to identify and address potential issues before they escalate. School resource officers, for example, should go beyond providing security. Their role should include building trust with students, parents, and educators as they become integral to the community they serve rather than a detached authority figure.

Mental health partnerships are another vital component of proactive policing. Collaborations between law enforcement, social workers, and mental health professionals help address crises at their roots. Officers trained in mental health response can de-escalate volatile situations with empathy and skill, demonstrating their commitment to the well-being of all community members. Such partnerships not only reduce harm but also build credibility, showing that law enforcement is dedicated to serving holistically, not just reacting to crises.

As society evolves, so too must the methods and priorities of law enforcement. Traditional training focused on physical tactics and rote memorization is no longer sufficient. Modern policing requires officers to navigate complex social dynamics, de-escalate volatile situations, and foster relationships with diverse communities, and all that demands innovative approaches to training and technology.

Virtual reality simulations, for example, immerse officers in realistic scenarios, allowing them to practice decision making and refine their responses in a controlled environment. Real-time surveillance systems and AI-driven technologies enhance situational awareness, equipping officers with the tools to act quickly and effectively during emergencies. Such advancements enable faster, more informed decision making, potentially saving lives and improving outcomes.

But no amount of technology can replace the human connection central to effective policing. Training must emphasize cultural competence, emotional intelligence, and communication skills to prepare officers to engage meaningfully with the communities they serve. Officers need to understand the histories, challenges, and aspirations of those they protect. Such an understanding fosters trust and helps build the relationships necessary to address concerns collaboratively and proactively.

The path forward for law enforcement lies in the balance between adopting new tools and reaffirming timeless principles. By embracing community engagement as a core strategy and equipping officers with the skills to meet modern challenges, departments can lay the foundation for a safer, more inclusive future. Trust is earned, not demanded, and consistent, thoughtful engagement is the key to earning it.

* * *

Every policing misstep, whether a failure in leadership, a breakdown in communication, or an act of avoidable violence, throws a spotlight on the urgent need for change. But here's the hard truth: law enforcement, as it exists today, isn't keeping up with the evolving demands of our communities. It's time to face this fact. The old way of doing things with its rigid hierarchy, reactive mindset, and outdated playbook, has no place in a society that demands trust, accountability, and results.

Policing cannot simply be about enforcing the law anymore. It must be about something bigger; acting as a force for good, a source of stability, and a partner in building safer, stronger communities. This isn't about minimizing the role of law enforcement. It's about improving it. It's about ensuring that every officer on the street understands their role isn't just to protect and serve. Their role is to lead and inspire.

Such a transformation must start at the top. Leadership isn't just about issuing orders or managing crises. True leaders don't just manage; they drive change, set standards, and hold themselves and their organizations accountable. They lead by example, knowing that their actions or inactions set the tone for their entire department.

A quote often attributed to French writer and aviator Antoine de Saint-Exupéry captures this idea well:

If you want to build a ship, don't drum up the people to gather wood, divide the work, and give orders. Instead, teach them to yearn for the vast and endless sea.

That's the kind of leadership law enforcement needs— leadership that inspires purpose and builds a culture where integrity, professionalism, and empathy aren't just buzzwords. They're the foundation for how the work gets done.

Quality control in law enforcement is about preventing mistakes. Every department should be conducting routine audits of security plans, operational protocols, and response strategies, not just in theory but in real-world applications. These audits should be random, thorough, and conducted with the understanding that no system is perfect, so there's always room to improve.

The best way to ensure objectivity in this process is through external oversight. Independent reviews bring a fresh set of eyes to help identify weaknesses before they become liabilities. More importantly, such reviews build trust by showing the public that departments aren't just policing themselves in ways that protect their own interests. Accountability isn't a burden; it's the foundation of credibility and trust.

One of the biggest mistakes law enforcement makes is waiting too long to address its own failures. When officers or departments misstep, the instinct is to go silent, minimize the issue, or deflect responsibility. But avoiding public scrutiny doesn't make a problem disappear; it only deepens the disconnect between officers and the people they serve.

Transparency isn't about giving up control of the narrative. It's about owning it. That means openly acknowledging mistakes, providing clear communication during crises, and laying out specific steps to rebuild trust when damage has been done. People don't expect perfection from their police departments, but they do expect honesty. Departments that embrace transparency as a strength rather than a vulnerability will be the ones that earn and keep public confidence.

This shift in policing isn't just about updating the same old plans. It's about reimagining police culture. The militarized mindset that teaches officers to see the public as adversaries, an uninformed citizenry that simply 'doesn't understand,' is outdated and ineffective. Authority that's built on imposed rationale and justifications no longer works. What does work is an approach that values empathy, partnership, and critical thinking. Effective policing isn't about exerting control. It's about maintaining order in a way that earns respect. Training should reflect that reality at every level, from the academy to ongoing professional development.

One solution is to create an independent body responsible for public communication during major incidents. Such a body would allow law enforcement leaders to focus on tactical responses while ensuring that the information shared with the public is timely, accurate, and transparent. Having an impartial entity collaborate on this responsibility would remove the political pressure from the equation and ensure that facts, not speculation or damage control, drive the narrative. Let's face it. Police executives are generally not equipped with the expertise, training, or inclination to effectively address the media in the complexity of our news cycles.

As the numerous incidents mentioned in this book demonstrate, police departments often struggle to communicate effectively in times of crisis. Leadership is torn between operational priorities and the need to manage public perception. The result? Muddled messages, delays in critical updates, and a lack of clarity that erodes trust.

* * *

Michelle Rupp, Emmy Award-winning broadcast journalist and Founder and CEO of Memorable Results Media, knows this firsthand. Her insight into how to improve crisis communication comes from 20 years in television news. As a journalist in Arkansas, one of the most defining moments of her reporting career came on the fateful night of June 11, 2010. That night, she was one of the first reporters on scene after a flash flood swept through Camp Albert Pike. Twenty people lost their lives in the middle of the night as rising water overtook their campsite with no warning. Michelle followed the coroner's team into the site, bravely reporting live from the aftermath.

The devastation lingered, reshaping Michelle's understanding of how crises unfold and how individuals process trauma. "I would meet people in crisis—whether they'd just survived a flood, a tornado, a house fire, or a workplace shooting," she recalled. But her encounters with tragedy didn't stop there. As a reporter, she frequently covered homicides. The emotional weight of those moments surfaced during a quiet reflection. "I remember my first dead body," she said, pausing. "I remember bodies two and three—it was a double homicide."

Through these experiences, she developed a deeper understanding of how law enforcement communicates in those early, pivotal moments. Like me, she has felt the frustration that comes when agencies struggle to communicate effectively after an incident, especially when clarity is most needed. Yet, she remains hopeful. "So much of how law enforcement is portrayed in the media," she noted, "begins with whether or not they've built strong relationships from the beginning." She continued, "That relationship can't be built in the middle of a crisis. It has to start long before."

Over her years as a reporter, Michelle built trusted relationships with police departments throughout Arkansas. One such opportunity arose after she built a strong relationship with the Public Information Officer (PIO) of the Little Rock Police Department, who invited her to take part in an active school shooter training exercise. Her reporting offered the public a rare, behind-the-scenes glimpse into how agencies prepare for school shootings, an effort that not only strengthened public confidence in law enforcement's readiness but also reinforced the transparency essential to building trust.

Having worked on both sides of the microphone, as a reporter and now as a strategist, she brings a rare perspective on the communication breakdowns that arise when strong media relationships don't exist. She puts it plainly with candid expertise: "It's a shame that more agencies don't prioritize building those relationships."

One solution she advocates, echoing my recommendation, is for law enforcement to engage an independent body to help manage the narrative during post-incident press conferences. Regardless of the agency's size, the insight of a media-trained collaborator can be instrumental in maintaining and strengthening public trust. The impartiality this provides helps to eliminate political pressure that influences messaging, ensuring that facts, not speculation or spin, shape the narrative.

These challenges aren't unique to law enforcement; they affect corporate executives and small business owners alike. Her breadth of knowledge has proven valuable across the board, supporting law enforcement and a diverse portfolio of businesses of all sizes.

Michelle said. "The modern media environment moves at lightning speed. Stories develop in real time, narratives take shape before all the facts are known, and a single misstep in messaging can ignite lasting controversy. In that environment, having a clipboard and a canned statement isn't enough. What's needed is a dynamic communications strategy run by professionals who specialize in transparency, clarity, and public engagement. Not spin. Truth."

Michelle recalled a recent example from Florida State University, where Tallahassee Police Chief Lawrence Revell led a press conference following a campus shooting. "The chief carried himself with a level of transparency and excellence." She recognized what her experience made undeniably clear. "When he stepped up to the mic, the reporters already knew him. They'd built a relationship with him. And that mutual trust was reflected in their questions," she said. "He didn't pass the buck, and they didn't try to catch him in a lie. He gave them what he could and promised to provide more when he was able. That's how you build trust."

This doesn't mean shielding police leaders from accountability. Quite the opposite. It means allowing them to focus on operations during a crisis while trained communicators ensure verified facts are shared with the public and the press. When handled properly, this builds trust. It also alleviates the burden on incident commanders, many of whom are already overwhelmed with rapidly evolving investigations. In pressure-filled moments, separating operational command from public communication ensures that the weight of one does not compromise the other.

Let's be honest. Some police leaders still view communication as a form of weakness. They default to silence, legalese, or tightly controlled messaging that does more harm than good. But silence isn't neutral. In the absence of information, people fill in the blanks themselves. They turn to social media, rumors, and speculation. We've seen time and again how that gap between silence and narrative becomes a breeding ground for mistrust.

We need to shrink that gap.

Michelle points out that law enforcement already knows how to run multi-agency operations. "We have playbooks for that," she said. "But when it comes to communication, those playbooks are missing or outdated." There is no shared protocol for who can speak, when, and what they can say. So instead, we get rushed press conferences, contradictions, and a barrage of 'no comment' statements that only inflame the situation.

"In this day and age, we don't just take what people say as truth anymore. You have to prove it," Michelle said. "If I can get you as much information as I can at this point in time and tell you I will give you more when I can, that builds trust."

We can do better. We must.

Departments that understand this, departments that invest in experienced communicators and integrate them at the executive level, are the ones that will weather the next crisis. They won't just lead with sound tactics. They'll lead with sound messaging, too.

Law enforcement cannot wait for another crisis to force its hand. The opportunity to evolve is here now. The departments that thrive in the coming years will be the ones that embrace accountability, rethink outdated practices, and lead with transparency. Those who refuse to do so will find themselves stuck in the past, watching as public trust erodes further and improvement is dictated to them instead of shaped by them.

Change is coming to policing, one way or another. The question is whether departments will take charge of that change or be forced to react to it.

* * *

To create meaningful change we must begin by acknowledging the weight of history. The journey requires an honest self-assessment of our cultural and systemic failures in order to move forward. Equally important is recognizing where we stand now. Policing is on thin ice, marked by both public skepticism and institutional inertia. The status quo has been incentivized for far too long, even when the need for change was undeniable. Standing still in this moment—failing to examine and address the issues before us—would be a disservice to the institution of policing and those we are sworn to protect.

The path forward won't be the same for every agency, every officer, or every community. But the guiding principles should be clear. The following questions are not meant to assign blame but to spark reflection, discussion, and meaningful action:

- How can law enforcement build a culture in which accountability is valued rather than resisted?

- Should police departments prioritize recruits with strong critical thinking skills, emotional intelligence, and moral reasoning?

- Does the increasing reliance on military-style equipment enhance public safety, or does it create unnecessary division?

- How can law enforcement acknowledge and address the historical impact of policing on marginalized communities while building a more just system?

- How can agencies balance the need for operational security with the responsibility of keeping the public informed?

- How can law enforcement actively recruit, support, and promote diverse officers to create a more representative and effective profession?

Everyone's answers will be different, and all will be valid. Whether you're a law enforcement officer, a policymaker, or a concerned citizen, the solutions lie in embracing an unflinching commitment to teamwork, accountability, and change.

Epilogue:
Bridging Thin Ice

"The best way to predict the future is to create it."
—Peter Drucker

Policing in America stands on thin ice, fractured by complacency, haunted by a legacy of mistrust, and strained under the weight of modern society's demands. Yet within these cracks lies an unprecedented opportunity to not just repair what's broken but to reimagine what law enforcement can and should be.

This book is neither a critique for its own sake nor a nostalgic call for the better days of policing. It's a blueprint, a roadmap for transforming law enforcement into an institution that earns and sustains the trust, respect, and partnership of the communities it serves.

As we end this journey, I ask you to consider what kind of society we want to build. Will we allow fear, division, and inertia to dominate, or will we rise to meet this historic moment with courage, collaboration, and commitment to lasting change?

This is the challenge—and the opportunity—of our time. The task ahead won't be easy, but nothing worth doing ever is. The effort will require bravery, not just in the face of physical danger but also in confronting uncomfortable truths about our systems, our culture, and ourselves. It will demand resilience, not just in enduring hardship but in pushing through resistance to change. Above all it will require hope, the belief that a better way is possible.

To my fellow retired and active-duty officers: Your badge is not just a symbol of authority; it's a promise, a promise to serve with integrity, to protect without prejudice, and to uphold the ideals of justice. Let your legacy be one of courage, accountability, and innovation. Be the leaders your departments need and the guardians your communities deserve.

To the policymakers and community leaders: Do not underestimate the power of partnership. Work with us, not against us, to build systems that prioritize safety and equity for all. Your decisions shape not just the structure of law enforcement but the trust that communities place in those who protect them.

To the public: Your voice matters. Hold us accountable but also support those who strive to do better. Law enforcement isn't just a policing issue; it's a societal one. Together, we can break the cycle of mistrust and create a system that serves everyone.

The thin ice of modern policing is not just a metaphor for its precarious state; it reflects the fragile social contract between law enforcement and the public. Once fractured, trust is hard to rebuild, but it's not impossible. Rebuilding that trust requires more than policies or protocols; it demands a cultural shift and a reimagining of what law enforcement means in a free and just society.

This journey has shown us the high cost of inaction. From moments of catastrophic failure to stories of quiet courage, every example in these pages underscores the stakes. Policing doesn't suffer from a lack of rules but from a lack of accountability, consistency, and vision. The time has come to move beyond complacency and to embrace transformation.

History has shown us the power of change. Just as policing evolved from its earliest, flawed iterations, it can evolve again. This isn't about erasing the past. This is about building a future in which law enforcement and communities thrive together.

Ultimately, this book is not just about law enforcement. This book is about the kind of society and world we want to create; a society in which law enforcement is a trusted partner, not an adversary; a society in which accountability is a core tenet, not a convenience; a society in which the badge represents integrity, service, and justice.

The thin ice we stand on is fragile, but it can be a bridge to something greater. Will we cross it together? The choice is ours. Let's choose courage. Let's choose accountability. Let's choose hope. Together, we can forge a path toward a safer, more equitable future for everyone.

Before we close, I want to share a few personal images that reflect the human side of this work. They capture not just the emotional toll of the job, but also the diverse friendships and creative influences that shaped how I see things, both in and out of uniform. One of these images appears twice: once as a photo, once as a painting. That contrast alone says something about how perspective can shift over time. Just as someone from the outside world once taught me to read, the unlikely influence of the art world has similarly shaped my outlook.

Growth doesn't always happen in training sessions or policy meetings. Sometimes it happens in the quiet spaces, when we are vulnerable, curious, and willing to listen. If we want to reimagine what policing and society can become, we must open our minds to it all: the humanity, the connection, the community, and yes, even the art.

A candid moment shared with my friend, celebrated British filmmaker and photographer Sam Taylor-Wood (now Sam Taylor-Johnson). Despite coming from vastly different worlds, our friendship highlighted the importance of influences that extended beyond my professional boundaries.

Captured by Sam Taylor-Wood, this portrait appeared in her 2006 book, "Jesus is Coming," produced while she was working on her renowned "Crying Men" project. The series explored a side of masculinity often hidden from view, especially for those of us in law enforcement, challenging perceptions that men, even cops, don't grapple with vulnerability and emotion.

A portrait by my good friend Juli Munson, whose law enforcement experiences were shared in this book. This artistic portrayal is based on a photograph by Sam Taylor-Wood, capturing not only the emotional strain of life in uniform but also the broader challenges of modern policing.

Acknowledgments

To Brielle Cotterman, Heather French Henry, Rachel Schenck, and Heather Glass, thank you for walking alongside me throughout this process. Your wisdom, insight, and steadfast belief in the power of my voice and vision reminded me of the importance of bringing these lessons to light.

To Juli Munson, thank you for sharing your unique artistic talent and creating the portraits included in this book of the most meaningful people in my life.

Each of you contributed in unique ways to ensure this book would resonate with law enforcement officers, leaders, and citizens alike. Together, you gave me the tools to share my message and purpose, and for that, I am endlessly grateful.

This book is also for the many individuals who have shared their stories, experiences, and lessons with me throughout my career. To my mentors in the Los Angeles Police Department to the officers I served alongside, your dedication and sacrifice have inspired every page of this book. It is my hope that this work honors your commitment and sparks meaningful conversations for the future of law enforcement.

Finally, to every reader who picks up this book, thank you. Thank you for caring about the challenges we face in policing, for seeking understanding, and for your willingness to engage in the difficult yet essential work of creating a better, more just society.

With gratitude,
Jeff Wenninger

Partnerships and Collaborations

Throughout my career, I've learned that meaningful change doesn't happen alone. It comes from collaboration with others who share the same commitment, drive, and mission.

That's why I carefully choose partners who align with my values and support the vision behind *On Thin Ice*. These partnerships bring additional tools, insights, and resources designed to help you put these conversations into practice within your own communities and agencies.

To learn more about these valued partners, or to explore partnership opportunities yourself, scan the QR code below or visit jeffwenninger.com/partnerships-collaborations.

Together, we CAN Reimagine Policing™ —*Jeff Wenninger*

About the Author

Jeff Wenninger is a Retired LAPD Lieutenant, Acclaimed Law Enforcement Expert, and Founder of Law Enforcement Consultants, LLC.

Jeff Wenninger brings over thirty years of frontline law enforcement experience to this discussion, having risen through the ranks of the Los Angeles Police Department to become a respected lieutenant. Renowned for his leadership in critical situations and his unrelenting commitment to accountability, Jeff's career is defined by a dedication to bridging the divide between law enforcement and the communities it serves.

As the founder and CEO of Law Enforcement Consultants, LLC, Jeff is a sought-after expert witness, consultant, and speaker, working alongside law enforcement agencies, legal professionals, and policymakers to reimagine policing for a modern world. His work focuses on fostering trust, raising professional standards, and advancing public safety through actionable, community-centered solutions.

In *On Thin Ice: An LAPD Veteran's Journey To Reimagine Policing,* Jeff offers a powerful and unfiltered account of his decades-long career and the critical lessons learned along the way. Blending hard-earned insights with a bold vision, he challenges readers to rethink what policing can be—and should be—in the twenty-first century.

Sources Cited

ABC News. (n.d.). *Police Training in the U.S. Falls Short Compared to the Rest of the World.* Retrieved from https://abcnews.go.com/U.S./police-training-us-falls-short-compared-rest-world/story?id=96729748.

ABC7 News. (n.d.) *"3 Bay Area police pursuits lead to serious crashes; law enforcement expert weighs in."* https://abc7news.com/post/3-bay-area-police-pursuits-lead-serious-crashes-law-enforcement-expert-weighs-safety-concerns/16100939

ACLU Washington. (n.d.). *School Resource Officers: When the Cure is Worse than the Disease.* Retrieved from https://www.aclu-wa.org/story/school-resource-officers-when-cure-worse-disease.

American Public University. (n.d.). *Policing diversity and why it should matter to communities.* Retrieved from https://www.apu.apus.edu/area-of-study/security-and-global-studies/resources/policing-diversity-and-why-it-should-matter-to-communities/.

APB Web. (2023, May). *Crisis Intervention Team Training.* Retrieved from https://apbweb.com/2023/05/crisis-intervention-team-training/.

Bakersfield Now. (n.d.). *LAPD investigates allegations of SWAT officers selling guns.* Retrieved from https://bakersfieldnow.com/news/local/lapd-investigates-allegations-of-swat-officers-selling-guns.

Board of Inquiry into the Rampart Area Corruption Incident. (2000, March). *Board of Inquiry into the Rampart Area Corruption Incident Public Report*. Retrieved from https:// lapdonlinestrgeacc.blob.core.usgovcloudapi.net/lapdonlineme dia/2021/12/boi_pub.pdf.

Browne, Malcolm. (2020, July 20). *The Invention of the Police*. The New Yorker. Retrieved from https://www.newyorker.com/magazine/2020/07/20/the-invention-of-the-police.

Bureau of Justice Statistics. (2018). *State and Local Law Enforcement Training Academies, 2018: Statistical Tables*. Retrieved from https://bjs.ojp.gov/library/publications/state-and-local-law-enforcement-training-academies-2018-statistical-tables.

CalMatters. (2024, May). *UCLA Protest: Palestine and Police*. Retrieved from https://calmatters.org/justice/2024/05/ucla-protest-palestine-police/.

Carte, Gene E., & Carte, Elaine H. (1975). *Police Reform in the United States: The Era of August Vollmer, 1905–1932*. University of California Press.

CBS News. (n.d.). *Police Accused of Selling Restricted Guns to Civilians*. Retrieved from https://www.cbsnews.com/news/police-selling-restricted-guns-posties/?ftag=CNM-00-10aac3a\.

Cillizza, Chris. *"Trump and Newsom Spar as California Grapples with Catastrophic Wildfires."* CNN, January 8, 2025. https://www.cnn.com/2025/01/08/politics/trump-newsom-los-angeles-fires-analysis/index.html.

City of New York. (n.d.). *NYPD Training and Specialized Units*. Retrieved from https://www.nyc.gov/site/nypd/bureaus/administrative/training-specialized.page.

Cleveland.com. (n.d.). *"Man killed, woman injured in fiery crash on Cleveland's East Side."* https://www.cleveland.com/crime/2025/03/man-killed-woman-injured-in-fiery-crash-on-clevelands-east-side.html

CNN. (2023). *Former Minnesota Police Officer Kim Potter Released from Prison After Serving Time for Deadly Shooting of Daunte Wright.* Retrieved from https://www.cnn.com/2023/04/24/us/kim-potter-release-prison-daunte-wright/index.html.

CNN. (2013, November 1). *LAX Gunfire Incident.* Retrieved from https://www.cnn.com/2013/11/01/us/lax-gunfire/index.html.

CNN. (2025). *Los Angeles Mayor Karen Bass fires Los Angeles Fire Department Chief Kristin Crowley.* Retrieved from https://www.cnn.com/2025/02/21/us/los-angeles-mayor-karen-bass-fires-los-angeles-fire-department-chief-kristin-crowley-and-appoints-interim-fire-chief?cid=ios_app.

College of Policing. (n.d.). *Official Website*. Retrieved from https://www.college.police.uk/.

Daily Mail. (2025). *Los Angeles Fire Department failed to deploy firefighters and engines during Palisades wildfire.* Retrieved from https://www.dailymail.co.uk/news/article-14286293/Los-Angeles-Fire-Department-failed-deploy-fighters-engnes-Palisades.html.

Defense Logistics Agency. (n.d.). *Law Enforcement Support Office (LESO) Program: How to Join.* Retrieved from https://www.dla.mil/Disposition-Services/Offers/Law-Enforcement/Join-The-Program/.

Equal Justice Initiative. (2019, August 9). *Five years after Ferguson, policing reform has been abandoned.* Retrieved from https://eji.org/news/five-years-after-ferguson-policing-reform-abandoned/.

Federal Bureau of Investigation. (2023). *2023 Active Shooter Report.* Retrieved from https://www.fbi.gov/file-repository/2023-active-shooter-report-062124.pdf/view.

Gartner. (n.d.). *Gartner's Top Strategic Predictions for 2024 and Beyond.* Retrieved from https://www.gartner.com/en/articles/gartner-s-top-strategic-predictions-for-2024-and-beyond.

Global News. (2022, July 12). *Uvalde School Shooting: Police Harassment Claims.* Retrieved from https://globalnews.ca/news/8957137/uvalde-school-shooting-police-harassment/.

Governing. (2019). *Chicago's Interim Police Chief Has a Tech Background.* Retrieved from https://www.governing.com/news/headlines/chicagos-interim-police-chief-has-tech-background.html.

Governing. (n.d.). *Why We Need More College Graduates Behind the Badge.* Retrieved from https://www.governing.com/security/why-we-need-more-college-graduates-behind-the-badge.

Government Technology. (n.d.). *Preparing for School Shooting Scenarios.* Retrieved from https://www.govtech.com/em/disaster/preparing-for-school-shooting-scenarios.html.

Griffin, Daniella. "California Wildfire Backlash: State Farm and Other Insurers Slammed for Dropping Coverage."

Fox Business, January 7, 2025. https://www.foxbusiness.com/lifestyle/ca-wildfire-backlash-state-farm-other-insurers-slammed-dropping-coverage.

Hadden, Sally E. (2001). Slave Patrols: Law and Violence in Virginia and the Carolinas. Harvard University Press.

Hewlett, S. A., Marshall, M., & Sherbin, L. (2016, November 4). Why diverse teams are smarter. *Harvard Business Review.* Retrieved from https://hbr.org/2016/11/why-diverse-teams-are-smarter.

History.com. (n.d.). *Black Codes.* Retrieved from https://www.history.com/topics/black-history/black-codes.

International Association of Chiefs of Police. (n.d.). *Enhancing officer safety and survivability.* Police Chief Magazine. Retrieved from https://www.policechiefmagazine.org/enhancing-officer-safety-survivability.

JAMA Network Open. (2021). *Impact of Armed Personnel in Schools on Shooting Incidents.* Retrieved from https://jamanetwork.com/journals/jamanetworkopen/fullarticle/2776515.

Kales, S. N., Soteriades, E. S., Christophi, C. A., & Christiani, D. C. (2003). *Emergency duties and deaths from heart disease among firefighters in the United States.* New England Journal of Medicine, 356(12), 1207-1215. Retrieved from PubMed.

KGOU. (2024, January 9). *Memphis committee recommends replacing police chief 1 year after Tyre Nichols' death.* Retrieved from https://www.kgou.org/2024-01-

09/memphis-committee-recommends-replacing-police-chief-1-year-after-tyre-nichols-death.

Larrabee, Benjamin. "Cold Comfort: The Latest Attacks on America Follow a Familiar Pattern." RAND Commentary, January 2025. https://www.rand.org/pubs/commentary/2025/01/cold-comfort-the-latest-attacks-on-america-follow-a.html.

Law Enforcement Action Partnership. (n.d.). *Peel's Principles of Policing*. Retrieved from https://lawenforcement actionpartnership.org/peels-principles/.

LinkedIn. (n.d.). *Why I Don't Like the Phrase "Defund the Police" by Jeff Wenninger*. Retrieved from https://www.linkedin.com/pulse/why-i-dont-like-phrase-defund-police-jeff-wenninger-svz0c/.

Los Angeles Police Department. (2022, February). *Final Consent Decree*. Retrieved from https://lapdonlinestrgeacc.blob.core.usgovcloudapi.net/lapdonlinemedia/2022/02/final_c onsent_decree.pdf.

Los Angeles Times. (2004, June 24). *Police Beating Incident Caught on Tape*. Retrieved from https://www.latimes.com/archives/la-xpm-2004-jun-24-me-beating24-story.html.

Los Angeles Times. (2007, October 10). *Police Response During May Day Rally*. Retrieved from https://www.latimes.com/archives/la-xpm-2007-oct-10-me-melee10-story.html.

Los Angeles Times. (2012, August 24). SWAT Gun Sales Under Scrutiny. Retrieved from https://www.latimes.com/local/la-xpm-2012-aug-24-la-me-swat-gun-sales-20120825-story.html.

Los Angeles Times. (2013, May 25). *LAPD Partnership with FBI Under Scrutiny*. Retrieved from https://www.latimes.com/local/la-me-lapd-fbi-20130525-story.html.

Los Angeles Times. (2024, November 9). *In MacArthur Park, Restoration Efforts of the Past Offer a Blueprint for a Way Forward.* Retrieved from https://www.latimes.com/california/story/2024-11-09/column-in-macarthur-park-restoration-efforts-of-the-past-offer-a-blueprint-for-a-way-forward.

Los Angeles Times. (2024, December 4). *LAPD SWAT "Mafia" Trial Verdict*. Retrieved from https://www.latimes.com/california/story/2024-12-04/lapd-swat-mafia-trial-verdict.

Los Angeles Times. (2024, December 4). *Memphis Police Use Excessive Force and Discriminate Against Black People, Justice Department Finds*. Retrieved from https://www.latimes.com/world-nation/story/2024-12-04/memphis-police-use-excessive-force-and-discriminate-against-black-people-justice-department-finds.

Los Angeles Times. (2025). *LAFD should have had 10 engines patrolling during Palisades wildfire, report finds.* Retrieved from https://www.latimes.com/california/story/2025-02-15/lafd-should-have-had-10-engines-patrolling.

Matter News. (n.d.). *"Something Has to Change:" The Police Killing of Colin Jennings*. Retrieved from https://www.matternews.org/community/crossing-the-line/something-has-to-change-the-police-killing-of-colin-jennings.

Metropolitan Police Department. (n.d.). *History of Policing.* Retrieved from https://mpdc.dc.gov/sites/default/files/dc/sites/mpdc/publication/attachments/1.4%20History%20of%20Policing.pdf.

Metropolitan Police Service. (n.d.). *Official Website.* Retrieved from https://www.met.police.uk/.

Murphy, Paul. "New Orleans Attack That Killed 14 Came amid Political Scrutiny and Security Failures." CNN, January 6, 2025. https://www.cnn.com/2025/01/06/us/new-orleans-attack-security-politics-infighting/index.html.

National Association of School Resource Officers. (2021, September 22). *National Survey Measures Strategic Fit of SROs in Law Enforcement, Education System, and Community.* Retrieved from https://www.nasro.org/news/2021/09/22/news-releases/national-survey-measures-strategic-fit-of-sros-in-law-enforcement-education-system-and-community/.

NBC News. (2024). *Murder charge reinstated for Philadelphia police officer who shot Eddie Irizarry.* Retrieved from https://www.nbcnews.com/news/us-news/murder-charge-reinstated-philadelphia-police-officer-shot-eddie-irizar-rcna122240.

New York Post. (2024, July 14). *Secret Service blames local police, says it was tasked with securing properties surrounding Trump's PA rally.* Retrieved from https://nypost.com/2024/07/14/us-news/secret-service-blames-local-police-says-it-was-tasked-with-securing-properties-surrounding-trumps-pa-rally/.

News 5 Cleveland. (n.d.). *Two Canton Officers Charged for Death of Frank Tyson*. Retrieved from https://www.news5 cleveland.com/news/local-news/2-canton-officers-charged-for-death-of-frank-tyson.

NewsNation. (n.d.). *Philadelphia's opioid crisis: The reality in Kensington*. Retrieved from https://www.newsnationnow.com/crime/fentanyl/philadelphia-opioid-crisis-kensington/.

Office of Community Oriented Policing Services (COPS). (n.d.). *COPS Hiring Program (CHP)*. Retrieved from https://cops.usdoj.gov/chp.

Origins. (n.d.). *May 2017: The 1992 Los Angeles Rebellion – "No Justice, No Peace"* Retrieved from https://origins.osu.edu/milestones/may-2017-1992-los-angeles-rebellion-no-justice-no-peace?language_content_entity=en.

Park, G., & Thayer, J. F. (2014). From the heart to the mind: Cardiac vagal tone modulates top-down and bottom-up visual perception and attention to emotional stimuli. *Frontiers in Psychology, 5*, 278. https://doi.org/10.3389/fpsyg.2014.00278.

PBS NewsHour Staff. "New Orleans Attack That Killed 14 Came Amid Political Scrutiny and Criticism for FBI." PBS NewsHour, January 6, 2025. https://www.pbs.org/newshour/politics/new-orleans-attack-that-killed-14-came-amid-political-scrutiny-and-criticism-for-fbi.

Police1. (n.d.). *Heart disease is the No. 1 killer of LEOs – Here's how to protect yourself.* Retrieved from https://www.police1.com/police-products/fitness-mental-health-wellness/

articles/heart-disease-is-the-no-1-killer-of-leos-heres-how-to-protect-yourself-LEtC4hJys1VsG1Xd/.

Police1. (n.d.). *The New Era of Law Enforcement Civilianization*. Retrieved from https://www.police1.com/police-recruiting/articles/the-new-era-of-law-enforcement-civilianization-jduO3jGF8MnIsa3Q/.

Police1. (n.d.). *Training Camden: 3 steps to creating a protector culture*. Retrieved from https://www.police1.com/police-training/articles/training-camden-3-steps-to-creating-a-protector-culture-bw3yHY1yoIksnJ2Y/.

Policing Institute. (2022, March). *Small and Rural Agency Crisis Response*. Retrieved from https://www.policinginstitute.org/wp-content/uploads/2022/03/Small-and-Rural-Agency-Crisis-Response_2022.pdf.

PolitiFact. (2022, May 26). *Research: Armed Campus Police Do Not Prevent School Shootings*. Retrieved from https://www.politifact.com/factchecks/2022/may/26/ted-cruz/research-armed-campus-police-do-not-prevent-school/.

Psychology Today. (2016, January). What Are Basic Emotions? Retrieved from https://www.psychologytoday.com/us/blog/hide-and-seek/201601/what-are-basic-emotions?msockid=1ce0e4d4ef67610f27daf03deee1607b.

Reason. (2021, October 20). *New Research Says Police in Schools Don't Reduce Shootings, but They Do Increase Expulsions and Arrests*. Retrieved from https://reason.com/2021/10/20/new-research-says-police-in-schools-dont-reduce-shootings-but-they-do-increase-expulsions-and-arrests/.

Roosevelt, Theodore. (1897). *The Law of Civilization and Decay.* The Atlantic. Retrieved from https://cdn.theatlantic.com/media/archives/1897/09/80-479/132123563.pdf.

Rydberg, J., & Terrill, W. (2010). *The impact of higher education on police officer attitudes regarding abuse of authority.* Police Quarterly, 13(1), 92-120. Retrieved from https://www. researchgate.net/publication/233468612_The_Impact_of_High er_Education_on_Police_Officer_Attitudes_Regarding_Abuse _of_Authority.

Sandy Hook Promise. (n.d.). *Facts About Gun Violence and School Shootings*. Retrieved from https://www.sandyhookpromise.org/blog/gun-violence/facts-about-gun-violence-and-school-shootings/.

San Francisco Chronicle. (n.d.) *"Police car chases kill hundreds every year. Most of the dead aren't the drivers fleeing police."* https://www.sfchronicle.com/projects/2024/police-chases-database

Savage, Charlie. "Tesla Cybertruck Explosion in Las Vegas Highlights Complex Security Challenges." The New York Times, January 2, 2025. https://www.nytimes.com/2025/01/02/us/tesla-cybertruck-explosion-las-vegas.html.

Scripps News. (n.d.) *"Police chase deaths reach record highs in the U.S., new data shows."*https://www.scrippsnews.com/us-news/police-misconduct/police-chase-deaths-reach-record-highs-in-the-us-new-data-shows

Security.org. (n.d.). *U.S. Gun Ownership Statistics.* Retrieved from https://www.security.org/resources/gun-ownership-statistics/.

Sigma Tactical Wellness. (n.d.). *Heart disease: The No. 1 killer of active and retired cops.* Retrieved from https://iamsigma.com/heart-disease-1-killer-of-active-and-retired-cops-1/.

Smithsonian Magazine. (n.d.). *Immigrants, Conspiracies, and the Secret Society That Launched American Nativism.* Retrieved from https://www.smithsonianmag.com/history/immigrants-conspiracies-and-secret-society-launched-american-nativism-180961915/.

SpringerLink. (n.d.). *Journal of Quantitative Criminology.* Retrieved from https://link.springer.com/article/10.1007/s10940-014-9236-3.

Stateline (States Newsroom).(n.d.) *"In reversal, more states allow high-speed police chases."*https://washingtonstatestandard.com/2024/04/15/in-reversal-more-areas-allow-high-speed-police-chases

Statista. (n.d.). *Distribution of police officers in the U.S. by sex and ethnicity.* Retrieved from https://www.statista.com/statistics/1357593/police-officers-sex-ethnicity-us.

Statista. (n.d.). *Number of School Shootings in G7 Countries.* Retrieved from https://www.statista.com/statistics/1155011/number-school-shootings-g7-countries/#:~:text=The%20United%20States%20recorded%20288,and%20France%2C%20with%20two%20apiece.

Statista. (n.d.). *School Shootings in the United States: Key Statistics*. Retrieved from https://www.statista.com/statistics/1155011/number-school-shootings-g7-countries/

Stelloh, Tim. "Conservatives Play the Blame Game for California Wildfires, Pointing Fingers at Democrats." NBC News, January 8, 2025. https://www.nbcnews.com/news/us-news/conservatives-play-blame-game-california-wildfires-pointing-fingers-de-rcna186983.

Stelter, Brian. "Trump Falsely Links New Orleans Terror Attack to Migrants after Erroneous Fox News Report." CNN, January 2, 2025. https://www.cnn.com/2025/01/02/media/trump-new-orleans-attack-migrants-fox-news/index.html.

Tandfonline. (n.d.). *Global Policing Abstracts*. Retrieved from https://www.tandfonline.com/toc/gpas20/current.

Texas Tribune. (2022, May 27). *Uvalde school shooting timeline: How the massacre unfolded and what we know about the police response.* Retrieved from https://www.texastribune.org/2022/05/27/uvalde-texas-school-shooting-timeline/.

The U.S. Sun. (2024). *High-profile Targets & Organized Crime: Coverage on Burglaries Targeting NFL Stars.* Retrieved from https://www.the-sun.com/sport/13429084/sick-crime-rings-targeting-travis-kelce-nfl-players/.

The Columbus Dispatch. (2024, August 15). *Takiya Young, Connor Grubb, and Blendon Township Police Officer.* Retrieved from https://www.dispatch.com/story/opinion/columns/guest/

2024/08/15/takiya-young-connor-grubb-blendon-township-police-officer-ohio-pregnant/74802431007/.

The Columbus Dispatch. (2024, February 28). *Columbus Suicide by Cop: Colin Jennings.* Retrieved from https://www.dispatch.com/story/opinion/columns/guest/2024/02/28/columbus-suicide-by-cop-colin-jennings/72760872007/.

The New York Times. (2007, May 4). *Immigration Marches and the LAPD Response.* Retrieved from https://www.nytimes.com/2007/05/04/us/04immig.html.

The New York Times. (2024, January 18). *Uvalde School Shooting Report by DOJ.* Retrieved from https://www.nytimes.com/2024/01/18/us/uvalde-school-shooting-report-doj.html.

The New York Times. (2024, July 28). *Trump shooting: Thomas Crooks and the Secret Service.* Retrieved from https://www.nytimes.com/2024/07/28/us/politics/trump-shooting-thomas-crooks-secret-service.html.

The New York Times. (2024, March 7). *Uvalde Police and City Under Investigation.* Retrieved from https://www.nytimes.com/2024/03/07/us/uvalde-police-city-investigation.html.

The New York Times. (n.d.). *Turnaround: How America's Top Cop Reversed the Crime Epidemic.* Retrieved from https://archive.nytimes.com/www.nytimes.com/books/first/b/bratton-turnaround.html.

The Texas Tribune. (2023, March 20). *Uvalde Shooting: Police and AR-15s.* Retrieved from https://www.texastribune.org/2023/03/20/uvalde-shooting-police-ar-15/.

The Violence Project. (n.d.). *Data-Driven Solutions to Reduce Gun Violence.* Retrieved from https://www.theviolenceproject.org.

The Washington Post. (n.d.). *Police Shootings Database.* Retrieved from https://www.washingtonpost.com/graphics/ investigations/police-shootings-database/.

Training Reform. (n.d.). *Not Enough Training.* Retrieved from https://www.trainingreform.org/not-enough-training.

U.S. Census Bureau. (n.d.). *Demographic Profile for Uvalde, Texas.* Retrieved from https://data.census.gov/profile? g=160XX00US4874588.

U.S. Department of Education. (n.d.). *Preventing Targeted School Violence: A U.S. Secret Service Analysis of Plots Against Schools.* Retrieved from https://www.ed.gov/sites/ed/files/admins/ lead/safety/preventingattacksreport.pdf.

U.S. Department of Justice, COPS Office. (2019, September). *Rural Law Enforcement Strategies for School Shooting Preparedness.* Retrieved from https://cops.usdoj.gov/ html/dispatch/09-2019/rural_le.html.

U.S. Department of Justice. (2015, March 4). *Investigation of the Ferguson Police Department.* Retrieved from https://www.justice.gov/sites/default/files/opa/press-releases/attachments/ 2015/03/04/ferguson_police_department_report.pdf.

UK Government. (n.d.). *Police Use of Firearms Statistics: England and Wales, April 2019 to March 2020.*

Retrieved from
https://www.gov.uk/government/statistics/police-use-of-
firearms-statistics-england-and-wales-april-2019-to-march-
2020.

Voice of America (VOA). (n.d.). *Are college-educated
police officers less likely to use force?* Retrieved from
https://www.voanews.com/a/usa_all-about-america_are-
college-educated-police-officers-less-likely-use-
force/6194798.html.

Weber, Christopher. "Los Angeles Mayor Karen Bass
Faces Leadership Test amid Catastrophic Fires." Associated
Press, January 6, 2025. https://apnews.com/article/mayor-
karen-bass-la-fires-leadership-
99e52cf69cc656ee7e0328c6b609be74.

WNYC Studios. (n.d.). *Policing Without Guns.* Retrieved
from https://www.wnycstudios.org/podcasts/takeaway/
segments/policing-without-guns.

World Population Review. (n.d.). *Global Police Killings
by Country.* Retrieved from https://worldpopulationreview.
com/country-rankings/police-killings-by-country.

World Population Review. (n.d.). *Police Training
Requirements by Country.* Retrieved from https://world
populationreview.com/country-rankings/police-training-
requirements-by-country.

ZeroNow. (n.d.). *National Center for School Safety and
Disaster Preparedness.* Retrieved from https://www.zeronow.
org/ncssd.